MEMOR
POTH
My Fight for the Legali

GONÇALO JN DIAS

Copyright 2021 Gonçalo JN Dias
Title: Memories of a Pothead
Author: Gonçalo JN Dias
Translation: Andressa Porto
Edition: Phoebe Zimmerer
Proofreading: Samantha M.
Cover: Printok
I Edition: August 2021
http://gjnd-books.blogspot.com.es

"Old men distrust the youth for they too have been young".
William Shakespeare

From left to right: Bora Bora; Boni; Eloi (Worm); Joey Nights & Crazy Gonga. In the bathroom of the Burrow in June 2000.

To the elements of the Burrow,
this subversive action of resilience to the instore powers.

I Turned 23 – Thursday, June 1st, 2000

Yesterday I turned twenty-three years old and it was, without a shadow of a doubt, the most spectacular of all of my birthdays. Just like every year, I kept my tradition and only did what I enjoy doing; therefore, I did not go to class.

I woke up at nine in the morning and decided to run a little to keep in shape, taking my uncle's dog, Penguin. The day was excellent, it looked like we had already got to summer, with a cloudless blue sky. I ran for almost an hour by the Agricultural School, got home, did some sit-ups, some push-ups and took a shower.

Every birthday, I like to revise my previous birthdays, and I was happy because yesterday I'd gone running in the grove of cork and holm oaks instead of being stuck in a traffic jam, unlike some other years, driving out of Cacém to get through IC19 to go to work in São Marcos as a security guard in a factory.

I had lunch with my aunt and cousin (who did not remember it was my birthday). We ate a delicious codfish meal and watched the news. After lunch, I took a nap, I think I deserved it.

I woke up lively and decided to start the festivities by going to the Burrow to smoke some pot. I went out of the house with no plan and decided to go see who was in that nefarious den known as the Burrow and maybe have some coffee by the Society coffee house. I dressed up, as usual, in my climber pants, full of side pockets to put hash, a lighter, wallet, the shrouds, etc. I put on a green T-shirt and went out. When I was about to arrive at the Burrow, right by the corner, I saw Ricardo and Mike in a car, passing by to greet me.

"Hey, stop, pull over! Today is my birthday, let's go for a joint."

Naturally, they were immediately up for it. Those guys are always ready to smoke a little Mary Jane. We climbed up to the Burrow and Elói was sitting alone, focused on the computer, as always. The rest of the guys were still at school.

Elói was surprised and, I would say, not actually very happy to see this bunch of junkies wandering into the place.

"Elói, today's my birthday, I invited the guys over to smoke some grass."

"Ah, right, happy birthday."

I gave the hash to Ricardo who made the joint. We were hanging out by the kitchen table.

"Where are the rest of the guys, Elói?" – I asked.

"They're at school. Have you been there?"

"No. What about you?"

"I only went to botany."

Afterward, Ricardo started talking about the bird recovery center in the Agricultural School, and how they have saved a black vulture and an owl. Elói looked quite interested in the subject and asked to visit the center sometime soon. I did not smoke much of the joint, because I expected it to be a long day and did not want to get crazy right at the beginning of the afternoon.

A while later, Ricardo and Mike took off and I was alone with Elói talking about some random subjects, that by now I don't even remember, because we were already high.

Around four in the afternoon the other elements of the Burrow have shown up: Boni, Joe Nights and Bora Bora. Joe threw me a recriminating look as if to say: "what is this guy doing here?"

"So, you skipped class, you bad boy?" – Boni asked me.

"Looks like I did."

Behind me, Elói was signaling to them that it was my birthday. They all greeted me.

"Fellows, since it's my birthday, I am here to smoke a joint with you guys."

"This early!" – Joe said and I noticed a little bit of judgment in his expression.

"Yes, I know it's late..."

Both Boni and Bora never say 'no', so we went back to the kitchen and made another joint. Elói and Joe didn't want to.

Afterward, the three of us went to the Society coffee house. When I got out of the Burrow I felt I would be considerably high if I kept it going, I would not be able to have dinner at home. I ordered a coffee, but actually, I felt like drinking some beers. In the Society there was Teodoro, this great personality of the neighborhood. Always friendly, he talked for a bit about something that, at the time, I did not take notice of, but I cracked up laughing just at the way he was gesturing. After the coffee, we started to order some beers.

I read a bit of the *Morning News*, and it touched me significantly; the first pages were all about crimes and blood and I, since I was already a little shook, thought I would be an easy target for killers. I set the paper aside and observed my surroundings in the coffee house. Everything seemed normal. Teodoro was talking to a client by the counter, some old women were drinking coffee, there was a drunk watching the TV that was showing a summary of a random match.

Quite a while later Joe Nights showed up, and he seemed to regret not smoking the playdough, asking Teodoro right away for a coffee and a beer.

"Yay, badass, you are thirsty!" – Boni exclaimed.

"Your eyes are pretty fucked up, guys." – Joe affirmed.

"It's just you, my dear friend." - Bora Bora said.

I kept quiet because I didn't know at what point Joe would agree to smoke hash in the middle of the afternoon, on a Wednesday. I wanted to ask if they all wanted to make a big dinner at their place.

Even if they didn't go for that, I couldn't show up in my uncle's house the way that I was, looking crazy.

"What is it gonna be, Gonga? Let's smoke some?" – Joe asked me and only then did I realize he was up for some mess.

"Sure, go on." – I answered.

We came back to the Burrow kitchen, but before we got in, we met the landlady of the house. Missus Gabriela – a woman of advanced age already, who was very fond of Bora Bora – started talking about the weather and then about the noise upstairs, that is, in the Burrow. Bora Bora was very polite and even keen while dealing with her, I was surprised for I figured he was already affected by the alcohol and hash.

When pulling the smoke up to my lungs on my third hash cigarette, I could feel I was getting really high. I pondered if I should stop, otherwise the night was going to be short.

"Fellows, can I have dinner with you? I'm already kind of fucked up and I cannot show up at home like this."

"No trouble, Gonga" – Boni said.

"Yeah, I'll make the appetizer" – suggested Bora Bora. - "The traditional hot dog rice."

"Great, I will pick up some wine and some beer." – I said.

Joe was kind of disoriented on the couch, staring at something. There were four bucks in my wallet and I wondered if it would be enough to pay for the drinks or if I would have to go downtown to an ATM. And how many bottles should I buy? It was hard enough to keep up with a sober line of thought. When I was about to walk into the coffee house, my cell rang. It was my folks.

"Happy birthday".

"Thank you, Mom." – I tried to make my voice sound as serious as possible.

"How was your day?"

"Well... Everything is going fine."

"I have called your aunt, but nobody answered. Are you at school?"

"No. I do not go to school on Wednesday afternoon."

The conversation had only lasted for a few more moments and my mouth already started to feel dry. I tried hard to concentrate on the dialogue with my mother, but my mind would fly in a ghostly fashion. At times I would look at a car that was passing by, then to a dove that sat and seemed to stare at me, then at someone who would pass by and I would wonder if they were an undercover cop.

I walked into the Society and waited for Teodoro to finish talking to a client and tend to me. When he did, I was blocked. What was I doing there? Ah, right, I was going to buy some wine and beer. I hesitated, not knowing what to do.

"So, speak up, boy" – Teodoro insisted.

"Yes... Give me some bottles of *Pelicano* wine and some beers" – the voice came out hoarse, I needed to drink something right away.

"And how many do you want?"

"Wine bottles?"

"Yes."

I could not help but notice that Teodoro did not have some of his front teeth and the remaining ones were quite yellow.

"Give me like four."

"Right, and the beers?"

Oh, so many difficult questions, I thought.

"Ten or fifteen."

"Big or small? Sagres or Super Bock?"

Fuck it! This guy sounded like KGB with all those questions. I was stuck. He went on:

"Is there a party? And I was not invited?" – he let out a sonorous laugh while glancing at the other clients.

"Yep, today is my birthday" – I said in a low tone.

"And you weren't gonna say anything? Happy birthday, buddy!" – he greeted me effusively. – "You should take at least fifteen beers, you guys are like wild animals."

He started laughing again along with the few clients that were there, while I was feeling nervous and ashamed.

"Teodoro, can you open a beer now so I can drink it here?"

"Sure, and this one is on the house. Did you bring any bags?"

"Bags?"

"To carry the drinks."

"Ah, no, I forgot."

"Then I will get you some."

When he handed me the drinks in the plastic bags, I asked how much it was for everything and worried that the money I had would not be enough; I could already picture myself apologizing for having to go to an ATM.

He did the math on a piece of paper and I tried to follow along with his twisted handwriting, but my mind was thick. I took a sip of the beer that he had opened and lit up a cigarette.

"1580 shields."

Good, I had enough money. I gave him one of my two buck notes. He gave me the change and told me to show up over there, after dinner.

I finished the cigarette, took the bags and took off. While making the small path between the Society and the Burrow, I worried that the bags were too weak and the bottles were going to smash into the ground. I stopped. There were three bags and I only had two hands, that math was not going to add up well. I thought of calling one of the elements of the Burrow, but my cell had no credit. I took the risk of walking slowly with the bags almost touching the ground. I was afraid someone I knew would pass by and see me with so much booze. While climbing up the stairs to the Burrow, this time I feared Missus Gabriela would show up and ask questions, but nothing happened. I climbed up the stairs, walked down the external hall of the house, and walked into the kitchen, where the door was wide open.

Boni was alone, in the kitchen, having a snack.

"Shit, man! You took too long! What the fuck, so much beer!"

"Well, alright... If there are leftovers we save them for some other day."

I had barely finished laying the beers in the fridge when Celia and Paula showed up.

"Happy birthday, young man!" – Celia said and gave me two kisses, then Paula did the same.

They laid their bags on the couch, taken off their coats and sat by the table.

"How did you know it was my birthday?"

"We saw Ricardo."

"Want a snack?" – Boni asked.

They said 'no' and I offered them each a beer. They took it, as did Boni, and I took another for myself. I pondered if possibly we were short of beers.

"So, can you make a joint?" – Celia was always ready, for sure she had already smoked some with Ricardo or with Paula.

"You make it." – I gave the hash to her. – "I'm terrible at making the playdough" – I concluded.

They laughed and I thought they were laughing at me for being clumsy.

The rest of the people living in the house, when smelling the joint, came out of their rooms and made their way to the kitchen, like vultures smelling dead meat. Soon there was smoke all over the house and beers all over the table. I was right, we were short on beer.

"You sons of bitches! So you have stolen some of the flowerpots from my building." – Celia shouted.

From what I understood, one of those nights, Joe and Elói were taking Celia home, since she was baked and could barely walk, and they literally took her inside her house. When climbing down the stairs of her building, they stole a couple of vases with plants, that were now garnishing the kitchen of the Burrow.

"Goddamn it! And I was saying it wasn't true, that no friend of mine had stolen anything and in the end, you are a bunch of thieves!"

Celia has a heavy northern accent and I enjoy hearing her say bad words.

Joe could not even answer he was laughing so hard. Elói, not hiding how proud he was for stealing the vases, was saying in his defense that the plants were fading and needed some care. He asked for my help. And I pretended I was knowledgeable in the field.

"Celia, my friends, Mister Elói, also known as Worm, and Joe Nights did a lovely thing. Take good notice of how those two plants fit like a glove in this kitchen, giving the apartment a nihilist aspect."

A short time later my sister called. She wished me a happy birthday and obviously heard all the noise around me.

"Are you at a party?"

"Yeah, kind of, I invited some friends."

After the conversation, I stayed out of the kitchen for a few moments, in the external hallway, answering friends that had sent me SMS. It must have taken quite a while because when I was back, Celia and Paula were already gone; they had something to do at home and Bora was already preparing dinner.

Bora has the best kitchen skills of all the guys. While he was cooking, I helped by opening another beer and giving some unnecessary tips on the preparation of the dish.

"Did you hear what Paula said, Gonga?" - somebody asked.

"What was it?"

"That she has some pot seeds she'll give us."

"Really? Cool!"

According to some rumors that go around the underground, Paula has a friend from her homeland who is a dealer, and hides hemp, hash and chips at her house. Due to that, she is always stocked and now apparently she even had seeds. We agreed that we were going to germinate the seeds and afterward some plants would remain in the Burrow and I would take some to my home.

Dinner was served, there was no more beer and two bottles of wine had already disappeared. Bora had a wine carboy from his homeland that he put to use. Celia and Paula had already returned and Paula left the seeds by the television. We stopped with the joints, by then it was just alcohol.

Boni, the most knowledgeable guy in the music field, picked up a cassette and played Portishead. Even though I kind of like that music, it felt a little annoying. This year I've been listening to a new rapper a lot: Eminem, who released an excellent album – The Slim Shady LP. However, here in Castelo Branco, almost nobody cared for hip hop. I think it is due to the lack of a suburban environment in the region. There are still a lot of people listening to heavy metal from the eighties. On that same note, it seems like Guns'n'Roses are really through and that's a shame. However, it seems like nobody likes them anymore and since it became mainstream, it is even considered tacky.

After Portishead, and by the request of the group, Boni put on some Moby, a new musician that released *Play*, an excellent album for background music, to be among friends.

In the middle of dinner, my cousin Toxic showed up. He knocked hard on the kitchen door and screamed "Police". At first, the guys thought it was Missus Gabriela complaining about the noise.

"Ouch, check out this scum." – He got in, and we all cheered up, like a fish back in the water – "Happy birthday Gonga, you're already high!"

I got a little awkward, I must have had a baked face...

As soon as he sat on the couch he began to make some playdough and somebody gave him a glass of wine.

After dinner, the kitchen had turned to an authentic pigsty, there was no more alcohol and I had promised Teodoro that I would have a beer at the Society. It was not easy to get those junkies to make their way to the coffee house.

Once out on the street, it felt like summer, an excellent windless night. We arrived at the Society's making a big mess. We decided to stay on the terrace, since it was too hot inside and there was too much light. Teodoro was all glad to see us and took a seat with us. There was beer coming and going. I was really happy and having the best birthday of my life, the event is still unfolding.

Bora decided to pick up his guitar back in the Burrow. These days, he teaches Sunday school in his homeland. He started playing songs from a band called Pólo Norte and we all sang along, already drunk and high, the song: *Aprender a ser feliz (Learn to be happy)*. Teodoro was so cheery he would not stop bringing more beer.

"This one is on the house." – he would say.

"One more! You are a killer, Teodoro."

"If we keep up this way we can't go to the Alternative" - Joe said.

"But you wanted to close down the Alternative disco!"

We all laughed, except Teodoro, who wanted to know the reason why the great Joe Nights wanted to close that hole down. Then, Joe told the story of how one night he was very drunk and got in a mess in the disco and the security guards, big as gorillas, dragged him out of the place. When he was already by the door of the disco, Joe swore out loud that he would go right away to the police and said that den would be shut down. However, when he got to the police station to state his complaint, in the middle of the night, clearly affected by a lot of alcohol, the agent advised him to go and get some sleep, saying: "if your sweet parents knew you would be around here at this time and in this condition, they would be very sad". And so, the Alternative disco is still open.

It was sure after midnight when Teodoro told us that the following day he would have to open at seven in the morning and asked us to continue the party someplace else. We were in a state of too much euphoria to go home and too drunk to go to the bars we would usually go to. Someone suggested we should go to the Mércoles Mount, where we could go on with the party, with no troubles about the noise. We took a case of beer from Teodoro's. I do not know who paid him if someone did. Today I'm going to have to go and ask him.

My cousin wanted to drop by home to pick up some more, in case we were short of beer.

"Short? You nutcase!" – I replied.

"Yep, we never know, Gonga."

Toxic really is a crude one.

I should have guessed that Bora Bora was in no condition for driving, when he took his car and, going in reverse, bumped into Missus Gabriela's car. It was a really small hit, but enough to make the guys laugh like crazy.

I was in the car with my cousin, who lately has been driving an old Ford Fiesta, two-seater only. The car still doesn't have a CD player, and Toxic put on a cassette of acid house music from a DJ that no one has ever heard of.

"Hey, well, today I can't stay late 'cause tomorrow I have to work early."

"Sure, just stay until about two." – I said.

The three cars went up the Mércules Mount, where tables were remaining from the last party, that takes place every year up the mount. Paula, who has a new Ford Focus, opened the trunk and put some music on the loudest volume. It was crazy. Bring on more beer and more joints. It was unbelievable! I had a hash in my hand and on the other side someone already giving me another playdough.

Bora Bora wanted to go away. All-day long his cell was vibrating and he was calling a friend that he had met on an internet chat. But to be able to talk to her on that chat, he would have to go to the Agricultural School, which was the only place where there was an internet connection that late.

"Hey, well, leave it behind, Bora! Talk to her tomorrow." – I said.

"Nope, nope, I have promised to go today, I will be there for a little while and then I can still come back here."

"But the school security guard will not let you in this late. Least of all, in this condition."

"I'm fine, he has to let me in, we are students in that school."

"Alright, it's up to you."

Charlie Big Potato by Skunk Anansie began to play. Those first chords are killer and the guys went crazy, to the point that Elói climbed up on a table and threw off all of his clothes. There he was, fully naked, dancing. Oh, well! I laughed so hard I couldn't even stand up and I just let myself fall. Already on the ground, I had such a fucked up coughing attack that I could not get back up. I looked around at the rest of the guys and they were all cracking up laughing.

A little after, Bora Bora showed up. I assumed the school security guard did not let him in. The guys were happy to see him.

"Guys, I drove the car into a ditch, come over and help me." – Bora said.

I assumed he had thrown the car into the roadside ditch, without any major damage. I followed him, along with Celia, with a beer in one hand and a cigarette in the other. I was relaxed, laughing at random silly things when I noticed we were going in circles around the mount and that Bora did not know where his car was. We got in a part of the mount in which there is a little convent and rumor has it that some priests were living there.

"But do you know where you left the car?" - I asked.

"Well, I think it is over here."

After some more rounds, we saw some lights far down, as we approached slowly, we confirmed that it was Bora's vehicle. The car was tilted against a sharp cliff like two meters high. How did the dude manage to get the car in such a place?

The vehicle is a Seat Ibiza and was posed perpendicularly towards the cliff. The front part of the car had hit the asphalt, where Bora was heading. The back part was kind of hanging over the bluff, and when we arrived there the motor was still running, the pilot door was wide open and the lights were still on.

There were all kinds of reactions. Celia and Elói were cracking up in laughter. Toxic became very dramatic and with his hands on his head would keep saying:

"Oh, Bora, what have you done? Oh, Bora!"

I thought the responsibility was mine. It was my birthday. I was the one who bought so much to drink and smoked so much hash that in the end, I was the responsible one.

"But, Bora, how did you place the car like this? Did you lose track?"

"No, there was a road up there. I saw a road."

"But there are only bushes all around. Where did you see a road?"

"Oh, well, I don't know."

As it seems to me at the moment, he must have gone off of the road and, without noticing, shoved himself in the middle of the woods and ended up on that cliff with the hood of the car hitting the road.

Celia, still laughing, was smoking a joint and offered some to Bora. He accepted it. It was only then that I realized my friend was in another dimension, in a galaxy far from the one in which I lived. For if I had been through the same, I would be looking to quickly recover my sobriety. However, Bora was in another wave and leaned himself on the hood of his car, smoking his weed.

Meanwhile, Joe and Toxic had gone downtown looking for a tow. Yesterday it seemed like the right thing to do, but today, already sober, where would they ever find an open garage at two in the morning?

There we stayed, the remaining ones, around the car without really knowing what to do besides comforting Bora, who did not seem to be much affected by the accident. And that is when the cops arrived...

There is no need to say we all went into a state of shock when we saw the police jeep in the same road where Bora's car hood was. Anyways, instead of coming towards us, they went up to where there was music and beer. We decided all of us should go up, except Boni and Bora, who stayed by the damaged car.

I was with Celia and Paula. Elói was some 100 meters forward, half-naked, he passed by the agents, said something and went on. We followed.

"Good night, what is going on around here?" – one of the cops said in a harsh tone.

Celia as well as Paula seemed soberer than me and started telling that we had come over to celebrate my birthday and one of our friends had run off of the track. I did not say anything. I had the impression that if I did say anything, they would notice how fucked up I was, and so the best thing to do was to hush-hush.

Both of them went along with the agents towards Paula's car, meanwhile, I went back to where Boni and Bora were. Arriving there, I come to notice that Boni, when aware of the fact that the police was coming, was trying to get Bora to stand up, but he was helplessly drunk. The police jeep came closer. Bora trying to show he was fine, got rid of Boni, took two steps forward and dropped down on the ground. The police jeep had to hit the breaks quickly to avoid running over him.

"Geez, what the fuss, it's been a while since I've seen someone so drunk." – said one of the agents.

Once more Boni was helping Bora to get up and he leaned against the hood of the jeep.

"Whose car is this?" – the other agent asked.

"It is mine." – he heard himself grunt.

He looked like he was going to puke.

"Watch it! Don't you throw up on my jeep..."

Too late, Bora puked over one of the wheels of the jeep and dropped down a little further ahead.

Meanwhile, Boni got closer to me and asked if I had seen his sandal. It was only then that I noticed that he had left home wearing sandals and by now he only had one on.

"Whose car was it that passed us by when we got up here? A Ford Fiesta."

"The car is mine." – Bora said.

"But isn't this one your car? The damaged one?"

"Yes, it's mine."

"I mean the other one which passed us by a little while ago."

"It is mine." – Bora said again.

I tried to organize the conversation a bit.

"The other one belongs to some friends who went after a tow."

"This late?" – the agent questioned.

Then Elói, Boni and Celia started talking very gently to both of the agents. They said we came over here since we wanted to avoid harming anyone. They said we were students of the Agricultural School and have been friends for quite a while. Elói, who is the oldest one of the group and is already kind of bold, gave the impression he was the most responsible one of the group and we only wanted to celebrate a birthday without disturbing anyone.

The two agents turned out to be very friendly and did not want any trouble either. They didn't even inspect us for drugs. They gave us a long lecture about the dangers of wandering around the mount that late, especially to the two ladies who were with us, for last month there had been a rape case or something alike.

Around three in the morning, Toxic showed up along with Joe Nights with no tow. Toxic, who already looked sober, took part in the chat with the agents and it was established that, on the following day, which is now today, they were going to remove Bora's car.

"Are you in any condition to drive?" – one of the cops asked.

Paula and Toxic answered affirmatively and walked up to their cars. Celia took Paula. I was kind of stuck, not knowing what to do and the agent walked me to the back door of the police jeep, along with the rest of the elements of the Burrow.

The seats in the jeep were quite uncomfortable. Three seats on each side of the van. The five of us sat down there and I must confess that, for me, it was the most epic moment of all of my adventures of the Burrow, the highest peak. There we were, the five of us, escorted by the police, with hash in our pockets and thoughtful faces. I noticed that Boni had recovered his sandal and that Joe was sending some phone message. I felt like saying some words at that moment, something like: "fellows, thank you for the magnificent birthday party" or "this was the best birthday party of my life", however, I remained silent, caught up in an enormous wave of happiness. The jeep had stopped nearby Missus Gabriela's car, one of the agents opened the back door and advised up to wise up.

I slept very loose, like a little angel, and woke up by ten, without any trace of a hangover. I took some breakfast and my aunt wished me a happy birthday and gave me a gift: a belt for my pants, which I needed.

I had promised to come over and do the dishes in the Burrow, so I showed up by that den before noon and spent an hour cleaning up that mess. I knew that Bora and my cousin had gone to pick up the car with a tow and it was already in a car shop.

What a wonderful birthday!

I Failed Physics & Portugal Lost to France - Saturday, July 1st, 2000

Although I am on vacation in Cacém, I arrived with a bitter taste in my mouth. The end of the school year went really badly. That's not even counting that Portugal lost to the French chauvinists by 2 to 1 in this year's European Championship in France. With a penalty by Abel Xavier... but I'll talk about that later.

I could only attend the 4th year of my course if I had been approved in everything or, at most, left two subjects behind. However, I blew it with four and it was particularly the subject of physics that brought up the announcement of this heavy loss. When my father got the news, he said right away to come back to Cacém in the 2nd semester, because I could not stay a whole semester in Castelo Branco only to pass one subject. He's right. This way, in September, I can go back to Castelo Branco; I have to get good grades for three subjects for the next semester and in February I will be back to my beautiful land of Cacém.

I was not slightly prepared to take the physics exam, which was really hard. I should have asked for help or even paid for a tutor, however, I ended up counting on a miracle and got screwed. I got a four.

All the other elements of the Burrow have been approved, which means, next year they'll remain together in the fourth year and I'll stay alone in the third... at least Celia blew it too.

On the day that I got the news that I failed, I went home depressed. Nelson was there and tried to cheer me up with a joint.

Then he told me he had to go and deliver some messages in downtown and I went with him.

He has a jalopy and missed a sign on the way; he was already kind of high, and almost hit a water delivery truck that kept on yelling for a while. When he was finished with the messages, we went to Dorali coffee for some beers. While we were there, his girlfriend kept on calling and he would either let it ring or reject the calls.

"Why don't you answer?" – I asked at some point.

"Oh, she is so boring, she's gonna ask too many questions."

"Tell her you are having a beer with a friend."

"I don't feel like it. You don't know her."

"But there is nothing wrong with that."

"Yep, but she's a control freak and she knows I get lost easily."

I remained quiet, I did not understand the explanation quite well, he must have noticed and said:

"Well, I'm a scatterbrain and if I don't have anyone to bring me back to earth, I remain adrift."

Though I appreciate the honesty, I had the impression that Nelson saw in his girlfriend a kind of a mother figure, someone that would take care of him and would give him limits. Next year he will not be in my uncles' house anymore, he's going to move to the girlfriend's parents' house, so she can control him at all times. It makes me sad to think about that, Nelson is really a nice guy and we would travel a lot with pot and alcohol. He is a guy with an excellent sense of humor. But patience...

After many beers, we went home. When we were going to the attic of my uncles' house, which is rented to students and is where I live, we heard the voice of Nelson's girlfriend knocking at the door and screaming "Nelson! Nelson!" What the hell! I decided to get away for I didn't want to hear the couple's discussion and let alone with Nelson kind of drowsy. I could get some of what he got.

I did not feel like having dinner at my uncles' nor did I feel like going to the Burrow to see my friends celebrating being approved in physics. I went to the Society.

I pondered all of my possibilities for that night. I kept on drinking beer and decided to call Célia.

"Hi, Célia, what's up?"

"It's good" – I noticed the lack of enthusiasm in her voice.

"Look, I already know you didn't make it. Me neither."

"Yep, I see, Elói, Joey and Boni have made it, right?"

"Yep."

We sat in silence.

"I don't feel like going home for dinner, wanna go somewhere?"

"Sure. Where?"

"I don't know... There is a taproom by the castle that's cheap."

"Oh, I know. Nice. What time?"

"By eight, I'll wait for you over there."

I would rather not go to her house for dinner, because she lives with her boyfriend and that guy makes a powerful joint anytime he sees me and is always ready to party.

I arrived at the taproom at eight o'clock sharp and she had obviously not arrived yet. She would take, at least, another half hour. While I was waiting, I remembered when I failed mathematics in prep school and, due to that, I had to take the subject again for a whole year in Gama Barros High School, in Cacém, at night.

When I was in prep school, I had bad grades in math and already knew I was going to do it over again. Since I would only go to classes to be with my friends, I wouldn't pay any attention to what the teacher would say. One day, I was playing a game in the back of the classroom, when me and Pinto (an inseparable friend) started to argue because he was saying that the octopus could be a domestic animal and I was saying that it was ridiculous. The teacher came by our table and said:

"Are you doing the exercises I have put on the board?"

"We were only taking a break, ma'am." – I said with some attitude.

"Why do you boys still come to class? Gonçalo, do you know how many classes you have missed?"

"Well, some 13" – I said without conviction.

"Wrong, you have missed 27 classes."

"What? What about the ones I have justified?"

"Your mother's signature is fake."

I remained silent.

"And what about you, Pinto, how many have you missed?"

"Like 10."

"It's 12, there are two left for you to fail due to absence, however, your last four exams put together don't add up to 10 points, therefore... There is no scenario under which you could be approved."

Afterward, she began some rigmarole that I don't remember very well, but I answered something like this:

"Look, ma'am, from what I can see, we've blown math, but we will be approved in all the other subjects, which means next year we will be having loads of fun and with only one subject to study."

I laughed and expected Pinto to do the same, but he remained morose.

"It is good, Gonçalo, that you think in such an easy and simplified manner. Life is so beautiful, isn't it? I hope neither of you shows up to my classes anymore and it is for the whole year."

This memory did not make me comfortable at all, so I had another cigarette, waiting impatiently for Célia to come.

She arrived one hour late, in her typical hippie style, with her face, as always, super white and her black hair. We complained about the exam for a while and then requested a meal for each of us, with a bottle of white wine. While they were preparing the food, we went outside for a joint.

"Have you talked to them already?" – Célia was referring to the Burrow.

"Not yet. They sent me some messages, but I don't feel like answering."

"By the way, have you planted the seeds in your parents' village?"

She meant the seeds that Paula had left us. At first, we germinated them in the Burrow and then the majority of them stayed there, but me and my cousin had taken home some. They grew so fast and since we couldn't keep them there, we decided to plant them in the Lentiscais, in our parents' land. Our idea was that some cousins who live over there would take care of the plants and, in the end, we could share the product. We were strongly convinced that they would accept because they lived alone and were our friends. However, when we knocked at their door, they said no right away, with unfriendly faces. Me and Toxic were stunned by their reaction, or better, looking dumb. Since it is the way it is, we decided to go to an empty land in the middle of nowhere, where there was a stream, and there we planted the pot. Afterward, we went to the People's House to drink some beers and watch Portugal beat Romania by 1 to 0 in the European, goal by Costinha.

"We planted them in an ideal place, they had heat and water, however, fifteen days later, I went back there with my cousin and the plants were already huge, but some bird or animal had eaten all the leaves."

"Fuck it... damn shit."

"Yep, but wait... there's more."

"Don't tell me."

"Bora brought some tricky compost from his little land and said: "this is very good, they are gonna grow a fucking lot". He laid the compost and some days later all the plants died."

"Really!" – Célia was angry.

"Yep, we don't have any plants anymore."

"That dude is a killer. How did you allow him to put down that compost?"

"I wasn't there."

"What the fuss, that's pretty unlucky."

"Bora should go to jail, straight, no trial."

"Agreed."

By the end of dinner, we had smoked another joint walking the streets of the old part of town and decided to go to Ti Jorge, as we were sure our rascal friends would be around.

When we arrived at the taproom, the door was closed; through the glass I could see that the whole gang was inside. I opened the door with attitude, with a strong swing. I did not notice that behind the door there was a customer of Ti Jorge, who took the swing from the door right on his back. The man did not like it and answered by throwing the door closed again. I came back and opened it again even harder and this time it hit the client in the face, dropping his glasses to the floor. After this triumphant entrance, I opened my arms like thy Lord Jesus Christ and awaited the ovation of the members of the Burrow and the rest of the scum.

I couldn't help but notice the reactions of the people around me. Joey, who was with his girlfriend, was intrigued trying to read my emotions after losing one year. Elói, always such a bad actor, would show compassion, one would say pity. Boni was already wasted.

"Congratulations, you pigs." – I said.

They fed me some clichés, like: "I don't know how I passed; It was unexpected; I've had so much luck; You will surely get it next time; You weren't the only one".

I only managed to stay there because I was already loaded and tried to change the subject.

At this moment Isaura arrived, unlike the other days, this time it was like salvation. She didn't even know anything about the exams, she was in another course and was only to Ti Jorge to check if I was there. In a general manner I try to be nice to her and to protect her from Elói's gross behavior, but this time I was even more welcoming to her. I stuck with her most of the time we were there, trying to unburden myself.

I am sincerely sorry for not liking her, I don't find her attractive physically or intellectually. But, she's been hitting on me since I was a freshman, despite telling her many times that there is no potential of having a relationship. In the end, I could still have a merely physical relationship with her if I found her attractive, but, really, not even that. And it's not as if she is ugly or fat, in fact, my cousin has already told me if he had the chance, he would do her, but she's not my type.

The Ti Jorge taproom is quite small, and I stuck together with Isaura by the counter, while the rest of the group was sitting by the few tables next to the wall.

"Hey, bald man, pay me a beer, will you?"

Isaura calls Elói bald man because she knows he does not like it.

"Go get some work, you rusted keychain" – Isaura is short and red-haired.

"Nobody gives me any work."

"You can get yourself to put that body to some profit, there's a corner right over there."

"You are the worst kind of gross!"

"Calm down, calm down! Let's not lower the level" – I said, still enjoying those mockeries.

Isaura, a little annoyed, said to me:

"I cannot stand your friend, he is so stupid."

"You started it."

"Yeah, but I was joking. Besides, nobody can make me think he's not gay."

Actually, there are a lot of people that think he is a homosexual, though it doesn't seem particularly feminine to me. Well, maybe when he laughs, his laugh may seem a little girly, but as for the rest, he seems to be quite a "normal" guy. Usually, I defend him and say he is a big macho man and that I have seen him having fun with many fine ladies, but it was not a normal day, so instead I said to Isaura:

"Yes, you're right, he is quite a sissy. Spread the word, tell all your friends."

"Yes, yes, I will put it in the news" – she said laughing.

I was laughing too, I always loved to shove myself in the mud.

"Isaura, you know what you could do? It would be funny to request the DJ in the disco a song to dedicate to your gay friend that is coming out of the closet."

Elói could not hear us, but he saw us leaving, laughing and looking at him.

By two-thirty in the morning, Ti Jorge closed up. It was not worth it anymore to go down the avenue to go to Coffee and Milk nor to the Rubro, so we went straight to the Alternative. It was only me, Joey and Elói. Paula and Célia went to Célia's; I don't know what for. Boni and Bora went home, they hate disco music. Isaura took off to find some friends and we would meet again in the disco. Joey sent, or better, advised his girlfriend to go home.

We were going down Nuno Alvares Avenue, talking loudly, when a guy from the Agricultural School from the same year as us that was in the Forestry course, approached. I don't know why he started teasing me. Although, later, Joey and Elói told me he was only joking.

"So, how come you two dudes from the north, hang out with this southern bugger?"

On any other occasion, I would have ignored the insult. Those are usually commentaries that I myself often make, but that night, I didn't like them. It might have been the alcohol, the joint, or simply the fact that I flunked that made that joke boil me over like lava from a volcano. So I ran in his direction, jumped, kicked out my leg and hit his back so hard that the guy spread out on the floor. At the moment

I started running in his direction, he even tried to run, but it was too late. Joey tried to help the guy up, while Elói was saying:
"What the fuck, are you crazy?"
"Yep, I'm Crazy Gonga."
We started laughing again while we were heading to the disco.
"But the dude was only joking."
"Fucking bad luck, I am not from the south, I am a bad motherfucker nigga from Cacém."
And I started to walk as if I was a rapper from a Detroit suburb. But actually, I felt regret at the moment I hit him. I'm not a violent man and I'm certain that if he was stronger than me, I wouldn't have done it, therefore, that makes me a coward, a piece of shit.

It was Thursday, and like all Thursdays, it was Ladies Night, which means the women do not pay for anything and they drink anything they want, while we have to pay 500 shields and still pay for each drink. Life is not fair...

We hold it as a tradition to stick around the women's bar, getting some drinks and hitting on one of them. This night was no different. There we were, the three of us drinking all that we could get: vodka with orange, rum and coke, whiskey with coke, etc. Célia and Paula showed up and gave us more drinks. Afterward, Isaura came around with some colleagues and acquaintances and all of them gave us drinks of questionable quality. About four in the morning, I was in a state of pitiful drowsiness.

Meanwhile, Joey started to laugh at something and leaned against a table, where two friends were sitting facing each other. When he leaned, he might have pushed, or slid, which caused the table to move and he fell to the ground on his back. It was hilarious! Joey, when he fell, must have hit his head on a chair or the table so he stayed for some seconds lying on the floor without moving. Both the ladies were stunned looking at Joey on the floor. Me and Elói, instead of helping our friend getting up, were laughing ourselves silly. Joey tried to get himself up, but he was too drunk and couldn't do it. He made me think of a crab with the carapace lying upside down. When he finally got up and joined his "friends", his pants and shirt were really dirty, stained from the drinks, but he did not seem to mind, if it wasn't him, Joey Nights, the Night Predator.

There was a moment in which one of them went to the bathroom, and the other went for a dance and I left. I couldn't stand any more of the terrible music the DJ want playing, there was Spice Girls and then Britney Spears. Currently pop is going through its worst phase. However, I also took off because I wasn't having fun. They could and should have fun, they passed physics. I did not. I made the way home alone, sad and with my head down. I thought I really have failed and I was the only one responsible for that, it wouldn't be worth it to blame anyone else. I didn't prepare for the exam and I expected that I could copy from someone or from my notes.

Moreover, I'd expected the other members of the Burrow to have flunked as well, like I did, with the slight hope that I would not be the only loser. But no, they were all approved, except me, which gave me even more of the sensation that I was a real failure. To make matters worse, I was feeling all the more ashamed for how I'd kicked that guy.

Anyways, I feel like some dark days are coming soon.

Since evil never comes alone, Portugal lost to France in the European Championship, in the overtime. I watched it in the Society with Elói, Joey and Toxic. Our table was filled with beers and the ashtray was full of cigarette butts. The environment in the coffee house was hopeful: this was the time that we were finally going to have our revenge towards the Gauls. All of the tables were occupied, people were watching the match standing up.

France had a better beginning over us, but in a counter-strike, Nuno Gomes shoved inside the first goal. Huge explosion! "Do you wanna see us going to the finals?" We got to the meantime winning, however, France has been on top the whole time, so in the second part nobody was surprised with their goal. Then the overtime came, the nerves coming through the skin, "do you wanna see it go to the penalties?" And afterward, that ridiculous moment will always be burned in the history of Portuguese soccer. Abel Xavier cut the ball inside the penalty area with his hand. At the moment, it seemed to me he hit it with his leg and even seeing it over and over, my eyes did not want to believe that the ball had touched his hand.

"That is theft."

"Cheat."

"There must have been a deal so France would win."

Those were some sentences at our table, me and my cousin went home really annoyed and drunk, but the one who took it the hardest was Joey. He went up to the terrace talking on the phone, quite unsettled, I would say he was crying; yelling at I don't know who. I hope it was with Zidane, that bastard.

Now that some days have passed, after watching that move over three thousand times, I have had to admit the penalty was fair, that the French played better and that Abel Xavier should be tortured for hours on end.

That week I went back to Cacém, on vacation, although I will work the whole summer in the Summer Camp of the Water Company, where my father works. I will be a monitor for the children, just like the last few years. It is something I enjoy doing and it gives me a little money.

I have plans to go with my cousin to the Southeast Festival, in the first weekend of August.

My Summer Vacation in Cacém (Kzen) - Wednesday, August 30th, 2000

My vacation is about to end and in a general manner, it was a bore.

I have been working in the summer camp as a monitor for the kids that are between six and twelve years old. It was better this time because I wasn't forced to take the train from Cacém to Lisbon downtown, to the headquarters of the company in Liberdade Avenue. This year they told me to go straight to the summer camp, which is located in Belas, which means, I would go in my father's car and it would only take like ten to fifteen minutes. Usually, I would arrive around 9h30 and prepare the material and activities for the day. The bus that would bring the kids would arrive by ten.

I have been to that camp as a boy and I have, in a general manner, good memories. It used to be a sleepaway camp, now the kids only spend the day. The facilities are great, there's a swimming pool, a soccer field, two playgrounds, an art studio, a library, a game room, a toy room, a huge dining hall plus the dormitories that are now empty and abandoned.

For the groups I monitor, I usually try to pour in some of the mysticism of the camp; I tell them about the stories that happened to me when I was a kid and what the camp was like back then. I always value the unity of my group: "one for all and all for one". We created a name for the group, we chose a flag and we used to sing an anthem. This year I got girls between six and nine years old. I think the girls are way tamer than the boys. I had a lot of fun and I think they did as well.

Some days we went to the beach, others to the gardens or parks and even to museums and palaces. The monitors were nice, especially one of them who used to go there every year like I did call Rui. He lives in the center of Lisbon and is quite peculiar, he's always trying to hit on one of the female monitors. This year the female monitors were about my age, there were some with nice bodies, but one of the few principles that I have in my life is: "do not eat meat where they give you the bread." Although, one of them, Filipa, gave me her cell number. She's got a good body, short, but with excellent curves, I was naturally temped to call her after the end of the season, however, I have come to learn that she has a boyfriend. So why did she give me her number?

I made some money and I want to save it in order to have a student life in Castelo Branco with a little less struggle. However, there was a day in which I went to work, and forgot my home keys inside the house and my parents as well as my sister were on vacation away from Cacém. None of the neighbors has a copy of my keys so I had to call the fire department and they came with the police to open the door, and this oblivion cost me the paltry amount of 5 thousand shields... fuck, that hurt me a lot.

I have had some quite healthy vacations; I was practicing a lot of sports in the camp when the kids would take the bus back to Lisbon, and I would go to the pool and swim for an hour or so. During the week, it was uncommon that I would go out at night, I would rather stay home playing on the computer. This summer I played *Championship Manager*, *Mortal Kombat* and *Sim City 2000*. By the way, I became quite addicted to those games and I spent so little time with my folks in the living room, that they would complain about my absence in the family conversations and my computer addiction. But the truth is that I get annoyed by the television programs that they watch.

I also read two books, the first one was recommended by my sister: *The Stranger*, by Albert Camus, that kind of let me down, it seemed slow and I did not feel any empathy for the main character. Curiously, the second one I read: *The Reincarnation of Peter Proud*, by Max Ehrlich, I enjoyed it a lot. I had no expectations regarding it, however, I found it full of twists and turns, with a very twisted love story. Unfortunately, the translation of the book is bad, but still, the plot was way more of my style. When I told my sister about this, she said I knew nothing of literature, that Camus was one of the best writers in the world, while "that Max" is unknown. Anyway, apparently we all have to like the same things.

In the field of arts, I watched *American Beauty*, by Sam Mendes, which seemed to me a great movie, with an excellent screenplay, a huge critic to modern society and traditional marriage. The scene in which the plastic bag flies through the street was so beautiful that I almost cried watching it. On the other hand, *The Green Mile*, with Tom Hanks, seemed to me like some typical American garbage, a familiar movie where a poor black man has special powers and touches everything and everyone. Above all, it is almost three hours long. Torture.

During the weekend, depending on what I felt like doing, I would hang out with my childhood friends from Mira-Sintra or with my friends from the Cacém theater group. When I was 19, my parents moved from the neighborhood. They traded the project housing of Mira-Sintra for the neighborhood of Tapada Mount, a middle-class area that is closer to the center.

Still, when I was 17 years old I enrolled myself in an amateur theater group at Ferreira Dias School under the influence of a friend of mine from Mira-Sintra, Pauley. Among the immense amount of people that I met, there was a lady, with whom I am still friends and that is maybe my best friend: Maria João.

Ever since, my group of friends from Cacém has been picking on the friendship between me and Maria João. In the beginning, our group of friends used to be the guys from the theater group and a few others, and we had the habit of going to the High Village and drinking some cups at the Beer House. Other times, we would hang out in a coffee house in Cacém, chatting all through the night. The group was changing, a great friend from high school, Bruno, showed up. Marco, my childhood best friend, would also hang out with us intermittently. Besides Maria João, there was also Sara and her boyfriend Pauley, plus Sara's twin sister, Nice. Many secondary characters would show up and disappear from the group, according to the plans. The guys would drink moderately, we all would smoke, however nobody would smoke hashish. We would often go to the beach or to Maria João's place, that is in Baleia (nearby Ericeira), where we would have parties, that were known as "hose parties" because we were all dudes. For me, those were the best moments.

There were a lot of great moments with that group. I remember once, at the International Exhibition of 98, me, Marco and Bruno have met some Swedish guys that were working there and we ended up spending all night with them, showing them Lisbon night life, where they would not let us pay for anything; we drank enough to collapse, literally. I threw up on the train when we were heading back to Cacém. Another time, the three of us went over to my parents' land for a weekend, in Lentiscais. We went in my father's car and, at the time, there was a festival in the Malpica do Tejo, nearby Lentiscais. The three of us were drinking a lot, smoking joints, laughing our asses off and we have watched a live show of "the Portuguese music prodigy", who was the hit of that summer: the little great Saul Ricardo, who was only 8 or 9 years old and would curse more than actually sing. It was a grotesque show!

We were set up to go to Algarve, to Albufeira, more precisely, to enjoy the summer. According to Bruno: "that place is filled with gringas that come on vacation and all they want is sex". However, Marco had found a girlfriend and disappeared. And worse than that, we met two lads that got in the group and turned everything upside down. First, it was Filipe, a friend of Pauley's, a very basic guy: manipulative, jealous, chauvinist, uncultured, greasy and always looking sweaty. He would wear white socks and short pants, very tacky. Maria João even confessed that she would feel disgusted just by looking at him. This guy barely saw Nice, before he fell in love and wanted to date her. Nice did not care for him, however, water-dropping day by day wears the hardest rock away. And after a weekend in which we had all been to his land in Pampilhosa da Serra or some other little land wherein the back of beyond, he had convinced Nice to give him a chance.

Another piece of work that joined the group was Renato. He was from the theater group and as everybody knew he was gay or, at least, bisexual. He would have never wanted to join the group if he was not enchanted by Bruno's personality, who is that type of guy that is so jolly and cheerful that he quickly becomes the center of any clan. Renato and Bruno became friends, almost inseparable and I felt that bit by bit, I did not have so much in common with them. Every weekend we would meet at a coffee house called 81, where there was a pool table and everybody would play, except me and Maria João. We would spend the whole night there and the conversations were, in a general manner, very basic, not very interesting, which would keep me from going to the place whenever I knew Maria João would not be there. There were so many moments in which I felt out of place in the group, so many! Sometimes I would only show up because Nice or Bruno would ask me, and when I was alone with them, I would feel ok, however, when the others would arrive, I could feel the level of the conversations, of the principles, of their prejudice, fall way too low for me. Gradually I took some distance from the group and got the habit of having coffee with Maria in the afternoons, only the two of us, where we would rant and rave about our group of "friends". Therefore, I decided that if my friend Maria was not around, I would prefer to play on my computer, watch a movie, read a book, or to visit my childhood friends in Mira-Sintra. Maria has a boyfriend, that would never want to hang out with us, so it became harder and harder to get to set up anything with her.

In the year 1998, me and Bruno planned for a long time to go to Albufeira, in the heart of Algarve, to do some of the drunken foreigners that come over on vacation. On the other hand, bit by bit, I had come to notice that Bruno was getting closer and closer to his friend Renato and further apart from me. Still, this August, we went to the camping site of Albufeira.

Albufeira is possibly the ugliest place in all Portugal, and bear in mind, I am from Cacém. Buildings of all colors and forms, over the cliffs, by the beaches, an urbanistic and architectural chaos. And the crowd that would go over there to spend their vacations was unbelievable, lines everywhere, people going everywhere, traffic jams, high prices, uproar, a mess. My God, never again!

I took the car trip with Bruno, and I noticed he was not as enthusiastic as I was.

"Hey, Bruno, our attack plan will be this: around four in the morning when the foreign girls are already very drunk and their expectations are low, then we show up and save their night."

Things went well in the first night, the two of us went out to check the habitat, we walked down Sá Carneiro Avenue, which was full of people early in the night, most of them blondes. We drank, we laughed, hit on some, we danced and came back to the camp after a while. Promising.

However, the following day, Renato had shown up, coming by bus.

"You invited him?" - I asked.

"Hum, well, no, but he invited himself."

His excuse was lame and, since then, they were always together in the nights, while I was alone. My hope of doing some of the foreign ladies has fallen way below expectations.

After being turned down by many ladies, I only had fun with one, an Icelander that I met in a karaoke bar, on the old side of town. She had short black hair, a very light complexion, black eyes and lips painted shiny red. She was almost my height, thin and not so curvy, however, in times of hunger, one cannot wait for the caviar. I hit on her in a bar, she found something I said funny and we started to talk, and shortly after she took the wheel and kissed me. She literally dragged me outside of the bar and we went to a quiet alley.

I thought I was gonna get lucky, we made out for like two hours. We started touching each other and I said:

"Let's go to your room?"

"I cannot, I am with my parents."

"Ah, I thought you were with friends. We can go to my tent at the camping site."

I had always thought that these people from Northern Europe were so independent, that going on vacation with parents was for kids.

"But you are overage, right?"

"No, I am 16 years old."

Since we were talking in English, I thought I did not hear her well and said:

"Eighteen?"

"No, sixteen."

I felt a little shocked. She looked as if she was my age, maybe a couple of years younger, but 16!

"I am 21, I don't know how things are in Iceland, but this can send me to jail."

"But I was not forced, it was my free will" – and she grabbed my neck. – "Do you want to go on or will you go away?"

In the end she was right, I had not forced her to do anything, we were just having fun. But, on the other hand, if cops came, or worse, her parents with the cops, then I could have problems. I'm a very weak man regarding the skirts and kept making out with her for over an hour, in that dark street in Albufeira. She would go away within two days, and she feared not seeing me anymore, so she gave me her address and I gave her mine so we could write letters. I never saw her again, and neither of us ever wrote any letter.

What hurt me the most regarding Bruno was his lack of trust in me. I used to consider him one of my best friends, I would tell him everything, however, he was ashamed of telling me that he was with Renato, that he was gay, or, at least, that he was bisexual. Maybe it was because we used to mock the subject: "the more gays the better, more girls will be left". He did not trust me and that hurt.

The vacation in Albufeira turned out below the expectations; except for the Icelander, I remember only a few nice moments there. Adding up to that, someone broke into our tents on the camping site and stole like 300 bucks from Renato. Well, it takes someone really stupid to go around with that kind of money in their pockets. And, in the end, I ended up paying for their part. Although Renato did pay me back quite soon, Bruno did not pay nor ever mention the subject again.

Bit by bit, I was getting away from the group, I did not feel good among them anymore. Later on, Bruno got upset with Renato and decided to leave the group; he denied his homosexuality and quit showing up. Renato, since Bruno was not around anymore, quit as well. The final strike was when Nice and Filipe broke up. Me and Maria were on Nice's side, while Pauley stuck by Filipe, even though two days later he was trying to date Nice.

The group came back to the origins, me, Maria and Nice. Our friendship was the basis of the clan, which would get bigger or smaller periodically, depending on the people with which we were hanging out at the moment.

In the Carnival of 2000, I met Rodas, a guy from the theater group whom I'd never actually talked to before. We were among a big bunch of friends in the High Village and soon I noticed he was from the *Legalize It* Team. In that Carnival, I was dressed as a vampire and he as a painter and we would walk down the alleys of the High

Village drinking beers and smoking hemp. I soon became his friend that night and since then we kept on making plans to hang out. He lives nearby my parents.

Coming back to this summer, at the beginning of August, as planned, I was with my cousin at the Southeastern Festival, in Zambujeira do Mar. He came by train to the Eastern Station and from there we went together to the festival. We still thought of staying over and camping, but we both had just a few days of vacation left. We went in my father's car, a Volkswagen Golf.

When we arrived at the festival, we parked in an empty space and got closer to the place. There were some stands selling beers; we took two and hung around enjoying the fauna surrounding us. The environment was very peaceful, it seemed everybody was in peace. It was hot and people had very few clothes on their backs; dark bodies and laid-back youngsters. Beyond the smell of baked meat, the smell of hemp and hashish was very strong. Everybody was smoking and no-one seemed to worry about cops, because it was a private place where cops could not get in. My cousin prepared a joint and we started smoking, watching people coming and going, the sun hitting our faces. There was a lot of dust flying around the place and loud music from the bands playing.

"Hey, Toxic, what a good vibe, dude!"

"Yep, believe it, what a cool place."

I imagined that heaven would be like this: there would always be good music, heat, booze, pot, young and healthy people. This was Eden.

We got into the room, more beer, joints, more music. The heads playing that night were: Morcheeba, Oasis, and Guano Apes.

The first ones were quite calm, they would fit well the relaxing environment, there was still some daylight when they began to play. I enjoyed it but did not find anything special.

I had good expectations regarding Oasis. Some years earlier, I had bought an album of theirs – (*What's the Story) Morning Glory?* And I had previously heard the album *Be Here Now* on a cassette. This night, they started with too much cocaine already up their noses, still I was enjoying them, they are good musicians and they were playing their most lively songs. However, a small percentage of the audience started to boo the band when they were playing *Some Might Say* which is one of the softest songs, and the rest of the public behaved like sheep, following the others and booing the band altogether. Other clowns put themselves to scream: "Guano Apes". Then, Liam Gallagher got fed up with the crowd and screamed:

"We're a pop-band, not a rock-band. Fuck off!" – and they left the stage and did not come back.

I actually think he was right. The crowd paid no respect to their work, if they did not like the song they should have gone for another beer, there were other stages, they could go for another joint and watch the stars, but they did not have to insult them. And I, who would care more for Oasis than for Guano Apes, had to stay and watch that nonsense.

It took almost a whole hour for the Germans from Guano Apes to show up. As soon as they came around, they started to play their most lively songs from their album: *Proud Like a God*. It was a good rock gig, even though I do not really like their style. According to the organization team, almost 50 thousand people were watching the concert. The crowd was hopping so much that at the end, such a cloud of dust had arisen which made it almost impossible for us to breathe. After the concert, me and Toxic went for another drink, smoked another joint, talked about the performances and went to sleep in the car.

We woke up in the middle of the morning, with an unbearable heat in the vehicle. We got out of there, hungry, and saw the car was covered in a huge layer of dust. We stopped in Vila Nova de Mil

Fontes for breakfast. I was going to take him back to the Eastern Station.

When we were already on the road, a car passed by us with a group of ladies, they were making signs as if they meant for us to follow them. We were taking turns and by this time I was on the wheel.

"Let's follow them, Gonga!"

"What for?"

"Perhaps, they want to screw."

"Yeah, right, Toxic. For sure they wanna stop over there in Palmela and fuck like rabbits."

"Yep, perhaps."

I do not know why, but that day I woke up in a bad mood, for no special reason. The previous day had been excellent, I loved the festival, but I had woken up on the wrong side of the bed, as it were. It might have been the annoying habit Toxic had of always giving opinions and hints on the way I drive. When he drives my father's car, he plays the racing pilot and automobilist expert, always rides at high speed, even though I have told him that the car consumes too much gas when faster than 120 km/h.

In those remaining days of my vacation, before coming back to Castelo Branco, I have been going to Mira-Sintra, the village in which I have mentioned I was born. I planned it with Miguel, who in his turn sets things up with Mota, Pelé and the Gypsy. The guys by now have a shack in the middle of the woods, built with plates, carpets, and sofas and chairs that they took from garbage containers. It's really nice, there is always someone over there to guard the place, plus there is a lock. The guys go over there to smoke hashish, even though some say that the older junkies, like Teixeira, also take heroin. If I drop by in day time, I take the car, however, even though it is still far, at night time I prefer walking my way over there. At night I always tend to be too paranoid and I am afraid I'll crash the car.

On the following day, I went there in the afternoon, it was Saturday, and I parked on A Street, near the soccer field. I went there with Miguel, smoking some joints, I bought some hashish to take to Castelo Branco and, around eight, I went home. When I was getting close to the car, I bumped into Pauley. What the heck! I have not seen him since Nice and Filipe had broken up. He barely knew they weren't dating anymore, when he had tried his luck with Nice, but since she turned him down, he'd started ranting and raving about her. I'd taken Nice's side and fell apart from him. Deep inside, I always felt as if I was for him as a second option as a friend: "I hang with Gonga if there are no other available friends."

"Pauley, what a surprise, you're here!"

"That is for me to say, you don't live here anymore! I saw your car here and have been looking for you."

I was high, but I thought I could hide it well. He is one of those guys that has never smoked pot, and is totally against drugs and alcohol. I noticed that he looked very white, and had possibly spent the whole summer without going to the beach. I imagined him secluded in his room listening to Pearl Jam and muttering with his father, as usual. According to rumors, he was upset with Filipe and Bruno. I do not know if it was because I was high but he looked a little fatter, he even had a considerable double chin.

"Where have you been?" – he asked.

"Well, around..."

"Around? Where?"

I could not say I was by the tent smoking hash, he would make a tremendous scandal.

"I was in Oliveira's coffee house, playing pool."

"But, Oliveira doesn't have pool anymore for about two years."

Fuck, he can catch a liar quicker than a lame one. Some time ago, Oliveira's coffee had a pool table and before that an arcade store, where I had spent a big portion of my childhood.

"Yep, I was around there, the old pool table" – I said with a little conviction that not even I believed. My mouth went dry.

He didn't even pay any attention to my lame excuse and started to talk about the misunderstanding between Nice and how Bruno was upset with Filipe and him. He talked and talked and kept on talking. As for me, I was only halfway listening, and I remembered when I was a boy and would spend hours in that soccer field playing. Then I remembered making out with this girl Sônia in that same place, by the field, when I was like 16 years old, and I wondered if she would have a boyfriend by now. Almost for sure, she was quite yummy. I miss those times so much!

"Well, Pauley, I have to go, my parents are expecting me for dinner."

"Sure, sure, let's see if we can set up some coffee with all of us together."

With all of us together he meant Maria João and Nice, but I doubt they would feel like seeing him.

"Yep, sure, we'll keep in touch" – I said.

Next time it would be better to park far from his street.

Soon I will be back in Castelo Branco. I can't wait to see the Burrow again and all the rest of the scums.

The Freshman's Burial – Sunday, November 26th, 2000

I am fed up with train trips between Lisbon and Castelo Branco. It is really tough having to take this trip every 15 days. I usually buy the ticket to the non-smoking area, because I don't like to breath somebody else's smoke and when I feel like having a cigarette, I go out to the hall between the wagons. I always find someone I know, but there are moments in which I have no patience for chit-chat and prefer to be sitting here, the way I am now, writing or reading a book. I started to read José Saramago, *The Gospel According to Jesus Christ*. The man really hits the church hard, so far I'm enjoying it, he did an excellent job researching Jesus' life, it's way more authentic and human than what they try to sell us. However, his writing is difficult to understand fully.

The way back to Castelo Branco was heavily anticipated, I can't wait to be back with my friends and partying the way I deserve.

There is a moment that comes to my mind right away: The Freshman's Burial. Typically, after the prank, the freshman's burial is performed, which consists of walking the city streets with a coffin that symbolizes the end of the prank. Me and Joey went out early to watch the burial, going up and down the streets, in the middle of the mess. Already tired, we went to Ti Jorge's to get something to drink and eat some of those rissoles that had remained untouched on the counter for 15 days.

It was a festive environment at Ti Jorge's, with a lot of youngsters going in and out. Joey and I were having a tame night, being philosophical about life, when two unique characters showed up.

The first one was Gasolines, whose name I actually do not know. Whenever I've been introduced to him, everybody always calls him Gasolines. There are two theories about the nickname. The first, as he tells: one night, after leaving Alternative, he and Elói had a disagreement, and dropping by a gas station, Elói filled the pockets of the other guy's jacket and pants with gasoline and started asking people around if they had a lighter. It's not hard to believe this story, because I have seen Elói drunk and he is quite a dangerous individual. The second theory, told by Elói, confirms the disagreement and that he threw the gasoline in his pockets, but that he never walked around looking for a lighter. The only thing that is one hundred percent certain is that the discussion between them was over the word "cassette", and if it was written with a single or double 's'.

The other character was Madeiras, quite a nice guy, who always makes me feel good since he is always more fucked up than me. According to some, he's the kind of guy that combines Xanax with alcohol and pot; they say he suffers from depression. He has long hair, a pale face, and always wears loose clothes and a Walkman, listening to heavy music from the eighties. All of his sentences, seriously, all of them, begin with: Yeah, kinda cool, dude

We were by the counter, in a tame chat.

"Well, I'd like to save up some money and go to the Netherlands, fill my head with good quality weed" – I said.

"I am saving up some money, but for something way nicer" – Gasolines said, expecting the guys to be intrigued.

"Like what?" – I asked.

"Doing the Trans-Siberian."

"Yeah, kinda cool, dude, that is really crazy" – Madeiras nodded.

"That means going all the way across Russia, right?" – I asked again.

"Yep, from Moskow to Vladivostok, which is a city by the Pacific Ocean. More than 9 thousand kilometers."

"Yeah, kinda cool, dude, but that is some serious cash, it's a *lot* of money."

"Yes, I am aware, but I'm saving bit by bit" – Gasolines said as if he was an expert on the subject. – "And obviously, I will not take the 9 thousand kilometers all at once, I will be stopping by the most important cities and places. Afterward, when I arrive at Vladivostok, I have two options: I either go over to the boundary with North Korea, which is nearby, or I jump over to Japan, which is on the other side."

"The North Korean boundary must be some load of bizarre" – I said, already cheering up about the trip.

"Yeah, kinda cool, dude" – Madeiras was going crazy.

"Yeah, the boundary is only 13 kilometers long and the countries are separated by a river, so there is only one bridge, where one train crosses over once a week. However, going to North Korea is forbidden. Although there is a village right by the boundary where I want to go, called Jasan. There are only some 500 inhabitants."

"What about ladies? What about bars?" – Joey does not talk much, but when he does, he touches on quite important topics, one could even say intellectual.

Gasolines pretended not to hear and kept on giving a lecture on the cities he wanted to see in deep Russia.

At that moment, a bunch of noisy people arrived, mostly ladies, and I checked to see if I knew any of them. Nobody called my attention, however, one of them came straight to me.

"Hi, Gongas, how is everything?"

At first, I did not recognize her and that "Gongas" did not sound good. Gonçalo for the acquaintances and Gonga or Crazy Gonga for the friends. "Gongas?" No, thanks.

"I have been looking for you for quite a while" – she kept on.

Who would it be? Her face was not totally unknown. She had some heavy glasses on and black curly hair. The long face, had some pimples, and was not particularly beautiful. She was thin and busty. After some over-human effort, I remembered her. Someone called Rita that I met one night in the Alternative and had been sharing drinks with all night long, during a *Ladies Night*.

"Look what the cat dragged in. How is it going, Rita, how long has it been?"

"Hey, I was afraid you would not remember my name. I remembered you a lot during my vacation and that thing you told me at the disco."

She had a strong alcohol smell and was getting closer and closer to me. It would take paranormal powers for me to remember our conversation months ago in a disco, I thought I might have given her the same chit-chat that I used to give others. My level of eloquence is very limited when I'm drunk.

"I've been asking the guys from the Agricultural if anybody could give me your cell phone or e-mail."

"Ok, remind me, you do not go to Agricultural School, right?"

"No, I go to the Education School."

Without even noticing, I'd left my friends and was in a conversation with her near the women's bathroom. She was grabbing me and, when she talked in my ear, she would give me little kisses. That started to turn me on. I thought to myself: "Gonga, not every day is Christmas, even if she isn't beautiful, she has a good body, don't ruin the moment, please".

The bathrooms at Ti Jorge's are a mirror of the rest of the place, two disease-infested filthy lairs. In the men's bathroom, besides an intense urine smell, there is a bucket nearby the toilet where everyone, and I really mean everyone, pisses in the bucket instead of the toilet. The women's bathroom is used with less frequency because there aren't a lot of women in that catacomb, so Ti Jorge has filled the place with stuff.

When she was about to say something in my ear, I kissed her. She not only consented to the kiss, but she would actually bite my lips and tongue. She had powerful alcohol breath. We started kissing slowly and making out. I looked at my friends, who were all cheered up and making me signs to go on. Ti Jorge was watching the scene sideways.

The entrances to the bathrooms have a screen partition, I opened the female room and pulled her in there with me. We dug in and kissed frantically, touching our intimate parts. I thought we were going to fuck right there. At some point, she touched my "killer vulture", which was as hard as stone and, with astonishing speed, she took off my belt, put my pants down and snapped it.

I got stoned, there, in Ti Jorge's bathroom, with a girl that I barely knew, on her knees, greedily sucking my penis. She would not stop, not even for air, and I was already thinking that it would not last long, I was almost having an orgasm. However, suddenly, someone tried to open the door, or rather, the screen. I yelled:

"It's occupied" – and slammed the screen hardly.

Although on the other side someone was trying to force it open, I thought, with that little discernment I had, that maybe it was Ti Jorge to complain. But it wasn't him, it was that bastard Gasolines that was trying to force it open, just to see what was going on. I threatened to break his face if he didn't leave. Rita, obviously, got scared with that scene, got up and fixed herself up to leave. But I couldn't leave, my "killer vulture" was in full vitality and I could not quite manage to shove it in my pants.

It was quite a struggle until I managed to leave the bathroom, my friends laughing in a corner like assholes. Ti Jorge was still looking sideways. Rita pulled me to the counter and kissed me.

"We'll finish later" – she said.

My God, how I hated Gasolines. Elói was right when he wanted to burn him. No, it would not be enough, he should have been tortured for hours on end. What a gross man!

I talked with her for a little while, she asked me if I was going to the Alternative, and I said it was quite possible.

"All right, I will meet my friends at Rubro and we'll meet over there, ok?"

"Yes, of course."

"Give me your cell."

We took each other numbers and she took off. I turned to my supposed friends.

"Gasolines, you are the worse bastard on the face of Earth, tell me why I shouldn't punch you in the mouth?"

Gasolines was laughing out loud hiding behind Madeiras, who possibly did not notice anything of what was happening, he lives in a parallel world. Joey asked in my ear:

"Was she sucking your dick?"

"Yep."

He looked at me in admiration.

A friend of Gasolines was passing by and the bastard took the chance to take off. That Gasolines is gonna pay big time.

I kept on the conversation with Madeiras and Joey, when Elói showed up, saying that Paula had her car parked, right there by Ti Jorge's door, to take us to the industrial polygon to smoke some pot. We went out of the bar and the three of us got in Paula's Ford.

Paula had a Bob Marley CD in her car, playing *Could You Be Loved*. We started singing out loud and Paula, in a jolly tone, said to us:

"Guys, I have some wonderful hash pollen that can drive you crazy."

In the back seat, we were howling with joy, the night was promising to be epic. We opened the windows, the cold wind blowing in our faces, and we kept on singing reggae, and growling like hungry bears.

When we arrived at the polygon, Paula parked nearby Brígida's jalopy. Boni and Célia were also there. When Brígida saw Madeiras she yelled in joy. They started school in the same year, in 96. The rest of them also hugged Madeiras, everybody likes him, he's a nice guy that never hurt anyone.

Paula opened the trunk, put the volume to the loudest setting, and made a joint with the aforementioned pollen.

There was beer in Brígida's jalopy and we all started to drink to the sound of Jamaican music, laughing, singing, talking about this and that, but nothing important. We were kind of in the dark, with only the lights of the street posts in the polygon.

At this point, I realized something that had a real impact on me, Joey Nights had made no commentary about what happened in Ti Jorge's, what seemed to me a classy act, an elegant gesture from a friend, who would not take part on other people's intimacies. And I reflected that if it was me, as soon as I arrived, I would have said: "guys, wanna know some good news, a random girl was going down on Joey in the bathroom at Ti Jorge's". I needed to be noisy, a loudmouth who would tell other people's private stories just so people would think I was funny. But Joey has some class. Sometimes when he drinks too much, a dark side comes out of him and he begins to put himself down, saying that he is a countryside simpleton, that he was born in a village in the middle of nowhere, that had no access to libraries or movie rentals but fuck it, the guy has very clear principles and doesn't have to be the center of attention. I should learn from him in this respect.

The joint was going from hand to hand, from mouth to mouth and got to my claws. I sucked it hard, inhaled the smoke, and let it stay a while in the lungs, then I let it out slowly through mouth and nose, did the whole process over again before passing the joint on to the next guy. What a crazy joint that was! It hit me in a few minutes. Then, suddenly, I wasn't feeling cold as hell, with the wind that came from Serra da Estrela. Instead, I was in a tropical country, maybe nearby a beach, the wind was just like a breeze, the beer felt like a refined drink, Paula's car had become a snack bar on the sand, and the four wet cats that were there turned into a hundred people, young and beautiful, all on the same trip, laughing. The world was a peaceful and happy place.

"Gonga, take it."

Somebody gave me the joint again.

"It's still alive, fuck it, I'm already too high."

Everybody laughed and, looking at them, I noticed they were all as high as I was. Squinty red eyes, smiley, and happy faces, kind of dizzy.

The sky was clear, there was a star that called my attention. It was shining brightly, I asked:

"Guys, do you see that star?"

"Which one?"

"Where?"

"Over there, that big one, see how much it shines."

"Yes, I can see" – Joey said.

I kept looking right at the star and it became even bigger, quit being a star and became a flying saucer, with a laser beam coming from below it. Oh, no, it's the apocalypse!

"Guys, it's moving towards us."

I looked at them, scared, but nobody would even mind me, they were all on their own trips and would not even notice that the Earth was going to be attacked soon, and that, maybe, we were going to be abducted by some species from some faraway country. I looked at the saucer again, but it was not there anymore, it was just a star that was shinning a little more than normal. Was it a hallucination? A little visual hallucination, but fuck, it seemed to me that I had seen a flying saucer getting closer at high speed! That pollen was really crazy.

The bunch of junkies wanted more revelry, they stopped playing Bob and Paula put on The Prodigy album *The Fat of the Land* and it was fucking crazy. There was another joint and nobody would stay still. I was hopping up and down, striking karate stunts in the atmosphere and, when *Breathe* was playing, I felt an intense need to run around the polygon, I had to spend my adrenaline. Somebody yelled my name, but I was already running nowhere like crazy, I went off the road and into the woods, I was swallowed by the dark and stopped running when it was pitch-black; I saw the lights of Castelo Branco in the distance. I remained quiet, catching my breath and watching the town asleep, with no thought on my mind. Nothing. I felt cold. I walked back.

"So, where did you go, asshole?" – Celia asked.

"What's gotten into you, dude?" – Boni said.

"Yeah, kinda cool, dude, what a trip" – Madeiras, of course.

"I needed to run, now I need a beer."

Bit by bit, without noticing, the environment began to fade. The music didn't give the same energy, the adrenaline was lowering. We started talking about classes, exams, some teacher or student that was more eccentric.

At this moment, my cell rang. Nobody besides my parents would ever call me and only in the daytime. I looked at the little screen and it was Rita.

"Yep" – on the other side there was too much noise. I got apart from the group for a little privacy.

"So, won't you come to the Alternative?"

"Yeah, yeah, soon I'll be there."

"Soon? They're closing. It's almost five."

"Five? Well..."

The noise on the other side was unbearable and she said something like "we'll talk later" and hung up.

The time had flown, and that late it was impossible to go to the Alternative, moreover, the spirit of the guys was already decreasing.

"Who was it?" - Célia asked.

"The cops. They are after some jars that disappeared from your building" – I answered.

The night was over. I arrived home and ate a ham and cheese sandwich while watching some TV, there was a documentary on History, about Stalin's rise to power. The documentary seemed impartial enough, exposing negative and positive features of the dictator. I got astonished to find out that he died owning only 900 rubles in his bank account. I went to bed and fell asleep as soon as I put my head on the pillow.

During this semester I only have three subjects, which gives me a lot of free time. However, I have been making efforts to go to all the classes, taking notes and studying a little before the tests. By doing it, I feel better, I feel less lazy and useless. My intention is to get approved in everything on the first try, not needing the exams and, by January, already be in Cacém to get a job.

Since I have been having more free time, I have been visiting my grandmother who is in a senior home, nearby Sé. I go there every week, usually on Wednesdays. She has her own bedroom and it looks like they take good care of her, although, she complains about not being able to be in her house and being in "that hole full of old people". I have been trying to cheer her up saying that the place is not so bad, and that there are people from Lentiscais in there, but she answers that they are all fools and that it is very sad to get old.

We would talk a lot about the times when she was young and I am always impressed to hear about how hard life was back those days. She did not go to school, doesn't know how to read or write and basically started working as soon as she had learned how to walk.

MEMORIES OF A POTHEAD

Whenever she tells me things about her life, I imagine everything as in the pictures from those times, in black in white. Some other times I feel bad listening about how hard and even miserable was her life and how I am a roublemaker. Often, I feel like I'm wasting my life.

"Your grandfather would always try to save money to buy some more land and plant olives, and now, nobody wants to yield them anymore, nobody wants to work. Nowadays people live in abundance, but in earlier times there was poverty."

Usually, we talk by her bedroom window, where the view isn't good, facing a cement wall. She gives me her hands, which are big and have many signs and marks, and always talks with her wrinkled green eyes lost in the distance.

"Do you have a girlfriend yet?"

"Not yet, gramma."

"You should get a skilled girl, from Lentiscais, who are good ladies. People say that those from the city go to hustlertheque."

"It's discotheque, gramma. And there are no girls in Lentiscais anymore. Only old people."

"Yes, you are right, the world goes around at an unbelievable speed."

After the freshman's burial comes the freshman's welcoming, which happened a few days ago. In the Agricultural school, this welcoming takes place in the cafeteria. Usually I walk with the guys from the Burrow. We jump over some wire fence in our neighborhood and cross over through the school; it's quicker and we avoid the road, where there is no sidewalk and the cars always go by at high speed.

This year I decided to ask for my cousin's car to go to the party. Going and coming back at night, in the middle of the Agricultural School, was something I didn't feel like doing, even so, I believe that it was the devil's idea that made me take the car, because I should have known that I would come back drunk and unable to drive.

Besides, her car is old, a Fiat Punto that, in order to turn on, one has to open the air, wait until the air gets to the engine and then start it. It is a difficult thing to do when you are sober, but almost impossible when one is soaked up, like I did when I went back home.

And if all of those signs weren't clear indicators that I should not take the car, there was another quite important situation that my cousin highlighted many times:

"Gonçalo, by five in the morning, I want the car here, because I have to take the first train to Lisbon."

Despite all the warning signs, I took the car.

After a quiet dinner with my aunt and uncle, I drove to the Burrow to pick up the junkies, who were already kind of high, and they washed down dinner with some cheap booze. They were fighting over who would get shotgun while pushing each other away; Elói won, who tends to get angry when drunk and I was afraid he was going to break something in the car.

I parked the Fiat in the Agricultural School parking lot that would require no maneuvers to exit. Before we got into the cafeteria, someone called us to smoke some pot. We could hear the music and the buzz coming from the cafeteria. By the number of cars parked, I imagined the party would be full.

Coming out of the dark and getting into the school, the lights hurt my eyes and, since I was wearing contact lenses, I thought one of them might have fallen off without me noticing. I would see people and things in a blur, I looked at myself in the mirror and saw my cloudy face. Already! I did not even get into the party yet and was already like that!

I walked into the cafeteria with my friends and noticed many eyes turning to us. I thought they were way better dressed than I was, they had come prepared for the hunt, while I was wearing cargo pants, a jacket and a very worn-out shirt that looked like second-hand clothes or like they belonged to a left-winger from the former Democratic Republic of Germany.

I felt thirsty and made my way to the place where the drinks were being served. I ordered a beer and the guy who waited on me requested a ticket.

"A ticket? No, I don't want a ticket, the beer is still not tax-deductible?"

"No, you have to take a ticket, it's prepayment" – and pointed, without much patience, to a woman behind the cashier.

I got in the line and checked the fauna around me. I found it really depressing. The people were mostly sober, in little groups, drinking water and juices. The music was the most horrible thing imaginable, a mixture of some bad American pop, with samba and old-fashioned Spanish music. Ugh! I was going to need a lot of alcohol and pot to stand that environment! And the light! Fuck it, everything was so full of light that the irises of my eyes were burning bit by bit, in a process of ruthless torture.

I joined my friends, already with a beer in my hand. The group was getting bigger, the crew of junkies from the Agricultural School was gathering up. The clan settled in one of the corners of the cafeteria, there were a lot of us. We are a kind of sect where only the ones who belong to *Legalize it* can join. It's mostly people that tend to courses related to Environment and Forestry, who wear rags like mine, that look second hand, but I'm sure that, in some cases, they buy their clothes in trendy stores. We, the *Legalize it* crew, look at the rest in a superior fashion as if we are better than them, but, deep down, our behavior is just for show. Actually, we are afraid of not being accepted by them. The ones who don't smoke pot do not belong to the group, although we are so comprehensive and tolerant that we would accept the others. As long as they are fanatic environmentalists like us and would listen to alternative music and watch European movies. In the majority they are people from the city, but many are from the suburbs, like me.

On the other side of the cafeteria, there were our antithesis: the dapper dans and the preppies. They are mostly from the Agricultural courses and Animal Production. They are from the south and try to give off the appearance that they are farmers and have big ranches, however, the majority don't even have a pot to piss in. They wear trendy clothes, listen to Paco Banderas and Spanish stuff and like bullfights. It is a group that cares a lot about looks and doesn't smoke pot, but they drink like there is no tomorrow. Some, on the low, talk bad of the 1974 revolution and vote for the catholic right-wing.

Someone called to go outside and smoke some hash.

"Yes, please, this light is driving me blind."

From this point on, there was a lot coming and going from the beer counter to the group of junkies and the garden of the school where we were smoking our devil's cigarette.

At some point, I was getting in the cafeteria to gather up my group, when Isaura appeared in front of me, with an unfriendly face.

"Look, I need to talk to you. Please, don't lie to me, is it true what people say happened at Ti Jorge's?"

In the beginning, I didn't get it, it seemed to me she was talking in Hiligaynon, a language spoken in the south of the Philippines. What happened at Ti Jorge's? She seemed upset. For sure she was already kind of drunk.

"What happened at Ti Jorge's? I don't understand."

"Don't play stupid. You and some lady in the bathroom at Ti Jorge's."

Oh! Right, now I was not so adrift anymore. I had found out why she was upset, she was probably jealous. But who told her? Certainly not Joey. Madeiras was in another galaxy, barely aware of what was going on. Gasolines, that asshole! That dumbass had let the cat out of the bag. Well, it is not that bad anyway, in the end this is kind of good for my reputation. An irresistible stallion, an enchanting Don Juan.

"So, is it true or not?"

"Oh! Yes, yes, it is true."

Her face turned very red and she said angrily:

"I want my CD, as soon as possible!" – and rushed out.

CD? What CD? I made some titanic effort to remember what CD she might have given me, and remembered it was Daniela Mercury, the album *Rice and Beans*. She clearly didn't know my taste, otherwise, she would never have lent me that musical outrage. Moreover, the songs in this album play ceaselessly in the nights of Castelo Branco; when I'm too soaked I even dance to them, but at home, sober, I almost puked when I tried to listen to it and I left it in some dark and dirty corner of my bedroom.

In a given moment I went to the bathroom and coming out I bumped into Cláudia. A lady from the same year as me and who curiously also flunked physics. Cláudia is that kind of person who loves to talk about her life and never listens to you. She also belongs to the *Legalize it* Crew and began to tell me about her current life. The topic really did not interest me at all, but since I was a little dizzy, I leaned against the wall and allowed her to finish her monologue. While she was speaking, I remembered that she always behaved like a chameleon. When she got in, she was an exemplary newbie, she would always go to the prank and to the night bars to be with the veterans. Afterward, she joined the group of preppies and wore trendy clothes and an expensive coat. Although she is from the north, she would force a southern accent, she belonged to the group of the rich ladies or at least tried to. Then she started going out with a vegetarian, left the preppies and started to hang out with us, smoking hash and wearing rags bought in fine stores. She became an extreme left-winger, a vegetarian and anti-prank.

"Wanna know, Gonga, now I paint."

My mind was really shortened and I thought she meant some building or construction site, like her boyfriend did.

"Oh, yes, at some building?"

"Building? No, I am learning to paint in an art school."

Then I laughed out loud because I thought she was a building painter and it would have never occurred to me that she could be an artist. She left me laughing alone and did not ask any questions, not even how I was doing. Typical of her.

When I put myself together, I went to the door of the cafeteria to gather with the horde of junkies. There was no one from my crew. Where would they all be? I went to the garden to check if they were in the dark smoking a joint. I did not see them, there were couples having fun, but none of my people. Had they all gone away already? But how long had I been listening to Cláudia? I looked at the clock: it was four in the morning. My cousin's voice sounded in my head, I had to get the car back to her by five.

I went to the car, with a beer glass in my hand and a cigarette in my mouth. It was really cold. I got in the car, opened the air, waited for a little while, and started it, but the engine did not turn on. I did the process one more time and then again, but nothing. Not a bit of noise would come from the engine.

"Oh, no, I am screwed, this old carcass will not start and I will have to tell my cousin".

I took the cell, but there was no credit. It's so hard to be poor! Again, I was trying to make the car work. Maybe on the fifth try I did it. Right, I'm safe. Although, when I picked my foot up, the car would die. There was something I was doing wrong, but I had no discernment to think calmly. I noticed that I had to always be stepping on the gas to keep the engine working. I was ready to leave. Despite that, I noticed that some dew had fallen and I could not see through the windshield. Easy thing, I turn the wiper on and trouble solved. In every car I have ever been in, the wiper is a handle near the wheel. It is not like that in that jalopy. There were two handles, one for the turn signs and another for the lights. It took me a while to try all of the handles and buttons that there were. I found the horn, the four flashing lights, but nothing of the damned wipers. Some days later, my cousin told me it was near the panel, a little hidden bar. As I would not find it, I took my hand out and cleaned the much I could, while stepping on the gas, because if I took my foot off of it, it was possible that the car would not turn back on. There was still a little bit of beer and I threw it on the windshield to take off some of the dew. I did not have the minimal conditions to drive a car, but I had no other option so I went on. I could not stop, otherwise, the car would die. I went around the school, very slowly, bumping a lot, and got in the road of Senhora de Mércoles. Since I had only been able to partially clean the windshield, I was driving with my head out of the window to check if there was no other car coming around so I wouldn't kill anybody. Moreover, I had the contact lenses on that were already dry and blurred my vision instead of helping me. I went on slowly, heard some voices, later on it came to my knowledge that Boni had seen me and yelled, asking for a ride. According to what he told me later, the Fiat passed by him very slowly, bumping and I had my head out like a dog.

 I got to the crossroads, to my right there was my village – the neighborhood of Boa Esperança – and to my left, it was downtown. I, obviously, should have turned right, with no need to stop or make a sharp turn. Anyways, there was a car coming behind me and I got nervous. Those were cops, for sure! Everything was lost, I would be without my driver's license, the car would be apprehended, my cousin would miss the train. I stopped at the crossroads where it was not necessary. I took my foot off the gas and the car died. The other vehicle remained behind me, waiting for me to start the car. I asked God and all the Saints for some help in this difficult time. I opened the fucking air, did the process all over again and the car started and I made a sharp turn so poorly that I got in the wrong hand and almost hit a car that was parked there. The car that was behind me turned in the opposite direction, but I imagine he must have been astonished by my driving abilities.

    I drove the car around my neighborhood, passed by the Burrow and, some fifty meters beyond, there was my uncle's. I parked the car. I got out of the car, confirmed that there was no scratch, it was intact, I could barely believe it! This must be the work of God. Providence had escorted me through those two or three kilometers. I swore, that same moment, that I would never drive a car drunk again. I went to sleep. The next day, my cousin complained that the hood smelled like beer. I didn't want to tell her the story.

Weekend in Mira-Sintra – Monday, December 11th, 2000

Another train trip between Lisbon and Castelo Branco, another trip in which I take the time to write down the latest happenings. Two ludicrous episodes deserve to be highlighted. The first one happened last weekend when I decided to visit my childhood friends in Mira-Sintra. The other is that, after months without getting some, I have finally gotten laid.

We shall begin with this weekend: when I was coming home to the beautiful Cacém on Friday, I was thinking that New Year's Eve was already close by and I did not know where to spend it. Friday, I was with Rodas and Nice and they suggested we should go to Lisbon, have dinner in some *fado* house, walk around the High Village and end up in the Looks Disco. A very interesting plan, although, it seems to be kind of inappropriate for the state of my pockets.

I wondered about the possibility of going to Mira-Sintra instead. It would certainly be cheaper. Hanging around the shack smoking hashish and drinking beer, listening to some heavy metal from the '80s. I decided to pay them a visit Saturday night.

I always have doubts about taking the car. If I take it, I cannot drink and if I don't, I have to take like a three-kilometer walk, which might be risky in the delinquent night of Cacém.

I called Miguel.

"Yep."

"Miguel, it's Gonga."

"Hi, how's everything?"

"All good, are you going to be around tonight?"

"Sure, show up, asshole."

"Yeah, sure. Are you going to Cacém afterward or is the plan sticking around over there?"

"We stick around over here, bro. At first..."

"OK, by nine I'm in Pereira's Coffee."

If the idea is to stay there, it would be better to take the car.

I put on a Fun Lovin' Criminals cassette, I had to rewind it a little to listen to the song I wanted: *Back on the Block*. For me this is the song that represents coming back to my origins, in the neighborhood where I was born, Mira-Sintra. I like this band a lot, it is possibly my favorite right now. They are unknown in Portugal, but some years ago they were here for a festival, as a secondary band, but since I didn't have any money I couldn't go. They play a sound style that I think represents my vibe, or I want to think it is my vibe: a suburban guy, born in a housing project neighborhood, a rascal, even a little bit of a delinquent, who is always at the limit of what is morally allowed.

By the time I arrived at my old neighborhood, I parked the car far from A Street, I did not want to bump into Pauley, like the last time.

I got into Pereira's coffee, and a man asked after my parents. I was nice to the gentleman and ordered a coffee and lit up a cigarette. A little later Gypsy showed up, whose name is actually Bruno, but since one of his parents is from the gypsy ethnicity, everybody calls him Gypsy. I like him a lot even though he is two years younger than me. He is quite a nice guy, also very unlucky, a lot of surreal things happen to him.

"What's up, Gonga?"

"Hi, Gypsy, what's up? Is everything ok?" – we had a hug.

"Sure, brother, always fine, and you, nutcase? Did you come to see your friends?"

"That's what it seems. Where's the rest of the gang?"

"They must be coming around. What about Castelo Branco?"

"All good, always on the groove, you know, right? Anything new?"

"Nothing, everything is quite the same. Check it out, Miguel and Pelé."

Bit by bit the bunch of scumbags was gathering up. The coffee house was always full, Benfica was playing with a random team, but our crew doesn't really care for ball.

It had been a while since I'd seen Pelé, there has been some improvement lately, the small boy that he has always been, now looks like a big guy.

"So, and Marco?" – he asked me.

It is a usual question and that already annoys me. Me and Marco would always hang around together, we were inseparable friends. Until one day he got himself a girlfriend and disappeared.

"Well, I haven't been seeing him."

"Yeah, he comes over to see the grandparents, but not often. And he looks very different!"

I did not want to keep on the subject, because I always get sad. He used to be my best friend all my life, now my parents' house is only 200 meters from where he lives, but we rarely talk. Earlier, when I would come from Castelo Branco, I would call him to check if he wanted to do something and he would always answer that he had some plans with the girlfriend and with other couples. They go to shopping centers and talk about buying a house and having children. It is depressing! He only comes to me when he and the girlfriend have some altercation, then he hangs around with me and unburdens and it makes me think our friendship is going to recover. Although, it is a short time of sunshine, and when they makeup, I am forgotten again. However, observing Marco's behavior now, through time, I see that is what he was always looking for: steady work, a girlfriend with plans to buy a house and have children. But why so soon? He is only

21 years old! One day he confessed to me that his biggest fear was to be alone when he got old. But why does he not give a shit about me anymore? Fuck, we were almost brothers!

"Let's go and have a smoke?" – I asked, with a low voice, to Gypsy.

"We'll go soon, let's wait for Mota" – he said to me with a complicit smile.

Mota was always the leader of the group, not that he is the strongest or the most intelligent, but he is smart and a boaster. I remember that when I was six years old, in the first grade, I used to sit by him in class. He would hit me almost every day and I, a mamma's boy, told my mother. She complained to the teacher and she set me with another boy, who had lice, but at least would not hit me.

"Mota is here!" – Miguel announced.

"So, guys, what's up? Only gangsters here! Gonga, you're back to the base?"

"Always. I cannot live without you guys."

"Yes, yes, you are a phony! Oh, Lord Pereira, give me a coffee and a piece of cake for my dinner."

"So, only business and you don't even have time for dinner?" – I asked.

"You bet."

Mota moves around the neighborhood as if he is the captain of a boat, like he is the lord of the manor. He knows everybody, everybody jokes around with him, but always with respect, he does not take shit from anybody. Mota is really ugly, with a long face and he is very thin; he looks a lot like Skeletor. Besides that, his front teeth are either rotten or have disappeared. He wears a short ponytail, with the hair very stretched and visible dandruff. Reminds me of the character of Jesus Quintana, played by John Turturro in *The Big Lebowski*.

As soon as Mota finished his "dinner", we went for a joint in the old mill that is currently being refurbished and is used for school visits. It seems, currently on Saturdays, the city hall performs guided visits inside the place and there is always a man making flour. Around the mill, they have built access facilities: staircases, sidewalks and many walls. So much cement along with the old mill made of rocks is kind of shocking, however, possibly the city hall did not have money for more. On the walls there is a lot of graffiti, the majority reads: "Mills Boys", which are us, the lads from the neighborhood, the lads that were born on those streets around the mill.

Earlier, to get to the mill, we had to climb a steep hill that had only one clay path, and it would become muddy in the winter. Behind the mill, there was an empty land that we, the Mills Boys", transformed into a soccer field with two goals made from eucalyptus branches.

"Someone make me a filter and get me a rolling paper"– Gypsy asked, while burning the hashish.

"I will give you the pall." – I said.

"Have you already been to the shack today, Miguel?" – Mota asked.

"I did, Quim and Teixeira were there."

"Someone should set that shit on fire with both of them inside."– Pelé stated with disgust.

"What? Teixeira didn't go to work? Miguel, did you hear it, shit?"

Mota asked Miguel, but he had the playdough in his hand and did not pay much attention.

"Yep, true, he didn't go to work. I think he had an altercation with the boss."

"Fuck it, that dude is a scatterbrain, he is already 30 years old and fucks up everything."

"Each person is the way they are, nobody is perfect, we all have flaws, now give that joint to Mota" – he laughed and spit on the floor.

"Oh Gonga," - Pelé seemed mad – "...but am I not right?"

"I think you shouldn't drink anymore. You are starting to sound like a gossipy old lady."

We passed by the old mill and went through the old soccer camp, by now it was already back to being empty land, with creeping grass. The new generation of kids would not use this site as a soccer camp.

I noticed some improvement in the shack since the last time I was here. There was a path with stairs and even a rail. The entrance was wider and they had put a little light outside. Mota knocked on the door loudly.

"Who is it?" – a voice from inside asked.

"It's the feds" – Mota answered with his eyes already red and a dizzy smile.

Inside, the shack was dimly lit. There was a table in the center and around it they had put some benches and some old sofas that, for sure, they had taken from the garbage. There were some people there. Quim was at the head of the table as if he was a patriarch. They say now he is the biggest drug dealer in Cacém. I don't trust him, he's a dangerous fellow, but he is always holding, even when the market is dry. So, sometimes I buy some from him. His wife, who is pregnant, was by his side, the only lady in the place. Also, Teixeira, Jajão and Aloísio were there. They were playing cards and listening to AC/DC. I took a seat next to Aloísio, who is my age while the others have all already crossed over 30 and I don't trust them much.

On a regular weekend night, around 20 lads might drop by, the smell of hashish is intense and every 10 minutes someone makes a joint. It is forbidden to consume other kinds of drugs in the shack, but I suspect the older guys hit some cocaine and heroin every chance they have.

"So, Gonga, 'round here?"

"Looks like so. 're you ok, Aloísio?"
"Yep. How are things around Castelo Branco?"
"It's cold as hell."
"But have you been getting lucky?"
"With the girls?"
"Yep."
"Nothing at all, I'm an ugly, poor junkie. None of them want me."

We started laughing and I noticed that Aloísio's front teeth were getting rotten too. When we were kids, he was the one who would get good grades, played soccer well, he was even good-looking, with blond hair and green eyes, but now, like the rest of the group, he worked in construction sites and was sleazy about his looks.

"Well, guys, I brought some hash from Castelo Branco" – and I gave a portion of hashish to Mota to make a joint.

Mota did not say anything, he already knows I am a disaster at making playdough.

They started talking about work, almost all of them work for the same boss, some kind of southern civil contractor. I was idle, it is a subject that I don't care for at all and I wished to go back to Pereira's coffee and drink some beers.

"Hey, Gonga, you had a future with the ball" – Aloísio said to me.

"Me! Fuck you, I couldn't play. I was a great crude."

"I'm not sure about that, you used to do some good organizing in the game, you had a personality in the field."

"Yep, but I lacked the most important thing: talent."

The conversation quickly died. The subject went from buildings to cars and bikes, almost all of them like high speeds. I started to feel a little uncomfortable in that site, like a fish out of the water.

"Miguel, let's drink some beer at Pereira's?"

I always ask Miguel because he is the one who likes beer the most.

"Eh, well, I don't know, I'm too high."

"With these eyes I can't go in there" – Mota said.

"No, this is psychological"- I tried to convince him.

"Fuck, I wish, I'm really fucked."

In the end, nobody wanted to go and we all stayed there. Bit by bit I noticed that I did not belong to the group anymore, that I didn't care for their conversation. Spending all night smoking weed and talking about cars or buildings wasn't for me. I decided, at that moment, that I would spend New Year's Eve with Nice and Rodas. But there is one thing I have noticed that broke apart that night, my own link with my childhood friends. They lived in a different reality than me. Suddenly I caught myself watching the card game of the older guys, just like when I used to watch them play the arcade machines or at the foosball table in Oliveira's coffee. At the time I would even look at them with envy, they would always have a 20 or 50 shields coin to play, always had big bikes and even Vespas, but now, bit by bit, more of them had gotten involved with heroin and turned into pure walking garbage. And now I was there with them. This thought got me even more annoyed.

I wanted to have a cheery hang-around like it was with the Burrow about music, European movies, politics and even religion, but, where I was, the subjects were boring. I pondered if any of them, any time, would have ever thought about the meaning of life. The reason for being here? What was the purpose of the planet Earth? I have that these were practical individuals, that would live their daily lives, and never have depression or existential problems. And maybe they were right, I was the one to turn everything over, I was the one that needed to find a meaning for everything, some logic.

I decided to leave.

"I'm going to the bathroom, be right back" – I said and left.

Once I was outside, I breathed the fresh air of the eucalyptus grove and took a piss in the dark. Afterward, instead of going back in, I went walked away. Again I walked through the old soccer field that now was just empty land, went down to the old mill and I thought that maybe, as the field and the mill, everything changes, everything modifies and I too was not the same boy that would play in that field and in the mill, I had changed and my friends did too. It is possible that I will not come back to the neighborhood very soon.

I got in the car, I looked at myself in the mirror and saw how pale I was and with red eyes. I started the car and the Fun Lovin' Criminals jumped up all screechy. I did not feel like listening to their grooves. I turned the radio off. I made my way in silence, sad, passing through the different streets of Cacém, where the urbanizations are huddled one over the other, everything full of inscrutable graffiti and full garbage containers.

Anyway, not everything is sad, not everything is fate. Last Tuesday, the Lord, in all his mercy, heard my prayers and gave me some candy fallen from Heaven. After some months without getting laid, I have finally made it with a lady again.

I was in my room, studying for a test that was coming soon in Environmental Impact Analysis. My cell rang, it was an unknown number.

"Yes."

"Hello, I'm Rita's friend, I don't know if you remember me."

Truth to tell, she might have introduced herself and said her name, but I do not remember. Indeed, I had to make some effort to remember who Rita was and connect her to the woman from Ti Jorge's bathroom.

"Ah, yes, Rita."

"Yes, she gave me your number and asked me to talk to you."

"Ah, right..." - this was odd.

"Can we meet?"

"Ok, no problem..."

She told me she had a car and would show up at the Society, around four in the afternoon.

I took a while to choose an outfit for the date, I wore a black shirt I borrowed from my cousin Toxic, I think it fits me well. I put on my old leather jacket and headed to the Society.

I took a seat strategically in one of the corners of the coffee, I wanted to have some privacy. Someone opened the Society's door, my expectations rose and an old lady walked in. Anyways, who was I waiting for? What did Rita's friend look like? I did not remember seeing her with any friends. And what kind of conversation were we going to have? Maybe, she might want to know about my feelings for her friend. Or tell me some personal subject about Rita, some trauma or disease.

I was waiting, flipping through the pages of the newspaper absently. A short young woman got in, dressed in black, looking for someone. Would it be her? I had never seen her before. As soon as our eyes crossed, she smiled slightly and came in my direction.

"Hello, how are you?" – she kissed me twice, took off the jacket and sat by my side.

"Well, fine and you?"

I looked at her carefully and, for sure I had never seen her before, at least not sober. She had quite a beautiful face, small, round, and her nose was kind of haughty. Her eyes and hair were light-brown. Anytime she would laugh, one could see she had small white teeth, and two canines were overlayed, but it looked good on her. She was curvier than her friend Rita. She had many cheap rings and childish bracelets. She had a strong vanilla scent, and had possibly dropped the perfume on herself. She had long nails, sharp, painted in light blue.

"So, you also study education? To be a language teacher?"

"Yes, I am studying to be a Portuguese and German teacher."

"German, ouch, that is hard!"

"Yes, it's complicated. My dream would be to study Russian, but there is no graduate program in Portugal."

"Russian? Why?"

"I am a great fan of Russian literature. I don't know if you know Nabokov, Tolstói and Dostoiévski?"

"God bless you" – I said, laughing.

"Excuse me?"

"No, you said some weird Russian names and it sounded like you were sneezing, that's why I said God bless you..." - I got a little awkward, she did not understand the joke and I had never heard of those Russians. – "It was a joke."

"Ah, yes, yes..." - she gave me a plastic smile. – "There are books of theirs in the city library of Castelo Branco."

"Is there a city library here?" - I started laughing again, and she did not care. – "It was another joke...".

That was not going well, I changed the subject.

"Would you like to drink anything?"

"Yes, a beer."

Good. I thought she was my kind of person, no teas or natural juices. Let the alcohol come!

"Teodoro, bring two cold ones when you can" – I yelled.

"I take it, you don't really like to read."

"I do, right now I am reading the *Gospel According to Jesus Christ* by Saramago. Lately, I have been reading Buddhist books, about Tibet and the Dalai Lama. That subject fascinates me."

"Ah, yes and why?"

Normally, it is not a subject I like to discuss with strangers, but I told her I have always had existential questions and, after the death of my two grandparents, I tried to find some answers in religion. I read many books about Tibetan Buddhism and found in them some logic, so for this reason I consider myself a Buddhist. She seemed interested in the theme.

"Then that is why you go around the Agricultural School with a notebook that says: Free Tibet."

What? How does this girl know about it? She goes to a different school and I didn't remember ever seeing her before. Indeed, I didn't even know her name. Who could tell me that she wasn't a German or Russian spy coming from some future like in *Terminator.*

"Yep..." - this was getting odd.

The beers arrived and Teodoro threw me a weird glance, like: "she's in the bag".

Then I wondered how I would react if any element of the Burrow came in? If they would sit at our table or another?

"And do you think someday they will have independence back?"

"Who?"

"Tibet."

"Ah, yes, it's possible. When the Chinese regimen falls down. The action pro-Tibet is gathering up more and more people."

The conversation went on about Buddhism, then we talked about the slight downturn for Catholicism in the west, but we never talked about Rita. Teodoro brought us more beer.

At some point, she went to the restroom. I thought about going through her bag or the pockets of her jacket for some form of identity. I pondered, hesitated and she came back.

"And music, what do you listen to, Gongas?"

"Gonga" – I corrected.

"Yes, what kind of music do you listen to?"

"I like many styles, but now I'm in a hip-hop wave."

"That is horrible! Black people music."

Ouch, already showing racist prejudice.

"In Cacém we listen to it a lot."

"Cacém? That is in Lisbon, right? I hate the Lisbonites, they are so conceited."

Well, what matters is that she was curvy, otherwise, I would have left already.

"Cacém is in the suburbs."

"Lisbon suburbs, right?"

"Yes. And where are you from? You have a northern accent."

"I don't have an accent" – she said annoyed. – "I'm from Carrazeda de Ansiães."

"Ouch, God bless you. Do you have a cold?"

"How unschooled! It's a village way more beautiful than Cacém, in the district of Bragança."

I thought it would be better to come back to the subject of music.

"And what do you listen to?"

She told me about Evanescence and some other gothic metal that are around. At this point, two more beers came and Teodoro passed behind her and made me a sign like: "she is in love".

I wondered about this possibility and thought it totally out of line, although, she seemed interested in something more, maybe some flirting, some fumbling. Because for what it seems, she did not come for Rita, she came to get to know me better. Maybe I would rather invite her home.

"Do you have any guilty pleasures?" – she asked.

"Guilty pleasures? What are those?"

"A pleasure in listening to some music or watching a movie that, in a general manner, is seen as corny."

"Ah, yes... I like Knight Rider, but the version that is dubbed in Brazilian Portuguese."

"Oh, that is really depressing."

"Gimme all ya got, kit! And what is your guilty pleasure?"

"I like Michael Jackson."

"Black or white version?"

She finally laughed. I tried my luck:

"Would you want to come to my house and see my sound system?"

"Sure, just let me finish my beer."

We left the coffee and made the short path to my home in silence. I tried to start a conversation, but it would only occur to me to talk about how cold it was and I preferred to remain quiet.

We arrived home and it seemed there was no one there. I got in my room and showed her the small stereo system that I have, with CD's and cassettes. One did not have to be very keen to notice she was not really interested in the subject and looked carefully around my messy room.

"What is this?"

Over my bed, there was a size A4 sheet of paper where I wrote: **Kzen – Born in the Ghetto**. It was a self-motivation statement. I got closer to her and answered:

"Kzen means Cacém."

"Ah" – she made a gesture of lack of interest and then gazed at me.

I decided to kiss her. If she said no, I didn't have anything to lose. Indeed, I did not know her, did not even know her name. She not only gave in, but she also kissed me back.

"Close the blinds. Turn the lamp on. Turn on the heat. Take your clothes off."

She took her clothes off and I noticed she was too thin. I prefer the chubbier ones, but in times of war (or hunger), one does not clean up the weapons. She shoved herself into my bed. I did the same.

"Do you have a condom?" – she asked.

"Yes, I do."

I brought a box when I came to Castelo Branco and I thought I was going to use them all in three days, but it had already been three years and there are still some left. I even thought they could have expired.

I fought with the condom packing to get it opened. It was hard. She took the wheel as well as the condom and put it on my "killer vulture" while my arms were hanging like a scarecrow.

We started the toil, I was on top doing some kissing. She grabbed my buttocks hard and then my back. The works were going well, she started to moan in pleasure, but the moaning almost turned into shouting, which distracted me, for I did not know if there was someone at home. My aunt and uncle live downstairs and they could be around. I pondered about asking for some restraint, but I did not have the courage and kept on the bustle. She was asking "faster" and I, like a good disciple gave her some more effort. She was screaming louder and louder and it was obvious that we were going to arrive soon to the climax. Then, at this very moment, she stuck her nails on my back in such a way that I screamed too, but in pain.

"Ouch, sorry, I have lost my mind" – she said, still gasping.

"You, your mind, and me, a load of my back."

"Let me see. Ouch, it is a little red. Do you have alcohol or povidone?"

"Alcohol is what we have the most of, but ethyl alcohol I doubt and povidone, not even any leftovers."

I got dressed and went downstairs, where my aunt and uncle live, to look for some povidone. I found a bottle and cotton. There was nobody there.

I came back up and she was already dressed. When she wiped the wounds with the cotton they burned a lot and I complained about the pain.

"It's not so bad, Gongas. For a guy from Kzen that is nothing."

I looked at her and smiled and she smiled back at me and, in this spare of a moment, I noticed that both of us were thinking that maybe we could even get to know each other better. Maybe we could go out and be a couple. However, the moment was gone, I put my shirt on and she headed to the door.

"Are you leaving? We can have a beer and smoke a joint."

"Sure, we can."

We went to the living room, which is beside my bedroom, where there is a television without a remote, from the time back when there were only two channels. I commented that next semester I was going back to Cacém because I was only going to take one subject. She told me she did not want to go back to live in her land, she had the intention of going to Oporto or going to Germany for some years, to improve in the language.

The conversation was kind, one could say we had some chemistry until my housemates came around. Messy, they came in the house like elephants, and as soon as they saw her, they made childish grimaces and she got scared. She finished the beer quickly.

"Well, I'm going" – she said.

"Already! Wait, have one more" – I insisted.

"No, maybe next time."

We stood facing each other. I thought of kissing her, I faltered, she noticed that hesitation and went down the staircase almost running. I wondered if I should have said something or gone after her.

My back still hurts and these past few days I have been sleeping with my belly down. Now, every time I sit down, I lean my back slowly. Although, the pain was really worth it. It is a shame that there are no more ladies like this one, that show up from nowhere and treat me like a sexual object. I pondered about calling her a couple of times, but since I don't know her name, neither do I know what she told Rita, the best thing is to wait and see them again on some night at Ti Jorge's or at the Alternative. Women are really bizarre beings.

New Year's Eve 2000/2001 – Sunday, January 7th, 2001

I made plans with Nice and Rodas to spend New Year's Eve with them. I was disappointed Maria João didn't want to come with us, but she preferred to have dinner with her parents and later to be with the boyfriend. A long time ago Maria and I would go together to the High Village and come back late in the dawn, always talking and creating philosophies about crucial themes of human existence.

The plan for New Year's Eve was: leaving Cacém early, by train, because we wanted to drink so it would be better not to take the car, we would go straight to the High Village, have dinner in a *fado* restaurant, spend midnight in a Beer House and later get a cab and go to Looks Disco. Yeah, that plan failed big time.

It looked like it was going to rain, but since walking around with an umbrella is for old people, I did not even raise the question of taking one. I spent a lot of time thinking about what clothes to wear; it's in those moments that I miss having a girlfriend to give me hints about clothing. I decided to go all in black, shirt, pants, boots and I put on my old leather jacket. I looked in the mirror and found it stylish. perhaps I would meet a pretty girl. That would be cool! It would be a great beginning for 2001. However, I know from my own experience, that one must not raise their expectations too high for this night, because, in a general manner, it's just one more night revelry, nothing more.

Rodas invited a friend of his, called Victor. He is a weird guy, he acts as if he's important and intelligent because he studies medicine and thinks he belongs to the cream of society. He does not talk to you, he is teaching you. Conceited is maybe the best adjective to describe him. The good thing is he is also shy, so he seldom speaks and never about his private life.

We took the train, already late, in Cacém station. We did not have reservations and started to wonder if it would be hard to find a *fado* house available. We were happy, feeling like we were on some spree.

When we arrived at Lisbon downtown, a drizzle began. We went up in the direction of Carmo Square and, on the way up, we saw an open Chinese restaurant.

"Well, should we go in this one?" – I asked.

"Weren't we going to the fado house?" – Nice complained.

"Have you checked the time? You wanna walk around, in the rain, looking for a place?"

The other two agreed and we went to the Chinese restaurant. We asked for a table for four and he took us to a table nearby the television. The last episode of Big Brother was on.

"Eh, well, let's see Zé Maria winning the contest."

"Go, Zé Maria" – Rodas howled.

We ordered and while we were waiting, we started to discuss the show.

"There's a before and after Big Brother. The soap operas have already lost their audience. In the future there will be only reality shows" – I predicted.

"They are already casting the second Big Brother."

"No, but this is going to get worse. They've opened Pandora's box! In the second one there will be even more scum. People who like to fight, girls that want to tramp with the first guy they see. There will be only human garbage."

"But this one is already only human garbage, now" – Victor said.

"Yep, but for this one they have cast kind of normal people, in the future there will only be pimps and whores." – I foresaw once more.

"Well, and what about Zé Maria? What is he going to do with all that money?" – Rodas questioned.

"All that money? It's only 20 thousand bucks. And a share goes to the Government. Afterward, you'd want to buy a car or make a down payment on a house and then end up with nothing."

"Yea, but they'll surely do advertisements, television or radio shows." – Nice said.

"I don't know. I agree that he has to exploit his 15 minutes of fame now, but within like ten years, nobody will remember him." – another omen of mine.

"He'll have to know how to sell himself the best he can, otherwise he'll end up working on construction sites. I believe when he leaves the house there will be many vultures trying to fool him." – Victor said.

"He seems frail to me." – Nice said like she was even worried about Zé Maria.

The restaurant was full, the food was taking too long and me and Rodas decided to go outside and smoke a joint. We sat on a bench, which was a little wet, by the Carmo Square, across from us was the headquarters where the bullets from the revolution of 1974 still remain. I said that I would have loved to be in the revolution, that during revolutions there is always a lot of hope for the future. He agreed and asked me if I would go on Big Brother. After thinking a little I said that I would if I could watch movies, read and smoke pot.

"Do you think Zé Maria is from the *Legalize it* crew?"

"Yes, without a doubt" – I answered.

We came back to the restaurant, but now, when we got in, everything seemed to me jollier and more colorful. The rest of the clients looked happy and the buzz we were hearing was even nice. I sat by the table, Nice and Victor, who do not smoke, would look at us with a little bit of judgement; however, I was happy and at the bottom of my heart, I wished everyone a 2001 full of health and joy.

The plate that I ordered came right away: rice with chicken and almonds sided with a quite light Chinese beer, that would pair well.

A little before midnight we headed to the High Village, more precisely to the Beer House. When we arrived there, there were a lot of people and we had to drill into the middle of the crowd to make some space to dance.

The Beer House is a mythical place to me. I started going there when I was 18 years old with Maria João, Nice, Marco, Bruno, etc.., bit by bit my friends were changing, many had left the group, others have quit going to the High Village, but I still go there. The music is excellent, there is always some contemporary rock'n'roll. The beer is cheap, the owners of the establishment are friendly and ask what kind of music we want to listen to. I have many stories in that House.

There was a swarm of people in the place, so after ordering beers, me and Rodas went outside to make some playdough. The environment outside was excellent, a crowd was going up and down the streets of the village, a huge mess that contrasted with the weather. It was raining again. We found shelter under an awning and we were chit-chatting with a group of German tourists that were there. They were smoking and we shared the joints. Before we noticed, it was already midnight and the joy broke out, people were beating on pots by the windows and fireworks exploding in the air, whistles, screaming, fuss.

"Hurray! Happy New Year!"

We were all screaming, we hugged the Germans and we came back inside the Beer House which had a little more space by then. Nice and Victor kept dancing and seemed quite sober. Starting then, there was a lot of coming and going to the counter to pick up beer and request some song, going outside for some joints and come back for some dancing. Somebody told us that Zé Maria had won the contest, I was glad.

The Beer House was getting empty and so was the High Village. Where did everybody go?

"Let's take a taxi to Looks" – said Nice.

"There are no taxis, we have to go to Chiado."

I was already too high, and felt neither like going to the disco nor walking in the rain. But since it seemed everybody wanted to go, I did not say anything.

When we arrived at Chiado there was nothing. The taxi square was empty. Somebody had the magnificent idea of going all the way to Terreiro do Paço because there, for sure, would be taxis.

The rain gave no quarter and when we arrived at the Terreiro do Paço we were soaked. The Commerce Square was, as usual, full of cars parked in the middle. Nearby the archway of Augusta Street there were two buses parked. The site where the taxis used to be was empty. Not a single taxi. We remained by the archways of the Commerce Square beside some Finance department.

"Looks like it will not be easy to get a taxi" – Victor said.

"Then what should we do?" – Nice asked. – "We cannot walk all the way there, we'll get even more soaked."

"We wait for a taxi to pass by."

"Meanwhile we may as well legalize the thing, Rodas."

"I agree, let's smoke another one."

One thing is for sure, I was glad to stick around that place. I did not feel like paying more than 5 bucks to get in the disco, which should be crowded, with extremely loud music. I have prayed that no taxi would show up. One could see that Rodas, as well as me, was having fun, however, Nice and Victor were bored. Indeed, Nice was wearing a skirt and high heel boots and it was cold as hell and she was already in pain in her legs and feet from standing up.

"Comrade Bolshevists, it seems we will be stuck here."

"Comrade Bolshevists? Don't say that you are a commie, Gonga!"

"I don't know if you guys want me to tell you the story of my life?"

Victor and Nice did not even answer, they were living an enormous lie.

"Would you please, mister Gonga" – Rodas answered enthusiastically.

"Right, comrades, you convinced me. When I was around ten, I went to the book fair with my father and asked him to buy me a book about the USSR. The book was written by a person who had gone out to see how the regimen worked and would say wonders about it. I was already fond of Socialist Realism, above all, the paintings and the symbology that there was on the walls in Lisbon after the revolution. Then, by the end of the '80s, the leader of the Communist Party, made a speech in Cacém. I asked my father to take me. He is a socialist and does not really like the commies, but he took me anyway. After the speech, at the age of twelve, I decided to subscribe myself to the communist youth."

I got really enthusiastic telling this story, I am only sorry there was no stand around, to order a beer and a snack.

"The CP board in Cacém is in the center, nearby Jardas riverside; the building is falling apart it's so old, and the walls are full of propaganda. After a little hall, to the right, there is a small bar. The man in the bar told me the president of the communist youth would only come on Tuesday afternoons. On the following Tuesday, I showed up there with Marco, who did not know anything about communism and was only there because I had convinced him that being a communist was cool and radical. We were both wearing sweatshirts. The mentioned president was a lady in her twenties, but to me, at twelve, she seemed very old. She smoked a lot and asked me why I wanted to join the communist youth and what was my idea of the ideology."

Rodas was cheery listening to the story and made another playdough, while the other two were wishing it was five in the morning to go to Lisbon downtown and catch the first train back to Cacém.

"And I told her I liked Karl Marx and Lenin a lot, while deep down, I didn't know much about them, and that I did not support Stalin. She told me literally: "I'm fed up hearing people talking bad of Stalin, some other day someone compared him with Hitler, he has done good things! It is all to blame on that shitty journalist Carlos Fino, who was placed on television by the party and now has betrayed us". They gave us flyers and took us to Cacém Station to hand them out. It was hilarious. Two kids handing out propaganda to the workers coming out of the train after a day of work. By eight p.m. they took us to Mira-Sintra. My mother, who was already worried because I was missing, was as astonished as she was ashamed when she saw me coming out of a Communist Party van."

Rodas was laughing his ass off.

"Although, shortly after I decided to join the CP, the world changed. The Berlin Wall fell, the people burned down the communist symbols, and the iron curtain vanished. Then I was in doubt if I had really chosen the best party."

"Check it out" – Nice said. – "Do you know they are going to tear down the CP board?"

"Really? Why?"

"By the Polis Program. They are going to fix that area and make an enormous garden."

"It's outrageous! Gardens in Cacém? They are destroying our traditions. We do not need gardens, nor sidewalks, nor trees. We want more buildings, walls, cement, bumpy roads. No green Cacém! Comrades, are you with me?" – I said, almost shouting.

"Yes" – Rodas howled.

"So, Legalize it. Make another joint."

"Let's go" – and started to make another playdough.

"But, check it, Gonga" – Victor was talking to me and I noticed that, besides being annoyed for being there in the cold, he did not really like me. – "The village Agualva-Cacém, which will become a city this year according to some, is formed by two parts: Agualva in which we all live and Cacém which is beyond the railway. This means we live in Agualva."

"Hold it," - Nice said – "I live on the other side of the railway, I am from Cacém."

"In this case, I am for building a segregation wall between Cacém and Agualva."

"I agree, comrade" – Rodas shouted.

"A wall to separate Agualva from the Cacém scumbags, from people like Nice."

"Watch out, you are this close to taking one on the nose" – Nice threatened.

"No," - Victor said – "what I mean is that, Gonga, you can say that you are from Agualva."

"Indeed, Agualva alone even sounds good. Someone asks: "where are you from"? From Agualva. "And where is Agualva"? In the council of Sintra. It is even classy" – Rodas agreed.

"Yes, but nobody knows Agualva alone. The name is weak, it sounds like some land in the countryside with four old people. Meanwhile you say: "I am from Cacém", people right away look at you like – "Ouch, watch out with this guy, he must be of the most dangerous scum. He might have been to jail" – I said.

The night went on, we remained by the archways, the rain did not cease a bit and we saw a taxi passing by, somebody yelled, but the driver did not even look. Some drunks came around us to scrounge a cigarette. Me and Rodas kept up supporting the *Legalize it* action.

"Rodas, Legalize it."

"Right, bro. One has to Legalize the stuff, here right by the Finance office. The government has to know that we want marijuana to be legalized."

"The people gathered up shall never be defeated" – I proclaimed. – "How can this country go on if there are no taxis and it is illegal to smoke pot?"

"That looks bad, friend. Legalize it."

"In this country, the people have no voice. Moreover, we just lost Macau."

"Agreed! We have to recover Macau."

"Nobody asked the Macau people if they wanted to quit being Portuguese."

"Ah, that's true, Gonga. Legalize it. And Cabinda?"

"Cabinda?"

"Yep, Cabinda does not belong to Angola. Cabinda was some offer from a king of a tribe to Portugal. Indeed, there is the Front for the Liberation of the Enclave of Cabinda."

"Holy crap, the things you know, Rodas! Legalize Cabinda."

"Without a doubt and Olivença."

"Olivença?"

"Olivença was Portuguese, the Spanish cheated us in eighteen hundred something."

"Uh, well, Rodas, it's contaminated now. It will be like Chernobyl."

"And why's that?"

"Well, after 200 years of being Spanish, that thing would really need a serious disinfection. Maybe it would take like 20 or 30 years to recover."

"Do you think, Gonga?"

"Sure, the guys from Olivença must enjoy bullfights and that gypsy music the Spaniards enjoy. Besides that, they only eat gazpacho, watch all the movies dubbed and say U dos instead of U2."

Me and Rodas laughed so much we were on the ground.

It was almost five in the morning and Nice, as well as Victor, were crazy to go to the Lisbon Station and catch the first train up to the beautiful Cacém, or rather Agualva-Cacém. We went through Augusta Street and me and Rodas were laughing, walking in the middle of the street, under the rain, talking bullshit. We arrived at the Station and noticed it was full of suburban rabble, heading to their dens.

"Oh, Nice, there are a lot of people, you might not get a seat" – I was mocking her because I could see she was suffering from the high heel boots.

"I have to get a seat, even if I have to pay for it."

We got four seats together, the buzz in the wagons was big. The cops came by. The people tamed down.

"Uh, well, I have a huge idea. With the money he is going to get now, Zé Maria could help with the Legalize it cause."

"Completely, besides Legalize it, he could even help recover Macau, Cabinda and disinfect Olivença."

Me and Rodas still had some energy and we even pondered going for a walk around Cacém to find an opened tavern to drink a few more beers. It was not necessary to ask if Victor had enjoyed it, his face showed that it was probably one of the worst New Year's Eves of his life. Nice only wanted her bed. I think she enjoyed the night until we left the High Village and started looking for the lost taxi. I must confess that it was the best New Year's Eve that I've ever had. In all the previous ones I would make great plans and have high expectations, this time I did not expect much, indeed I even imagined myself in the disco, annoyed, however, being by the archways in the Commerce Square was a great turnaround.

Return to Kzen – Tuesday, March 20th, 2001

I have finished the three subjects I had for the first semester with no need to take any exams, therefore I could go earlier to Cacém. I took my father's car to Castelo Branco and brought a big amount of my stuff. It was a strange kind of sensation coming back to my homeland, even knowing that it was just for half a year. My objective was to get a job, save some money and take a trip abroad in the summer. I would like to go to the Netherlands, but I saw a documentary about the Way of Saint James and it seems cheap and interesting.

The huge problem I bump into is being approved in the only subject I have for this semester: physics. I am not going to attend the classes, therefore I will have to take the exam. Studying on my own does not seem very practical, so it would be best to find a tutor. However, until now I did not lift a finger regarding the subject.

I arrived near mid-January and after settling down in my old bedroom, I started looking for work. The first option was to hand in my resume at Blockbuster movie rental, which is nearby Cacém Station. From time to time I notice they are looking for people, therefore I have been there personally to talk to them. They accepted my resume and did not say anything. I started looking in the newspaper job offers, I was open to anything, except being a waiter.

Three days after handing in the resume at the movie rental, they called me from the Blockbuster in Massamá, to have an interview. I was very glad, I was sorry it was not the store in Cacém, but Massamá is quite close.

I was well dressed and combed, took the train in Cacém Station and, in the following one, Massamá, I got off and headed to the shopping center which is nearby. Blockbuster is in the outer part of the shopping center, in a store at the street level. It looks more like a village shop than a store inside a shopping center. As soon as I got in I noticed the movie rental was way bigger than the one in Cacém, twice as big possibly. I got in by the exit door and one of the employees called my attention.

"The entrance is on the other side."

"I apologize. I have an interview with Cristina."

"Oh, just a moment."

While I was waiting, I walked around the movie rental. The store was in the shape of a perfect square, on the walls there were the newest movies, in VHS as well as DVD. In the middle there were many racks, filled only with cassettes, of older movies, some classics, sorted by genre. There was a little game section and near the counter there was the popcorn and other delicacies.

A lady introduced herself as Cristina and asked me to come with her to proceed with the interview. We went in an enclosure reserved for the employees. There was a restroom and another room, kind of big, a bit messy and full of boxes. That place smelled like tobacco and sugar. I imagined the employees would go in there to smoke and that some of those boxes were for candies.

"Are you looking for work?"

"Yes, this semester I only have one subject, so I am looking for a job."

"Part-time?"

"No, full time."

That Cristina seemed old to me, not elderly, but definitely in her forties. She was a little fat, had rabbit teeth and when she spoke a gob would accumulate in one of the corners of her mouth. She was not a bit attractive.

"And would you like to work here?"

"Yes, I am a client of the Cacém rental and a constant customer, I really like the style of the store and I am a cinephile. It was my first option when I started looking for a job."

"Have you ever worked directly with the public?"

"Yes, I have worked in many bars and restaurants."

"Do you intent to stay any longer, or is it just for this semester?"

"If I like it and you like me, ma'am, I can even stay for some years."

I obviously only wanted to work until September, tops.

"Don't call me ma'am, you make me feel like an old lady. I am not much older than you. I'm only 35."

I was astonished because she looked quite aged. She was twelve years older than me and I have wondered if when I got to be her age, I would look that old myself. I preferred not to think about the subject. She started to talk about the internal rules.

"Each employee has the right to two days off, but if you prefer, you can accumulate them. You can take home 10 movies a week. The net salary is around 100 bucks. There is no cleaning lady, so we have to vacuum the carpet and the racks ourselves. The shift is seven or eight hours long with a one hour break for a meal. You always have to wear a blue T-shirt, which we will give you and a name tag. Are you interested?"

"Yes, I am."

Is that it? Am I hired?

"When can you begin?"

"Tomorrow."

"Great, bring your security card and a copy of your identity. You begin on Wednesday."

I left the store very glad, I told my parents right away and they appreciated the news too. Afterward, I went for a coffee with Maria

João, who was happy that I'd found a job so soon. Right away she said she was going to visit me to scrounge movies.

Now that I have been working for almost two months, I can analyze the good and the bad parts. The positive points are many. I really enjoy the cinematographic environment in which we live. Above all, some of the clients are great enthusiasts of the seventh art. The work itself is not hard, although it is physically tiresome since I never sit down, but one can take it well. I can spend the morning in bed, because I normally begin at four p.m., I take a one-hour break to eat and at eleven we close the store, midnight on weekends. My workmates are nice, not all of them, but the majority. The place is ideal to meet some chicks. I can see right away, if they go to the movie rental alone is because they do not have a boyfriend, and based on the movies they take I can enter a conversation. Sometimes I suggest one or another movie and I have even said: "take this one, on my bill. And later you tell me if you like it".

The negative part is the discussions with the clients that bring movies in late and don't want to pay the fees. Or that scum that only come in to steal so you have to play cop.

Now on to reviewing my workmates:

That Cristina is the boss of all the stores between Lisbon and Sintra. Rarely shows up and is a nice person. I think she likes the way I work.

The boss of the store is Ana Paula. She is a chubby lady, tall, her cheeks are always red and she has an attitude of superiority, but deep down, that is a defense mechanism to gain the respect of the employees. She does not smoke, does not drink alcohol, is an only child and very protected by her parents. Some of my workmates say she has a crush on me. I believe it might be true, she treats me differently. When I took the training with her, she was wearing too much makeup and putting off some vulgar perfume so much I was retching. Sometimes we hit each other (joking) and the darn lady is strong. I get along with her without being her friend.

Christiane is Ana Paula's right arm, she is a simple employee like me, but she is an ass kisser. She is lazy, always tries to find a way to avoid attending the clients. She does not like to close the store and always makes efforts to get the morning shift. She is friendly with me, although we do not have anything in common and quickly run out of things to talk about. She is short, very dark and skinny. Her mother is Brazilian, so she pronounces her name with a Brazilian accent. Her boyfriend is a former employee of the movie rental, a phony fellow, careless, his only intention is using other people. Both of them are short and we call them "keychains".

The person I get along with the most is Hugo. He's taller than me, a couple of years younger, wears a ponytail and he has a big build. He is quite a nice fellow, knows all the clients and half of Massamá. After Ana Paula, he is the one who has been in the store for the longest, like two years and according to what he says, he is fed up and wants to leave as soon as possible. He helped me a lot with the procedures, he knows a lot about movies, music, and belongs to the *Legalize it* crew.

The other one is Luís. He is a really ludicrous fellow. He is always playing, has a really dark sense of humor, and doesn't like the work or the clients. He just waiting to be fired. He has been working there for a year. When the bosses are not around, he plays heavy metal out loud, and some clients even complain. I feel ashamed, but he and Hugo sing and, since I do not want to be a party pooper, I do not say anything. Luís does bodyboarding; due to that has a very tanned skin and uses paraffin in his hair to turn blond. He likes to get near me and compare the colors of our complexions. By his side, I look like a ghost. He is very childish.

At last, there is a lady, called Ana, who only works weekends. She is like two or three years younger than me, short, has a bit of acne, black hair and clothing, likes metal and gothic music. She is a very nice girl, intelligent, loves movies, has a cool boyfriend, but she often cheats on him. She is also part of the *Legalize it* crew.

In my early days working there were two employees that were fired because they were stealing from the cashier. The first one is called Tico, a lad with a heavy suburban accent, tricky, dangerous, experienced. He got married to a girl, against her father's will, because they got married after being together for only a few months and Tito looks like he has just been released from jail. Still, since he is friends with Hugo, he shows up frequently and always tries to scrounge something. One night I went with Hugo to smoke pot at Tico's house, they were playing PlayStation and it was very annoying. I have never gone there again.

The other employee who was fired was Dália. A mulatta who was also stealing. She was the typical curvy mulatta with a guitar-shaped body. She had a five-year-old son and was a single mother. She would lasciviously look at me. One of the few principles I have is: "do not shit where you eat", but I was willing to skip that principle in case there was an opportunity. But she was kicked out and I have never seen her again.

I usually have my days off during the week because on the weekend there is more work. Normally, I like to begin the week vacuuming the floor and cleaning the dust from the racks in my area. This way I get my tasks fulfilled and the boss does not yell at me.

In one of the racks there is a section that says: "employee favorites". I love this corner. When I was a client, I used to watch the movies that the employees would put up and I would imagine what kind of people they were. Now there is my name and the five movies I recommended. At first, I put my favorite movies until Hugo told me:

"It is funnier if you recommend unknown movies. The movies you laid out are all too well known."

He was right, I had:
- *Pulp Fiction* by Tarantino
- *Platoon* by Oliver Stone
- *The Godfather* by Coppola
- *Annie Hall* by Woody Allen
- *The Shining* by Stanley Kubrick

So I decided to change it. I laid out more unknown movies, wanting to give off some intellectual cinephile aspect. This is my current proposal:

- *Gattaca* by Andrew Niccol – excellent science fiction movie, about obstinacy and persistence.

- *Bananas* by Woody Allen – one of the master's early movies, a political satire.

- *Rashomon* by Akira Kurosawa – to me the best movie by the Japanese director, approaching the different angles of a crime.

- *Hate* by Mathieu Kassovitz – the story of this movie takes place in the suburbs of Paris and reminds me of Mira-Sintra.

- *Pulp Fiction* by Tarantino – this one I could not replace, it is the best cinematographic work of all time.

The movie rental lacks many classics, indispensable movies that would give the house a good name, so I made a list of some 20 or 30 classics and handed it to Cristina.

"But nobody watches those movies! People want new things."

"Yes, but a big share of the new ones are pure garbage, only entertainment. There are masterpieces in this list, works of art, Cristina."

"But no one is gonna rent them!"

"Of course they are, the people who see movies as a form of art will rent for sure."

"Yes, sure, the weirdos from the neighborhood. I'll see what I can do."

For sure she has thrown my list in the garbage.

One of the things I like to do in the store is to put movies on the two televisions that are placed in the middle of the establishment. Generally, I put the movies from my list, but, sometimes, I put on something new so I can watch. The funny thing is that some people sit down on the floor to watch the movies.

They have already started to teach me to close the store. First, one has to do the accounting, make the billing report, put the money in the vault, organize all the VHS and DVDs and, obviously, close the store. Usually, Hugo is the one who does it. He is teaching me the tricks and when we close, sometimes, we smoke a joint, other times we go for a draft beer, but, most of the time, we are tired and want to go home. Sometimes he smokes a joint when he takes his dinner break, he even offers to let me join him, but I take work too seriously and I know that if I smoke I can screw up and I attract attention when I'm high.

At night when I arrive home, I eat whatever and go to my room to watch a movie – I always take some with me from the Blockbuster. I put the VHS and the kitchen television in my room. Occasionally, I fall asleep watching a movie. When I smoke a joint with Hugo, I prefer to watch a comedy or science fiction.

One thing is for sure, I've reduced my hashish consumption a lot. First, because I quit going to Mira-Sintra to buy hashish, then because my workmates, like my friends from Cacém, smoke less. Also, I have not been going out at night too often, and the times I do go out are usually in Massamá, after work, with my workmates and since I go around with my father's car, I prefer not to go crazy. I have to say that the night environment in Massamá is way better than Cacém. There are more bars open and the people are better than your average scum. It's because the neighborhoods in Massamá are newer and for the middle class. While in Cacém the neighborhoods are old and occupied by a lower-middle class. In the bars of Massamá there is a ratio between lads and ladies of 50%, while in Cacém the bars look like hose parties, there are 10 vultures for each woman.

I have not been seeing my friends in Cacém, because during the week, when I have a day off, they are at school and I work the weekends and finish late and without much will to stay outside smoking, in the cold, or going to a bar full of scums.

Coming back to my parents' house was a little bit strange, but not at all negative. Since I usually work from 3 p.m. to 11 p.m., we only see each other on my days off or on the weekends. Sometimes, they wake up in the middle of the night and as they see I am awake watching a movie, they knock at my door and we chat for a while. But mainly we just talk on the weekends. My father is always worried about me and gives me advice as if I was a ten-year-old. My mother has been tired, her work is very hard and she is over fifty. She gets sick suddenly, and frequently has insomnia. She worries about my eating habits. Often, she cooks extra food for dinner so I have something to eat for lunch the following day and to take to work. She tries to teach me quick and healthy recipes, but, to be honest, I do not like to cook and I do not pay much attention to her "classes". When I don't take food to the movie rental, I usually go to the mall, there is a Chinese restaurant, a sandwich store, a pizza place, etc., though I try to save money and I eat out only as a last resort.

One of the big changes that happened after I went to Castelo Branco is that my sister left home. One can notice a big void, there's less life in the house. She bought an apartment in Algueirão and only comes on weekends for lunch or an occasional night for dinner. It's amazing how she has accomplished all the goals she had set up. She studied in a private college and to pay for it she got a job, she pursued work in her field and after getting it she did not settle, she took tenders to City Halls until she got hired to the City Hall of Cascais. And now she's bought a new house, in a nice neighborhood, well placed. One has to bow down for what she's reached at this point. I get along with her pretty well, we talk a lot about movies and music, sometimes she goes to the movie rental to rent some movie on my bill and we chat for a while.

I enrolled myself in a gym again, but I must confess I am not really motivated. Going back to the gym after three years was weird, above all because most of the clients have changed and I do not know anybody there. Besides that, I used to go with Marco and we would work out together for hours. Now I'm alone in the mornings, most of them sleepy, and I end up feeling I do not have the same discipline anymore. I have a simple objective to gain a little muscle volume and lose a little stomach fat, which basically is summer preparation. However, many times, I stay up late watching movies and then I do not feel like waking up early to work out.

Weekend with Luísa – Thursday May 10th, 2001

I want to write about this past weekend, which I spent with Luísa, but first I have to share some news that happened at the movie rental.

The first is that Luís has left Blockbuster. He got himself fired, something we all knew was coming. He was a terrible employee, so it was only a matter of time. The bosses did not trust him and they did not even let him close the store or have the keys. However, the funniest part is that everything collapsed because he got a girlfriend. I should point out that the spirit in the store went down a little when he left, mostly from Ana and Hugo, who used to like him a lot and would laugh at his drollery. I was sorry myself; when the two of us were alone we even had some nice conversations, we almost become friends.

There is a pair of sisters that used to rent movies, called Margaret and Anaisa, who have French-ish names because, according to what they say, their parents were emigrants in France and, according to what it looks like, they are very corny. Both of them were always very friendly, they would joke around with us and chat often. At this point Luís started going out with Anaisa; truth be told, I have never paid much attention to her, but she looked like a little girl, around 16 or 17 years old and was neither ugly nor beautiful. On the other hand, her sister had called my attention. She is my age, has a beautiful face, blue eyes, light complexion and a curvy body, she is not fat or thin, she was ripe for the picking.

When the dating began, the two sisters would show up even more often to the movie rental. Luís was so in love and I must confess

I even felt a little envious of his happiness. Margaret, the older sister, would always flirt with me and was very lovely, I started to think she could be interested in something more. Indeed, she even invited me to go out with her and the loving couple and we all went to some bars in Massamá. I must say the conversations were too childish, the little couple only talks bullshit and Margaret is no scholar. Although, she was wearing some jeans that gave her an ass to put a man on his last legs. In a given moment we were alone, she told me she had ended a many year's long relationship and wanted to fall in love again, I thought it was a hint for me.

Before Luís went away from the store, I asked if he thought I would have any chance with his new sister-in-law, he said yes and encouraged me to invite her out. I thought she was already in the bag, so he gave me her cell and I called her from the store.

"Hello, Margaret, it is Gonçalo, how are you? Look, I just wanted to tell you that you have some movies with fines to pay for."

I started to laugh.

"Ah ah ah" – she said, she did not think much of the joke.

"Look, I was wondering if you would like to do something one of these days?"

"Oh! I don't know, I don't think I can."

"Oh... Right, ok, no problem, we'll talk later...".

I hung up with my mouth opened. She was so cold, so distant. After all this, had I misinterpreted her signs? Not that I am the last coke in the desert, but I doubt that she could get a nicer guy than me. While I was digesting this punch in my stomach, Luís was laughing his ass off at my dumbass face. What an asshole! He probably already knew she was going to say no, but still encouraged me to call her.

Since that day, Margaret doesn't go to the movie rental as often and when she does show up, I despise her plenty. I was fucked up, my ego was on the ground. She tries to be sweet and asks to be attended only by me, but I barely look at her and pretend not to listen. Deep down, I don't understand her behavior and I think she wanted to make me her puppet, that I would crawl for her, but she was very wrong. She had a nice ass, but not that nice.

It is in those moments that I remember my friend in high school, Pinto. He is a kind of guru regarding skirt matters. He would say wise words like: "One would rather get a no than not try" or "In a hundred years nobody is going to remember you, so forget the shame". And really this guy had not a drop of shame in his face, he would always throw the mud at the wall to check if it would stick. He must have been dissed dozens of times, but water-dropping day by day...

I am sorry we did not keep in touch. He is one of those people who's always joyful, with contagious laughter. I have never seen him sad. We were good friends in school, mostly in the last years of high school. He was a popular fellow, one of the most known in the school, I, on the other hand, was his shadow: a lad full of pimples in his face, with the oddest hairdo (I had the habit of straightening my fringe) and would be incognito. If there were people that influenced me in my teenage years, Pinto was possibly the one who did it most. He was a sportsman, didn't smoke, but did take proteins and supplements to gain muscles. He had a goal of becoming a policeman, going to the intervention brigade like his father. He didn't care for soccer, he preferred the martial arts and was a big fan of Van Damme. He would listen to Bruce Springsteen and Rod Stewart. He was a womanizer and used to say he would never be loyal to any woman. When we finished high school, we lost touch bit by bit, I left Mira-Sintra and went to Castelo Branco, he became a cop. We changed, our environments and groups of friends have changed too. The last time that I saw him was downtown Cacém, he was with his gym friends and I with Maria João, smoking a cigarette.

"So, you smoke now?" – I understood he was judging me.

"So, you are a cop now?" – I said, smiling.

"Well, when are we going to do something?"

"I'll call you."

And I did. One weekend I came from Castelo Branco, I thought of setting something up with him, I wanted to see what he would do. Although, he had set up an all-nighter with his gym friends and said he was going to talk to me soon. However, he never said another word and I did not persist.

Letting the nostalgia aside and coming back to the present, I have to mention that with Luís leaving, a new lad called Eduardo came. The guy is my age and from the get-go he seemed to be a cool guy. He's a little shorter than me, thin, his front teeth are a little twisted and quite yellow, it's pretty noticeable that he doesn't keep good dental hygiene. He smokes compulsively, but only tobacco, as he says pot makes him sleepy. He lives in Massamá and has a blonde and chubby girlfriend. They seem like a very steady couple. I like his vibe better than Luís, he is a better professional, more grown-up and curious. I think Hugo and Ana like him, but would prefer Luís' drollery.

Well, now I must talk about the weekend I have spent with Luísa, but first I have to explain who she is.

Right in my early weeks at work Luísa had gotten my attention, she would go to the movie rental on the weekends, usually wearing a sweatshirt or any homelike clothing. She would only carry a small wallet, a pack of cigarettes and her home keys in her hand. It was obvious she lived nearby. She would greet the older employees and, right the first time I saw her, I asked Hugo:

"Who is that girl who greeted you?"

"That's Luísa, she used to work here."

Even with the sporty outfit, she got my attention. She is not a flashy woman, instead, she is short, a little over 5'3, noticeably flat-chested and I would not say she is chubby, nor is she slim, she might have a couple of extra pounds, but it seems to me they fit her perfectly. What called my attention the most was her face. She looks pretty, but I have come to find out that many disagree. She has a dark complexion, one of those people that become tanned after a week on the beach. She has big brown eyes, with very curvy eyelashes. Her hair is dark-brown, straight, very loose, cut at shoulder-length. Her nose is a little like a potato. She has a wonderful smile, jolly, contagious. When she laughs she shows her little teeth and it makes her look like a child.

Sometimes she would come to the movie rental with a guy. At first I wondered if he was her boyfriend, but by his age and the way they treated each other, I have realized he is her younger brother. I searched her client form for information about her, and confirmed she lived very close to the mall and is one year younger than me. She used to rent thrillers, sometimes some romantic comedies or horror movies. Many times I thought of starting a conversation with her, but she seemed so self-assured, so reliant in the way she would come into the store that she made me awkward. Besides that, she would greet my colleagues and barely look at me.

One day she got in and the store was almost empty, she was picking up a movie, a thriller, *The Pelican Brief*, with Julia Roberts and Denzel Washington. She got close to the counter, in her light-colored sweatshirt.

"Hello" – she greeted me.

"Hi" – I took her associate card, got her client form and passed the VHS through the code reader. I gathered up some courage.

"I have watched this one, it's not bad, but it lacks some energy."

"Oh, ok."

"Maybe you will like it. Do you like thrillers?"

"Yes, but I watch other genres too."

"There is a classic thriller I watched recently that has a lot of energy, is full of plot twists, called *No Way Out* with Kevin Costner."

"Oh, ok, and where is it?"

I went around the counter and picked it up from the thriller section. While I was heading there, I thought things were going well.

"It's this one. Would you like to watch it?"

"Yes."

"OK, but it's on the house, I'll put it on my list."

"Oh, thank you, but it won't be necessary" – she smiled and her smile was enchanting, I noticed she started looking at me differently.

"No, seriously, I can take home 10 movies a week and I never take that many. Watch it and then tell me what you think."

She left, smiling, and I said to myself: "yes, you are the greatest, Gonga."

I didn't have to wait too many days for her to come back to return the movies and she commented that she loved *No Way Out*. Although, this time she was not wearing homelike clothing, she was elegantly dressed, wearing make-up and perfume. I got nervous, I wanted to act naturally, but I started to sweat and stutter, and avoid visual contact. She had dressed up for me, she was certainly interested in me, but I went down to the ground. I got kind of dumbfounded, pretending to be working, while she was walking around the movie rental waiting for me to approach her. However, Luísa came to the counter and said:

"No suggestion for me today??"

"Sure I do..." – finally I smiled and joined her. – "Have you seen my favorites list?"

"Not yet."

"Well, if you don't know, my name is Gonçalo and those are the five movies I put out."

She looked at me and said:

"I can see you have a refined taste. I have only watched *Hate* and *Pulp Fiction*."

"And did you like *Hate*?"

"Very good, excellent."

"Then take one out of these other three. What would you like?"
"Something light, not very dramatic."
"The movie *Bananas* by Woody Allen is a political satire, very funny."
"Right, you've convinced me, but this time I want to pay."
"No, please, I insist."
"Me too, I insist on paying."

I was with Ana and asked her to be alone for a while in the store so I could go outside for a smoke with Luísa.

She smokes a giant SG, while I smoke a Camel. I was still nervous, my hands were shaking, but I was trying to hide it, talking about movies. Although, she changed the subject.

"I used to work here."
"Oh, really?"
"Yes, didn't Hugo tell you?"
"No" – I lied. – "And did you like it?"
"Yes, it's right by my home. The environment was nice, but I found another job and I left."
"I'm from Cacém, but I am studying Environmental Engineering in Castelo Branco. Since I have only one subject this semester, I'm taking the time to work a little."
"I'm in college too, but it's kind of abandoned."
"Oh, yes, and what do you study?"
"Physics."
"Physics?" – I couldn't believe it. – "The subject in which I am late is physics!"

She laughed.

"You could give me some lessons on physics, really! I'll pay you with movies."

Both of us started laughing and I could tell by her gaze, by her body talk that she felt attracted to me.

"The offer sounds interesting to me."

The conversation went on, we smoked another cigarette and I started to think I had been out of the movie rental for too long and I should go back.

"Well, the conversation was nice, but I have to go back."

"Right."

"Look, would you like to go out for a drink one of these days?" – I risked.

"OK."

"When would you like?"

"On the weekend."

"Right, on Friday I get off work at 11 p.m., we could go somewhere."

"Deal."

We exchanged phone numbers and said goodbye.

I got in the store with a smile from ear to ear. After Margaret's bucket of cold water, I had the guts to invite another lady and, this time, things went well. Pinto was right: "within a hundred years nobody is going to remember you, so forget the shame".

Ana had noticed my joyfulness and commented:

"So, don't tell me you are interested in the girl?"

I did not know what to say.

"Well... I think maybe."

On Friday at the end of the afternoon, Luísa showed up with her brother. I thought she was going to cancel our date, but no, she came to rent a movie and confirm that at 11 p.m. she would be waiting for me, by her car, at the exit door of the movie rental.

"Would you like to go somewhere specific?"

"No, maybe we could go to Sintra, there are some nice bars over there."

"Right, but I planned to go to Lisbon afterward with a girlfriend."

"Ok."

All night I was watching the clock, anxious. How long had it been since I had gone out with a girl? I prefer to not even think about that, it gets me depressed.

By 11 or so I left the movie rental and looked for her outside. I didn't see her. She called me. She was very elegant and wearing makeup. Her car was a brown Ford Escort, two doors, I got in and it felt small, my knees were bumping in the glove compartment, she told me to pull the seat back, but I couldn't find the damned handle and we were there for a while trying to move that seat, until I got to feel minimally comfortable.

We left Massamá and went down through IC19 heading for Sintra. We were cheerful, I was nervous. She was looking so attractive.

"So, where do you work?"

"At an informatics company in Lisbon."

"Oh, yes, and what do you do?"

"I'm a programmer, I help with informatics."

"Really? You must be gifted. You take physics in college and you are a programmer!"

"It's no big deal."

"And you quit school so you could work?"

"Yeah, I had a good offer to start working and now I'm thinking of changing jobs."

"Oh?"

"I have another offer from another informatics company and I am seriously thinking about leaving. I've been really nervous about all this, because it's a huge step in my career."

I felt tiny, this lady, one year younger than me, was already talking about her career, there were already companies competing for her work, she even gave herself the luxury of quitting college. I see my professional future totally cloudy. When I finish the course what am

I going to do? Where am I going to work? For sure nobody is going to fight for my work.

"And you? What precisely do you study?"

"Environmental Engineering, in Castelo Branco."

"And do you like it?"

"Yes, I enjoy it. I also like the city, it's small, has good services and is surrounded by nature."

"And what are you going to do when you finish?"

"I don't know, I'd like to work in a natural park. Do you like nature?"

She hesitated a little.

"I'm really urban, but I like to wander around here by Sintras's Mountains or to go to the beach, there are not too many people and there is more forestry."

We arrived at Sintra downtown and she parked the car nearby the Village Palace. The weather was cool and we put our coats on, we went to a bar close by. I ordered a beer, she ordered a rum and coke.

"Do you live with your parents?" – she asked me.

"Yes, I also have a sister, but she left home a little while ago. And you?"

"With my brother, who you already know, and with my mother."

I wondered if I should ask about her father, but did not want to sound nosy.

"And in Castelo Branco, do you live in a student residence?"

"No, I have family in the city. My aunt and uncle have a big house and on the upper floor they rent some rooms for students so that's where I live."

"With other students?"

"Yeah, three or four other guys. But I usually have lunch and dinner at my aunt's. I have an easy life."

"And over there don't you have a girlfriend?" – she said with a suspicious smile.

"Not a girlfriend, but I have a wife and three kids."
We laughed.
"Are you still going to Lisbon tonight?"
"Yes, I'd already planned it with a friend. We are going to a disco in the old town."

There was some silence and I thought that, maybe, she was so elegantly dressed up to go out with her friend and not with me. Perhaps, she could even have a boyfriend or someone in sight. She did ask me if I had a girlfriend so I made the same question:

"And you, do you have a boyfriend?"

"No. I had a very quarrelsome relationship a short time ago and now I want some peace. Besides that, with the opportunity of changing jobs, I am not looking for a relationship."

We left the bar and went for a walk. Though it was cold, it was ok to walk in the street.

"There is a fountain over there I would like to see" – she told me.

We were walking through the street that linked the Village Palace to the City Hall, until we arrived at the fountain she wanted to see. It was an Arabian-style fountain, with three pillars by the entrance and a lot of blue and white tiles. There was a little white bench nearby the fountain that was throwing water. We stayed there for a while, observing the details of that monument and I thought it was high time I kissed her. I tried to get close, but she decided to get out of the fountain and crossed to the other side of the street, climbing onto the little wall that divided the sidewalk from a garden, and I followed her and climbed the wall as well. It was only half-meter tall, and I kissed her.

We were on that wall kissing for a while, we got off and kept on caressing each other, her breath smelled like rum and tobacco, but her neck smelled good, I have come to notice that, as well as me, she was nervous.

"Let's go somewhere?" – she asked me.

"OK."

"Do you know any quiet places around here?"

"Yes, nearby the Hockey Arena."

"How can we get there?"

"Through the road that leads to the beaches, follow me."

In that area, there is urbanization and houses for rich people. Once I was there for the birthday party of a friend of Maria João's, a lady that even used to hang out with our group, but she was so much of a nutcase that bit by bit she managed to cast away all her friends, including Maria João.

It didn't take much longer than five minutes to find the urbanization. It was a quiet area, with no traffic at all, there were some cars parked on the street and the lights were dim. She jumped on my lap. We started making out, we had been working for quite a while until I tried to go to the next level, starting to slide my hand under her shirt and reach for her bra.

"No, no" – she said, laughing, while she was kissing me. – "It's still early."

"It's almost two in the morning."

"Maybe next time."

From time to time we would stop our works, smoke a cigarette and talk for a few more minutes.

"You know, Gonçalo, I am going to meet my friend in Lisbon because she is having troubles with the boyfriend and asked me to go out with her tonight. I told her about you and she got curious and went to the movie rental to check you out."

"Really? When? Today?"

"No, yesterday."

"Nobody told me anything."

"Of course not, I told her you look like Edward Norton."

And both of us laughed.

"Edward Norton! Well, that is very nice, I really think the dude is stylish."

"My friend said you had gorgeous eyes."

"Give me your friends' number... Just in case."

We laughed again, finished the cigarettes and went back to the works, but she was always setting up limits, not being less than eager. Hours later she said:

"Gonçalo, it's already too late, I have to go see my friend."

"Right, take me to Cacém, please."

"Sure."

In the car we started to talk about music, she enjoyed contemporary rock, some hip-hop and was a big fan of Jorge Palma. She turned the radio on in Antenna 3 and there was some dance music on.

She parked the car nearby my parents' building and we made out a little more.

"Will we see each other again?"

"Sure, silly, tomorrow afternoon I'll drop by the movie rental."

It was almost five in the morning when I got home. I laid in bed and from so much cuddling my "killer vulture" was hard as a rock. I needed to rub it off, for my testicles were aching too much.

Before sleeping I sent her an SMS saying: "I had a lot of fun tonight".

She did not answer right away and I fell asleep. When I woke up the first thing I did was to check the cell for some answer or missed call. She had answered: "Me too, see you soon. Kiss"

Since then we started seeing each other almost every day on my dinner break, she would show up at the movie rental, she would wander around, pick a movie and, afterward, we would have coffee at a bar. We would barely leave the store and start kissing right away, we would walk hand in hand and in the coffee house we would kiss and caress.

Some mornings we would meet in the garden area in North Massamá, we would sit on a bench and make out. Afterward, we would smoke and chat.

"Look, Gonçalo, what if we went for a trip on a weekend?"

"Great, where would you like to go?"

"There is a friend of mine that has been to Almograve, to a youth hostel, and told me it is an impeccable site."

"Almograve? Where is it?"

"In Alentejo, nearby Mil Fontes."

"Oh, great, it's a very beautiful area."

And that is how it went, she made the reservations, I took the chance to set up my vacations with my boss, for this weekend as well as in June to go a few days to Castelo Branco.

I was very happy those days, I prepared some music cassettes for us to listen to in her car. I packed up. I chose my best clothing and many condoms. With the map I had in the car I made a little itinerary of how to get there and what we could visit around Almograve Village.

On the day of the trip, Luísa arrived later than planned, we left after 10 o'clock. My mother, who is a professional gossiper, went to the window to check how she looked. She saw her coming out of the car, waiting for me, taking the time to smoke a cigarette and greeting me with a kiss in the mouth. Later on, when I got back home, she told me:

"Oh, Gonçalo, so that lady is your friend or girlfriend?"

"Friend, mother" – I answered without making a big deal out of the conversation.

"Then you kiss your friends on the mouth?"

"Only the cute ones, mommy."

"She is not so cute."

"Don't you think she is beautiful?" – I was intrigued.

"Well, besides smoking, she has a big forehead, is short and chubby."

I am glad that her beauty is not unanimous, but for me she is, without a shadow of a doubt, quite curvy and attractive.

The first part of the trip was up to Sines, then we decided to wander around the city and have lunch in a restaurant. She had some music cassettes that I was putting on:

Staind – *Break the Cycle*, during which she commented that she many times felt like the song *It's Been A While*.

Incubus – *Make Yourself*, in which I love the song *Drive*, it is really motivating and full of hope.

Jorge Palma – his best songs, in which she told me that she many times sees herself in the song *Frágil (Frail)*.

Passing the 25th April Bridge, Luísa commented:

"Now every time I cross over a bridge, I remember the Entre-os-Rios accident."

"Well, yes, what a horrible thing."

"How can a bridge fall down?"

"Only in this country really. Sometimes I think about the anguish of the people in that bus the moments before they died."

We were talking the whole time:

"Have you been without a girlfriend for long?"

"It's been three years, more or less."

"In Castelo Branco didn't you have any?"

"No."

"It's hard to believe..."

"I've had fun with girls, but I didn't have a relationship. And you?"

"As I told you, I ended some months ago an almost three-year-long relationship with my ex."

"Ouch, three years is quite a while."

"Yes, I let the relationship roll, but there was a long time I didn't like him anymore. He was very manipulative, jealous and a liar. He hurt me a lot."

I remembered my first, and up to now, only girlfriend, Elsa. I thought she would say the same about me, and would effectively be right. I was a terrible boyfriend, full of insecurities, fears, I would always try to show I was better than her, that she was a redneck from a lost land and I was a wise guy. Remembering now the things I have done to her, I feel very ashamed. I would like to see her again and plead for forgiveness. I would like to tell her that boy from before wasn't the same anymore, he had grown up, gained more self-assurance and maturity.

"It's possible he only treated you like that for being a kid with no trust in himself" – I told her thinking about myself.

"No, he was eight years older."

"Eight? Do you have any daddy issues?"

I asked as a joke, but she threw me such a furious gaze that I realized I had hit the bull's eye. The relationship with her father must be complicated.

"Do you see her?"

"Whom?"

"Your ex-girlfriend?"

"No, I worked with her in a coffee house, in Cacém Station, she was the niece of one of the owners. She had come from a small village, nearby Coimbra. We started dating, but we worked together in the same place and would argue all the time. Most of the time it was my fault. I was a very insecure boy..."

I made a pause because I did not even like to remember her nor the stupid things I have done.

"The environment in the bar was unbearable, at least for me, when I left, we broke up. We still kept in contact, sending letters, calling each other, but we have moved on. She wanted to serve in the army, went to Oporto as a volunteer, afterward, she even went to Bosnia and I think she is a policewoman now. I'm not sure."

"Was she your first girlfriend?"

"First girlfriend, but I didn't lose my virginity to her."

"To whom?"

"So, do you work for the KGB? I don't want to know about your boyfriends."

"Why not?"

"Because it's not my business."

"Are you afraid of getting jealous?"

"It might be that too, but I don't know, I'd rather not know..."

There was a pause and, deep down, the subject made me uncomfortable. First, I remembered Nicole, the girl with whom I lost my virginity and I asked myself how she'd be. Did she remember me as I remembered her? Then, I thought of Elsa. What I felt for Elsa was something big, new, the first time I was in love for real. For me every relationship was very deep, I remember once writing: "If I cannot be with her, I don't want anybody" or "I would never love anyone the way I have loved her". My God, how I suffered! I did not know how to manage that new feeling, everything was so intense and so brilliant. Sometimes it even seems it happened in another life, that I will not be able to love like that anymore or, at least, with so much ingenuity and innocence.

"Were you never unloyal to her?" - she came back to the subject.

"No."

"I would not forgive someone for cheating on me."

"Is this a hint?"

"Well, we are not a couple..."

"We have a thing..." – I said with a Brazilian accent.

She laughed, then got a little more serious and I already knew she was going to say something important.

"We are still getting to know each other and, besides that, I'm changing jobs, this moment is very important to me, right now I can't give priority to anyone else."

"Which means, I can go out with other girls."

She smiled maliciously.

"Do you want to go out with other girls?"

I pondered a little. Truth be told, I only wanted to go out with her, be her boyfriend, but she had already been very clear about it: "right now I can't". I wanted to say something funny, but nothing came to mind and I remained quiet.

"Is that a yes?" – she insisted.

"No, right now I'm fine with you. I can wait until you want to be my gal."

She did not laugh, I noticed she was apprehensive.

When we arrived at Sines, we could not find the old part of the town, so we stopped on a random street and I, from the window, asked an old man how to get to the castle. He came closer to the car and explained the path we had to take. Afterward, in the parked car, Luísa grabbed me by the neck and gave me a long kiss. However, she had not pulled the parking brake, and, without noticing, she took her foot off the brake. I noticed the car seemed to move backward, but I thought it was the ecstasy from the kiss. Suddenly, that old man was complaining, we opened our eyes and saw the car was moving backward on its own, Luísa quickly put her foot back on the brake, the car blew hard and then turned off. The old man kept on yelling. Luísa turned the car back on and we left the place laughing our asses off.

"Did you hit the old man?" – I asked.

"I think I rubbed against him" – and we laughed again. – "But I did not hurt him."

I opened the window and started screaming:

"Watch out with this woman! She is a killer, she almost killed an old man."

"Shut up, dumb ass."

I got closer to her again and started to kiss her on the neck, on the ears and lips.

"Stop it, please, we will have an accident."

We parked nearby the Sines Castle and went sightseeing. The castle was kind of in ruins, but it had some impressive views of the ocean and the sea harbor. We asked a tourist to take some pictures of us. We kissed again and I noticed in her eyes that she was happy.

We ate in a restaurant near the castle: a traditional tavern, with not many clients. I ordered Alentejo pork and she ordered cod with cream.

"I'm on a diet" – she said.

"Really?"

"Don't you think? I ordered cod with cream! But I have to start a diet."

"Why?"

"I feel fat."

"Really! You are yummy."

"Ouch, you're so romantic"– she said ironically.

"And eloquent" – I said with my mouth already full of food.

We left Sines heading to Almograve. Leaving the town, we got to the Natural Park of Alentejo Coast, which had a simple landscape, a little tame: the fields were yellow, there were some trees, mostly pines, and in some farms there were cows. The road did not have much traffic and in less than half an hour we arrived at the destination.

The youth hostel was right by the entrance of the village. It was kind of a weird building, low, long and apparently windowless. We went into the building and the reception was right by the door but there was no one there. While we waited, we looked around. On the lower pavement, there was a kitchen, a dining hall and a living room. It took like 10 minutes for the hostess to come by; she gave us a key to the room, asked if we wanted to take breakfast in the dining room, and gave us a load of touristic flyers of the region. She had a very heavy southern accent, so much so that it seemed like she was doing it on purpose.

We took our luggage to the room, closed the door, closed the window, and took our clothes off. While we were kissing and touching each other, we got in the bed and it was the hunger and the desire to eat put together. Right away I was already on top of her, ready to penetrate her. We started the works, me on top and her on the bottom, but the will was so strong that after a few thrusts I came. So soon! I felt a little ashamed and noticed she expected some more. However, the voice of my guru spoke to me once more.

When I was in high school, I had a similar experience, only then, there was not even any penetration yet and my "killer vulture" was already spitting fire. I asked Pinto if that was normal, he said yes and advised me to rub one off before the date or to keep on the works when the accident happened without giving it any importance.

And that is what I did, I rolled her over and started kissing her neck, her back, went down to the legs, rolled her over again, kissed her breast, her belly and then her vagina. She squirmed in pleasure. The "vulture" got back up and I penetrated her again, this time it had legs. We had been on the job for quite a while and finished tired, exhausted, sweaty, but very satisfied. We were hugging and holding hands. At first in silence, then she said:

"We should have worn a condom."

"Yep" – I still thought of asking if she was on the pill, but the answer seemed obvious.

"I am waiting to have my period by now, but I prefer not to risk."

"As a matter of fact, I even brought condoms..."

"Maybe we would rather go to a pharmacy and buy a morning-after pill."

"Yeah, but maybe there aren't even any pharmacies in Almograve."

"Let's try."

We left the hostel and went for a car ride in Almograve, which was really small, there were quite a few bars, a supermarket, a drugstore, a pharmacy and some stores that would only open in summer. The houses were typical of the Alentejo region, all white with a blue or yellow stripe, the roofs very red, the white chimneys, the architecture of the balconies in the Arabic style.

She stopped 50 meters from the pharmacy.

"Will you go in there, Gonçalo?"

"Me?"

"Yes, please, I'm ashamed. Perhaps there is an old man there who would give me a lascivious gaze."

"And what do I say?"

"That you want the morning-after pill."

"Right... but you think this pharmacy lost in the middle of nowhere will have this?"

"Let's try. Wait, I'll give you the money."

"No, let it be."

I headed to the pharmacy. I have always thought of Luísa as a strong, modern woman, but, on this occasion, she seemed so frail and insecure, I got a little deluded. Instead of what Luísa thought, the person at the counter was a woman about 30 years old, quite curvy by the way. Fortunately, there were no clients.

"Hello, good morning" – I said forcing a smile. What an annoyance! – "Well... I want a morning-after pill."

"Right, is it for your girlfriend?"

Well, technically she was not my girlfriend, but the pharmacist did not need this detail.

"Yes."

"Do you know if she had her period short ago?"

"She says she is waiting for it for the following day."

"Then, look, the pill works until 72 hours, which means, three days after the intercourse. If you see that the time comes and the period does not drop, then you come back. Above all, the pill is very heavy and has many side effects that can be quite harmful."

"Right, it's a deal, thank you."

We exchanged a smile and I left the establishment. I got in the car.

"They have the pill, but she advised to wait for 3 days and then we see if the period comes, because it seems that it has side effects."

"Right" – she said looking unconvinced.

"Let's see the ocean?"

She agreed and we took a walk to the beach. The village was tiny, some of the houses seemed new and big, all of them white. We were wandering holding hands, through the typical Portuguese pavement. After the last house there was a green field, where there were some cows grazing and right after: the dunes. The dunes were huge, certainly the biggest I have ever seen. The stone pavement gave way to a wooden path all the way up the dunes.

"How beautiful are those dunes!" – I affirmed.

"Yes, it's well preserved."

The path climbed subtly until reaching the top of the dunes, then there was a little more vegetation and one could see the ocean. We climbed down, hand in hand, until we arrived at the beach parking lot. There were only a few cars, though it was already May the temperature had barely reached twenty degrees and the sky was cloudy.

We sat on a bench to contemplate the sight. There were the typical steep cliffs of the Alentejo coast, the sea was agitated and the waves hit against the rocks. We could hear the seagulls. A couple of fisherman were throwing their fishing rods into the water.

She was touching me nicely and, afterward, she was sliding her hand inside my t-shirt.

"Have you ever thought of getting a tattoo?"

"Not really."

"Isn't there any design you would like to see on your skin? I got one."

I already noticed that on her shoulder blade there was a rose and a weird design around the rose.

"Maybe I could put it on my chest, something like: *Born in Kzen*."

"Cacém is really horrible."

"Says a lady from Massamá!"

"Don't compare Massamá with Cacém, please."

"Of course not, Cacém is one of the corniest areas in Lisbon, we are leveled with the worst: Chelas, Musgueira, Amadora and Amora. Massamá is for the rich kids."

She laughed.

"I am not from Massamá."

"And where are you from?"

"From Alcântara, in Lisbon. My maternal grandparents are from there. I've grown up in Alcântara village and only went to Massamá when I was six-years-old."

"Ouch, look at me! I am Lisbon to the bone, I am no commoner, I am not from the suburbs" – I said ironically. – "I am from Cacém, I am proud of being raised in a poor slum."

"I think it's just for show."

"What?"

"Being from the ghetto, a suburban scoundrel, from Kzen. Deep down you are a boy who had the opportunity to study in a university away from home, you ride around in daddy's car, you are a dapper dan who has never been deprived of any basic needs. You use it to showcase for the girls."

We started to laugh.

"All right, you already took my mask off."

"You don't fool me."

"I will tell you the story of my life. See, my grandparents were four illiterate farmers from a lost village. My parents came to Lisbon and started from nothing, they didn't have money even to get a blind man to sing. They got a little place from a housing project. The block was far from Cacém in the beginning, there was no bus, schools, health center. Before going to college, I was working as a guard for a year in a factory in São Marcos and lived in the attic in my uncles' house who gave me a discount. Yes, I was born in a ghetto, I was raised in a slum and I am proud of being from Kzen."

"You are a swaggerer! Have you ever robbed anybody?"

I laughed.

"Are you recording this conversation? Are you a cop? Where is the microphone?"

I started to touch her, pretending I was looking for a microphone.

We went to dinner in one of the two restaurants in the neighborhood, which was close to the hostel. The place was big and was expecting the tourists who would spend the summer in July and August. Now it was almost empty. We ate in the outer part of the restaurant, wearing our coats because it was getting cold. We ordered mahi-mahi with potatoes and broccoli, paired with the house's green wine. We shared dessert.

When we were done, we ordered two cups of coffee, smoked cigarettes and stayed for a while, chatting.

"Would you be able to live in a village like this one?" – I asked.

"No, it's terrible! So boring!"

"I would."

"And what would you do for a living?"

"If I could get a job here in my field. Here in the Alentejo Coast Natural Park."

"And wouldn't you miss Cacém?"

"It's not that far away."

"You could have some cows here" – she joked.

"Or I could be a gigolo in the summer for the tourists."

"Yes, you kind of look like a gigolo. You only lack a mustache."

"Maybe I should bulk up a little."

"No, please! You already have too much muscle."

"I am skinny, I have almost no muscles! Don't you like my muscles?"

"I do not like men who lack confidence and have low self-esteem, so they go to the gym to work out."

"Ouch, this one hurt. You took my mask off again."

She laughed, me not so much.

"I like thin men, with no muscle, with an intellectual touch. Romantic and, if possible, with money."

"Bingo! That's me."

We were silent for a while and I thought that in her workplace there would be many lads with the characteristics she described. In the world of informatics it is the easiest thing to find dullards, with no muscles, with glasses and possibly with a rich daddy. I got jealous. Was it be true that she was looking for someone like that?

"And you? What do you look for in a woman?"

"Nothing special. Thin, fat, old, young, rich, poor, one can get laid with all of them. It's all grist to the mill."

"I see you're unrefined."

"I'm from Kzen, baby."

"Please, I want to leave."

"Only after paying the bill, sweety."

"You are not funny, Gonçalo. Enough!"

I shut up. After a moment I asked:

"Was this our first argument?"

We both smiled.

"Let's go to the hostel, I want to abuse you."

"Oh, what a romantic girl!"

We kissed slowly, in the middle of the sidewalk, ignoring who was around us and we went to the hostel.

When we arrived in the room, she got into the bathroom and I did not know how to get into bed, if naked or wearing a t-shirt and underwear. It was a tough doubt, because if I was naked it would give the impression I wanted a little party, but if I was wearing the t-shirt could give the opposite idea. I decided to wear the t-shirt and shoved myself under the covers. I turned a dim light on and waited for her to come out of the bathroom.

Coming out of the bathroom, my jaw dropped, she had put on a sexy nightgown, short, purple, that fit her like a killer. My heart was pumping. That was for me! Oh, so fortunate!

"Do you like it?" - she said and I noticed she sounded kind of embarrassed.

"A lot, I am speechless."

She slid into the bed and we started the works.

"You have too much clothing."

"I thought I should be naked but didn't want to look like a maniac."

"Shut up and kiss me."

In short, while I was already naked on top of her, I tried to take her clothes off and she said she wanted to do it with the gown on.

"No trouble, proceed for bingo" – I said with my teeth clenching.

And we started the deal, the bed springs were creaking, our breathing was quickening, the will was growing. Things were going well until I felt all wet in the private parts. I did not care and kept focused on the procedures. However, while she was riding me strongly, I started, bit by bit, to notice some liquid run down my "vulture".

"Something is wrong" – I pondered.

Luísa finished, hugged me, kissed me and at this moment she too felt something weird herself.

"Ouch, my period!"

Oh, then that is what it was. She got up and a squirt of blood fell to the floor, she ran to the bathroom.

Looking down, I was astonished. It looked like *The Texas Chainsaw Massacre*, the sheets, my belly, penis and legs were covered in blood. It was kind of coagulated, with some solid chunks. I got up and there was another squirt on the floor. I went into the bathroom.

"Look, I'm really sorry, Gonçalo, seriously. I didn't notice."

"Don't worry. It's nothing."

I got into the tub and that looked like the movie *Psycho*, a river of blood running to the drain. Then she got in the tub and I got out. I dried off, put on my underwear and t-shirt, put my glasses on and checked the damage. It was considerable. The inner sheet had a big bloodstain, the outer one had a little one. The floor, which had a carpet, had two red strikes. I would have to clean that up.

I collected the sheets and put them in the tub and brought toilet paper to clean the floor.

"We have to buy some sheets."

"Excuse me?" – I asked.

"Those stains won't come out even with bleach."

"And how are we going to buy sheets? Do we ask at the front desk where do they usually buy the sheets?" - I said with a sarcastic tone.

"Then what do we do?"

We washed the two sheets in the tub and left them there to dry. The stains on the floor did not come out fully. We decided to drag the bed so it would cover the spots.

"How are we going to dry the sheets?" – I asked.

"Maybe if we put the air conditioner at the highest setting."

"Good idea. Tomorrow we hang them near the air conditioner and run at the highest."

We laid down without any sheets.

"Good that the mattress doesn't have any stains." – I said.

"Gonçalo, forgive me, I'm a little ashamed of this situation."

"Don't worry" – I got closer and kissed her.

"You weren't super disgusted?"

I smiled a little.

"No. It was weird, a little gory, but I'm not disgusted."

We turned the light down and she fell asleep quite soon. I did not feel sleepy and I noticed I was a little agitated. I got up and went to the little balcony we had in the bedroom. I smoked a cigarette while contemplating the dark field we had in front of us. The sky was still cloudy and one could hear the sound of the sea from afar, sometimes a dog barking. There was a lot of humidity and a cold breeze froze me. I considered going in and putting some more clothes on, but I did not want to wake her up. I thought about Luísa and felt what I already knew, I was falling in love with her, there was already no way back. I remembered the last time I felt like that, with Elsa and I wanted to erase the memory from my brain. Although, I considered that a lot of water had passed under the bridge, I was already more mature, more experienced and now I was prepared to fall in love.

I went into the room almost shaking, I looked at Luísa, who was sound asleep. What a beautiful face she has! I lay close to her and tried to fall asleep.

On the following day, I woke up to Luísa telling me to get out of bed because we were supposed to take breakfast before 10 a.m. She had already showered and was getting dressed. I opened the curtains, opened the door to the balcony and saw it was a spring day, the sky was almost clean, the humidity persisted and so did the cold breeze.

We had breakfast among many couples with unwashed faces wearing sweatshirts. I filled my stomach, Luísa mostly had coffee.

We went back to the room. Luísa was changing her clothes.

"Gonçalo, you are going to put something else on, right?"

"So, do I look bad?" – I complained.

"Seriously, we are going to wander around Mil Fontes, we are going to a restaurant, I will be wearing elegant clothes and you could put on something a little better."

I was wearing a red t-shirt with the letters "CCCP" in black. I had bought it in Castelo Branco's market, on a gypsy stand. Reluctantly, I put on a shirt.

Before leaving, we hung the sheets between two chairs and a table and turned the air conditioner to the highest. That should work, I thought.

Already in the car, heading towards Vila Nova of Mil Fontes, she asked:

"Are you a commie?"

"No, but I have a communist rib. I'm quite fascinated by the former Soviet Union."

"Why?"

"The idea they had of creating a perfect State. Think about it, when the Chernobyl center exploded, they would not accept there was a problem with the soviet nuclear centers, that would be impossible. They blamed it on a human mistake and they found a scapegoat."

"Did you know that in 1991, a little before the end of the USSR, there was a referendum to know if the people wanted to continue in a renewed Soviet Union or to cut it off?"

"Oh, I didn't know."

"Well, yes, and they won in all of the republics, with an overwhelming majority, the ones who wanted to continue."

"Gee! Do you like politics?"

"Not really, I'm a left-winger, but I don't really care for politics" – she made a pause. "My father took me some years ago to the Communist Party Celebration."

"Is he communist?"

"No, he likes parties" – she said in disapproval.

Afterward, she told me her father had a family before marrying her mother, from this first marriage she had a half-sister. Then she and her brother were born and her father left them to live with a younger woman. I was glad she trusted me with that story.

Vila Nova of Mil Fontes is a tame township, with a lot of typical Alentejo style, with the houses all white and the yellow and blue stripes. There is a lot of touristic urbanism that seems to grow like mushrooms. In one of the main avenues there are many stores, where we wandered slowly, she went in a shoe store and bought a pair, she confessed she had more than 30 pairs of shoes, which was her perdition.

We saw a poster indicating the movie the theater had playing: *Cast Away* with Tom Hanks.

"Have you watched it?" – she asked.

"No, it wasn't released on VHS yet."

"Would you like to watch it?"

"What time is it showing?"

"There is a session at 6 p.m. and another at 9."

"Yeah, all right. We can have lunch here, wander around some more and then watch the movie."

And that is how it was, we had lunch in one of the many restaurants there was in the avenue with all the stores. I ordered ribs and she had the bass. We had wine, dessert and coffee. She has asked me if I was a Catholic and I bored her talking about Tibetan Buddhism. As far as I can tell, she is not an atheist, but not by far.

After lunch, we went wandering by the river mouth. The landscape of the two shores of the river is quite beautiful and we sat on a bench to contemplate it while smoking some cigarettes and kissing.

At five in the afternoon, we went looking for the theater, called Cineteatro GiraSol, and by the aspect it has on the outside, it seemed to be a kind of homely amphitheater. There were a lot of teenagers. When we got in, we noticed the building had been restored, we bought popcorn and got in the theater, which was small, but the seats looked new, were comfortable and the screen was big. I was surprised.

"The movie might be boring" – she said.

"In that case we can make out."

She laughed and she really has a seductive smile.

The movie was also a positive surprise, indeed I must confess I was moved and I even cried a little. The story is full of messages about what really matters in life. The part in which Tom Hanks talks to the ball, representing his conscience is genius. However, the sentence he says: "I have to keep on breathing, tomorrow the sun is coming up, nobody knows what the tide is going to bring", moved me in such a way I did not resist and, in the darkness of the theater, I dropped a tear.

When we left, we both agreed we had watched a masterpiece, though I noticed that I was more touched than her. We went to have dinner in the Almograve restaurant, talking about movies the whole time.

"Have you noticed we always have things to talk about?"

"Yes, it's true. We have a lot in common" – she confirmed.

We were silent for a moment, then I said:

"Tomorrow we are already going away, it was so fast."

"Yes, true. Good things end fast."

"What is your plan for tonight?"

"We can watch TV, spooning."

After dinner, we went to the bedroom. It was cold and it would be pleasant to be in a warm place, however, when we opened the door to the room, a wave of heat hit us ferociously.

"Fuck it…"

"Turn the air conditioner off, quick!" – Luísa ordered.

The heat inside the room was unbearable. It was pumping heat all day long and we had totally forgotten about it. The sheets were extra dry and we had to open the window and the balcony door to cool it down.

"One can barely notice the stains."

"Great, we've done a good job" – I said, very glad.

The room cooled down quickly, the breeze that came from outside was cold and loaded with humidity. We made the bed with those sheets, she put on pink pajamas and we got in bed. We checked what was on TV and ended up watching a documentary on channel 2 about UFOs. I fell asleep halfway through.

On the following day, after taking breakfast, we packed up and left.

We were chatting all the while through the trip, I put on a cassette I had of the rapper, Sam The Kid, of the album *Sobre Tudo (Above All)*, and in the song *Não Percebes (You Don't Understand)*, both of us were singing out loud:

You don't understand what I say,

You don't understand what I tell,

You don't understand what I live,

You don't understand what I chase.

Learn the mission is not being on top,
It's empty, shit on it, you don't understand the Hip-Hop!
You don't understand the Hip-Hop, you don't understand!
You don't understand the Hip-Hop, you don't understand!
You don't understand the Hip-Hop, you don't understand the Hip-Hop!

At that moment, while we were singing, I knew I was deeply in love with her. She has everything I look for in a woman. She is intelligent, attractive, modern, suburban like me, and likes music, movies, and theater. She is a left-winger, is curious, feminine, seductive, drinks alcohol, smokes, and has no trouble with pot. Fuck! This woman was perfect for me! I started to imagine that it could turn out right, that we could live in a suburban middle-high class area, have a happy family, united. On weekends we could go to Cacém or Massamá for lunch with our parents and then we would make plans to go out for a coffee with our friends. Maybe we would have a beach house in Almograve and we could go, sometimes, spend the vacations abroad. She would be a well-paid programmer and I would work in a renewable energy company.

It even seems like she guessed my thoughts and tried, subtly, to tell me, once more, that at that moment she could not have a relationship because she was in a process of changing jobs and was overwhelmed. I said yes, however, I was convinced the feeling was mutual. Unfortunately, that is not how it was.

She took me to Cacém and we said goodbye with a long kiss. I was really happy, it had been a remarkable weekend.

On the following day, I went to work and had hopes of seeing her, but she did not show up and didn't send any news. The same thing on Tuesday and I started to think that there was something wrong. I did not want to pressure on her, we were not a couple. However, I started to feel some anguish. Wednesday was my day off, I had been up and down with the subject and I sent her an SMS:

"Would you like to have dinner with me tomorrow on my break?"

I waited anxiously for the answer, but she did not say anything the whole day and I was checking the phone over and over.

On Thursday I went to work all agitated, I did not have any news and was getting more and more confused. Every time someone would come into the movie rental, I would look, hoping to see her. By dinner time there was an SMS from her:

"Sorry, I have been a little busy, when I have some spare time, I will call you right away".

It could be worse, I thought. At least she was not ignoring me totally. Still, I was sad, it would not cost her to come to join me for a coffee. Her house was only five minutes away.

She did not call and I, on Saturday night, after another anxiety attack, took the cell and after a long time pondering what to write to her, decided on this:

"How was your week?"

She did not answer that night and I was wondering what had changed? Right, she could be busy at work, but she didn't have five miserable minutes for me? Last weekend we were both happy, or at least that is what it seemed to me. It never crossed my mind that she would disappear like that. It was hard to fall asleep.

On Sunday I had lunch with my parents and I was morose. They tried hard to find a subject that I would respond to, but I was down, depressed.

I went to work and it was almost dinner time already when I received an SMS from her:

"Will you be working tomorrow afternoon?"

"Yes, from 3 to 11."

"Ok, see you tomorrow, kiss."

My mood was lifted up into the air. Oh, such splendid happiness! I spent the rest of the day well-disposed, cheerful and willing to see her again. After all, she was not upset with me, she just had too much work.

On the following day, I went to the gym in the morning and then I dropped by a florist and bought a red rose. I had lunch with my mother, who was on sick leave for the whole week because of a backache, she made me dinner, although I thought Luísa was going to invite me to have dinner with her.

I took the red rose inside my backpack, I did not want the colleagues from the morning shift to see the flower. I changed my clothes and left the backpack partly opened to keep the rose from withering. However, those gossipers saw the rose when they were changing their clothes, they took it from my backpack and put it in a small crystal vase.

"Look, we put your rose in a vase, otherwise, it would die."

I was ashamed, red as a tomato.

"Ouch, look the boy is in love" – Christiane said mocking me.

I tried not to care and finally, they left the store.

In the middle of the afternoon, there was me and Eduardo in the movie rental. He was on the counter and I was laying out the new DVDs that had arrived when she showed up.

"Hello" – Luísa said.

She was wearing some elegant clothes, from her work, she had her face a little flushed from the heat.

"Oh, hello, I am so glad to see you. I was already thinking you didn't want to see me anymore" – I said joking but she did not laugh.

"Can we talk?"

We got in the dressing room, I saw the rose in the jar and I thought of giving it to her but she started to talk. She had an anguished posture.

"Look, Gonçalo, I have been thinking a lot during this week and I think you are a great guy, but" – oh no, I could already see the storm that was coming – "at this moment I can't give priority to a relationship, we can't date. I'm sorry."

Somebody had thrown a bucket of cold water on me.

"I don't want you to hate me, can you hug me?"

Someone else punched my stomach.

I gave in, hugged her and said:

"I bought this flower..." – and gave her the rose.

She took the rose, looked at me with wet eyes and left the room quickly. I stayed quiet, feeling the most stupid, dumb, failed man in the world. Once again I misinterpreted the signs, she was not in love, she just wanted an affair.

I left the dressing room with my head down. If somebody wanted to shoot me at that moment, I would thank them. Eduardo asked.

"So, what happened? Luísa left the store crying."

I told him what happened and he cheered me up. He was giving me support the whole afternoon, he is really a nice fellow. He asked me if I wanted to go for a beer after we closed the store, but I did not feel like it, I wanted to be alone, licking my wounds.

I closed the movie rental and headed towards my father's car, which was parked close to Luísa's street. I got in, started it and the song from the cassette I had put on earlier jumped up: Moby from the album *Play*. I made it all the way from Massamá to Cacém, going through the same streets as always, however, when I got close to the garden of North Massamá, where me and Luísa would meet to make out, and it started to play: *Why Does My Heart Feel So Bad?* Then my eyes got cloudy and I could not hold back the tears, crying with drool and snot.

Academic Week in Castelo Branco – Friday, June 22nd, 2001

I had set up with my boss to be on vacation for the academic week, however, there were some mishaps at the store. Hugo has gotten fired; he has been very fed up with working there and many of his friends were already gone. I was sorry. I hope we can keep in touch in the future, because I consider him a friend, I told him to come to the movie rental and take some movies on my bill. It was a sad farewell.

There is a new lad, an 18 or 19-year-old fellow, who seems nice. One can tell he takes quite a while to learn things, but he is making progress. The other day Ana, the colleague that only comes on weekends, told me he was gay.

"No way..."

"Shit, didn't you notice yet?"

"No, he seemed like a 'normal' dude."

"Are you blind? You can see it from miles away."

Since then, I have been trying to observe if he really does have some effeminate ways; nothing has called my attention, but now I try not to change my clothes in front of him.

Ana Paula, the store boss, got sick leave. She had a fever and flu and stayed on bed rest for a whole week, precisely the one I had set up to go to Castelo Branco.

Cristina begged me to move my vacation, but I said I had to be gone for at least a couple of days to talk to my physics teacher and the most I could do was to make my vacation a little shorter, which means, going on Monday and coming back on Friday. She took it.

Luísa has been to the movie rental from time to time and, in a general manner, always with her brother or a friend. I treat her with kindness, sometimes I ignore her, I always ask my colleagues to be the ones to attend to her. Indeed, once I went to the dressing room to smoke a cigarette until she was gone.

I do not want to talk to her. I think she has to be the one to take the next step, if she feels like it, otherwise no problem. In September, I'm going back to Castelo Branco and I will never see her again. However, my feelings cannot be that easily erased. I still like her, whenever she walks in the store my heart skips a beat, I get nervous and anxious. I still have many unanswered questions, many doubts to clear up. I have been sad because things didn't go well.

The only person to whom I can open up honestly is Maria João. She is possibly my best friend. She is a good listener, she knows me well and is sensitive to my problems. When I told her the story, she said that possibly Luísa does not want to fall in love because she is very focused on work or she is afraid of getting hurt. There is also the possibility that she sees no future in the relationship.

I have always unburdened myself to her, when I was with Elsa I told her briefly how the relationship was and the reasons that caused it to fail, however, I never told her the huge dumbasseries I made with Elsa, I have always kind of played the victim. Maria João does the same with me about her relationship as well, and tells me it seems more like a friendship with benefits than a commitment. They only see each other on weekends and not even all of them. She confessed that she, many times, thinks about that song by Caetano Veloso called *"Sozinho"(Alone)* and she feels that is the way her relationship goes. She could even cheat on him and he would never notice. Talking to her always makes me feel better, it's like cleaning my soul and I love to listen to her opinions. I am afraid our friendship will end as it has with Marco, my childhood friend.

I turned 24 years old this year. It was on a Thursday and I could take the day off. I went to the Carcavelos beach with my sister and a friend of hers. It was fun, I talked to them and I had time to answer some SMS' that were coming in and also to the people who were calling me. Luísa did not say anything, I think she does not know my birthday, as I do not know hers either.

In early June, I went to a travel agency in downtown Lisbon to buy flight tickets to Holland. I already have everything set up, I will leave on September the 4th and come back on the 14th. The only trouble is that I will have to go to Oporto to take the flight. I have already booked the accommodation. I will be in a hostel downtown. I have already bought a book about the city and have been studying the maps and places to visit.

I was really ready for the academic week to come. I missed my friends from the Burrow, our conversations and the craziness. I felt like getting out of the movie rental routine and getting away from Luísa. However, I had barely gotten on the train at East Station before I felt I did not miss taking that trip again at all.

My vacation was only four days. I left on Monday and had to be back by Friday, because that day I had to close the store. Besides being with my friends, I had three important goals: talking to the physics teacher about this year's exams; visiting my grandmother in the senior's home and setting up with Célia for our physics classes from September 17th until the final physics exam on October 3rd.

I arrived at Castelo Branco at the end of the morning, it was hot as hell already, like a glimpse of summer. I took the straight line from Carapalha to my uncles' house and arrived sweating already. I went to the Burrow and it looked like there was no one there. When I got to the house, my aunt was there and she welcomed me joyfully, she told me to go take a shower and, afterward, we would have lunch together.

After the shower, I put on some clothes and had lunch with my aunt. She told me the news about the neighborhood and Lentiscais. I told her about the day-by-day at the movie rental, about my mother's sick leave and my sister's new house. She was very happy to see me and so was I. I already missed her.

After lunch, I went to check if my despicable friends from the Burrow were in the den. Only Boni was there and he welcomed me with a huge hug and some weed. Afterward, we went to the Society. He was telling me the news from the guys, whom he had been seeing, what had changed, who was going out with whom. We talked about movies and music. Afterward, we went to the Agricultural School, he had a class and I wanted to talk to the Physics teacher. I found him already on his way out and he told me to drop by his office on Thursday around 4 o'clock. Then I headed to the school cafeteria and chatted with some of the guys who were around. I waited for Boni's class to be over and met Elói and Joey, who were happy to see me, even though Joey is a very restrained man. They had an exam the following day, therefore, they did not want to go out that night, besides that, the parties of the academic week would begin on Tuesday.

Therefore, Monday night, I stayed upstairs at my uncles' house, with my cousin Toxic and the rest of the students who were living there by then. We played cards, drank some beers and my cousins even made a couple of joints. It was really nice to come back, the overnight was pleasant and I was glad when I went to sleep.

On Tuesday the parties began, the elements of the Burrow had to take the exam in the morning, and told me to show up by two o'clock for some coffee. On the other hand, me, Célia and Cláudia went to talk to a teacher in the physics department for him to give us some private lessons by the end of September. After we talked to that teacher, everything was set up and I went to have lunch at Célia's house, where she used to live with her boyfriend and, by then, was also sharing the place with Cláudia and her boyfriend, who was coincidently from Cacém and naturally from the *Legalize It* crew.

Célia is a good cook and made a good tidbit. We had some wine that was not good, but it was either that or water and we smoked five joints. The elements of the Burrow were fed up with sending me SMS telling me to show up, but by four p.m. I was already too high and I had difficulty keeping up with the schedule. Actually, I have behaved very well since I arrived in Cacém, I did not drink much and I would rarely smoke hashish. When I arrived at the Burrow it was already six p.m., and I was high as hell. I got in through the kitchen, which was opened and said:

"Hello, my name is Crazy Gonga and I bring drugs and alcohol."

The elements of the Burrow came by, one by one, everybody glad and laughing.

"Great Gonga, you are finally back!"

"We said two in the afternoon" – one of them complained.

"Let's go to the Society" – another one said.

In the Society there was some coming and going of beer bottles to our table, Teodoro would keep on bringing peanuts, lupines and some beers, on the house. The guys were getting all fucked up, it was promising to be an epic night.

"Gonga, your birthday this year was calmer than the last one, right?"

"Quite tame, nothing like last year. Indeed, I haven't been drinking and smoking much in Cacém. Ah, it's true, I have already bought the flight tickets to Amsterdam. Does anybody want to come?"

"I'm out of money" – Boni said.

"When are you going?" – Joey Nights asked.

"I go on the 4th and come back on the 14th. Ah, another thing, the flights for going as well as coming back are in Oporto. Elói can you get me a place to sleep on the 3rd?"

"Yep, you can count on that. You can come on the 3rd in the morning and we can get around in Oporto."

"Nice."

Joey and Elói were going to check flights and accommodations and see if they could go to Holland too.

We went to the Burrow for dinner, already quite drunk. Boni put on the Trainspotting soundtrack and then we started to smoke more hashish and drink more wine, more nonsense conversations, laughter. We told old stories, talked about girls, more tobacco, more addictions, more laughter, we talked about music, movies, tv series, soccer games. We had dinner, more hashish, more tobacco, more wine. Ouch, we went out of the Burrow like a bunch of wolves, hungry for meat and debauchery.

Before going to the city park, which is where the academic party takes place, we stopped by many stations and alleys, having a drink here and there, a beer here, some smoke there, some conversation with someone, some flirting with someone else.

The Burrow has a tradition of not paying for concert tickets and I believe that traditions must be respected, which implies we have to jump over some fences. And anyone would agree, playing Spiderman drunk could obviously have a twisted end. And it did.

The city park was full of students and nasty old men seeking fresh and easy meat. There was a trailer parked by the park entrance, selling snacks and beer. We stuck around, ordered some beers and were planning to skip the bill. The method would be the one we always use, jumping over the fence beside the public restroom. Boni and Bora Bora dismissed that hypothesis, they preferred to pay rather than to risk their asses on trickery.

The iron gates to the city park were wide open and inside there was a mess of voices and people. By the back end of the park there was the concert facility, by the right side of the public bathroom.

The three of us headed to the site, as if we were professional thieves. Elói, who is the deftest of us, was the first one to climb up. He clung to a small tree, a beech with a thin trunk and with our help he climbed up the wall. I followed and then Joey Nights. Upon the wall there is a fence, like a meter and a half of plain wire and beyond that there is another one, and this one is made of barbed wire.

Carefully, me and Joey bent down the plain wires as much as we could, Elói jumped up, did a flip and got in. On the other side there was a slab roof of a hatchery. It was my turn, I jumped, tried to flip like Elói, but it did not work out so well, I scratched my knee on the barbed wire and then I fell defenseless on the roof of the hatchery, moreover, I had hit the same knee on the roof. Fuck it, the pain was awful! Anyway, I was too drunk and drugged to get upset about it.

"Are you ok?" – someone asked.

"Yes, it's just a scratch."

We jumped from the roof to the ground, with the impact from the jump my knee was hurting again. We walked like 50 meters, bent, hidden and got in through a side of the concert site. In the middle of the crowd, we were howling in joy, the wolves had entered the haystack.

It was *Tunas* Day, so there was no music band. Due to that, the place had a lot of people wearing scholastic gowns.

I was coming and going from the beer stand and the center of the site, sometimes behind the stage to smoke some hash. From time to time I would stop to talk to some acquaintance, who would almost always ask what I had been doing and comment on not seeing me for a while.

In one of those comings and goings, I saw Rita and her friend, the one with whom I have tramped without knowing her name. They were alone, looking at the stage. This moment was like a comparison between perspective and reality. When I saw them, I imagined that, if I came by, they would be euphoric for seeing me and would hug and kiss me, and they would ask questions, worried about my knee, and they would take me home, heal my wound and the three of us would make love, a *menage a trois* in style. Oh, that would be my great chance to make one of my most sordid fantasies come true.

I approached them full of hope and one could even say nervously. However, the reality was way more bitter than the expectation.

They saw me, and were surprised, but at no point could I say they were glad.

"Ouch, check out the missing man!" – Rita said.

"Hello, how are you girls?" – and I greeted them with two kisses on the cheeks.

"Everything all right, what about you?" – Said the nameless – "You've been gone?"

"Yep, I'm working in a movie rental, nearby Cacém."

"Ok, nice. What happened to your pants?"

My pants had a considerable hole, and since they were yellowish, one could see a darker color around the hole, which was the blood.

"I fell from a wall, but I'm fine."

I thought they would ask questions about the movie rental or the return to my parents' house, but they had not the slightest interest in me, they looked at the stage and then talked in each other's ears. So, did they not remember me? Did they not remember what we had done? Had they already found another guinea pig? Please, use and abuse me, please!

The situation was getting awkward, I was trying to find something in common to talk about and they barely answered, until they said:

"We are going to gather up with our friends, bye Gongas."

"It's Gonga, not Gongas." – I still complained.

And they were gone. The night was really not going well, although, when I was meditating about what just happened, the

Agricultural School tuna began to sing. I went to the front row to support our boys. When they began to sing the anthem, I put my hand on my chest and started to sing with determination. Gasolines, who is a member of the tuna, yelled:

"Gonga, you bastard, come up on the stage and sing with us."

So I did, I climbed up to the stage, my knee hurt but I was in complete ecstasy and I hugged Gasolines. Someone gave me a plastic beer cup, more arms hugged me and I sang the anthem from the top of my lungs and got all emotional:

"Nobody shall get in our way, because we are the plows,

And 'cause we are the plows, 'cause we are.

In the morning we go to class and at night we flirt,

And at night we flirt.

We cultivate carrots, but we also have nuts..."

The night was passing by, my knee was hurting more, it was already four in the morning and I did not feel like drinking or smoking anymore. I looked around myself and the people were going away. The *tunas* had been replaced by a DJ who was putting on some techno music. I looked for the Burrow and saw Joey dancing and it was here that the comparison between perspective and reality came back up. I was expecting to tell Joey that my knee was hurting, that I was going home, and my great friend would say "I'll help you, you might want to go to a hospital. We haven't been hanging out in such a long time, let's talk, unburden." For that too, the reality was different.

"Joey, I'm going, my knee is hurting too much."

"Right, bye."

"You're staying?"

"Yep."

"Do you know where the others are?"

"Nope."

And he disappeared in the middle of the crowd, making a pose like a macho predator.

When I was leaving the park, I pondered over going to an emergency room, but I was drunk and high, so I decided to go home. It was painful and torturous to make those two kilometers from the park to my uncles' house. Each step I took was like somebody would prick my knee with pins, I started walking with my leg stretched, I could not bear to bend it. The path seemed to last forever. I arrived home sweating, almost without any of the alcohol effects.

I climbed up the stairs of my uncle's house with difficulty, it seemed I had a wooden leg. I went in the bathroom and looked for the povidone, I put my pants down and then I saw the wound. That really looked bad. It was a hole. I put some povidone on a piece of cotton and laid it over the wound. Fuck it, it burned like hell, I had to restrain myself from screaming and waking everybody up. I came back upstairs to my room, in the attic. I laid in bed and fell asleep almost instantly.

I woke up in the middle of the morning. I didn't get enough sleep, but any slight movement I made with my leg would hurt terribly. I tried to get up but my leg hurt even more. *I am fucked*, I thought. I heard some noise coming from downstairs, who would it be? My aunt and uncle would be at work already, it should be my cousin. I put on some trunks, with tears in my eyes from the pain, and literally dragged myself to the stairs and yelled to her:

"Tête, Tête, come here, please!"

After a while, she opened the door that linked the two halls and said:

"What's going on?"

"Yesterday I fell and I can barely walk, help me here, please."

She climbed up the stairs, looked at my knee and uttered:

"Holy crap, how did you do this?"

I told her the story briefly and she left to pick up the first aid case. My cousin had been taking care of the pilgrims on their way to Fátima and knew how to heal wounds.

"Gee, Gonçalo, I'll have to take you to the hospital, this looks really bad."

She helped me down the stairs. I got in her red Fiat Punto, the same one I took to the freshman reception. She gave it some air and started the car in a few seconds. Shortly afterward, she left me in the emergency room and said:

"I have to go to work, I cannot wait for you, try to grow up!"

I waited for like half an hour until I was called. I was attended by a nurse who, seeing the wound, said I would have to get some stitches. I waited for another half hour, I was hungry, I hadn't eaten in hours. A doctor showed up, he looked at the wound and asked:

"How did you do it?"

"I was drunk and jumped over a barbed wire fence."

He looked at me astonished and then smiled.

"Right, I'll have to give you a few stitches and local anesthesia. Are you allergic to anything?"

"No."

"Do you take any medication?"

"No."

"So, in like 30 minutes I will treat your leg, now the nurse will come and prepare you."

I had been waiting for over an hour for the surgery to begin, and meanwhile, my hunger grew. I was in a hospital hall and that was depressing. All there was to see were sick people with sad faces.

The surgery went well. The doctor, while he was sewing me, told me when he used to be a student, he also took some monumental guzzles, but afterward, he had met his ex-wife and got adapted to her habits. They had two kids and have been divorced for two years, though he had a kind of affair with one nurse. The fellow was clearly given to chit-chat and I was afraid he was not focused on his task.

"Well, you will have to wear this bandage on your leg for a week, the six stitches I have given you will fall on their own, you'll not have to come back here. When you shower, do not get the bandage nor the wound wet. Here, you have a crutch to lean on, use it during this week. Walk carefully now, the effects of the anesthesia will still last. Try not to bend the knee too much. Have fun, you are at the right age for it."

He smiled, slapped my back and went away.

A crutch? Really? Are we not over-reacting? Is it really necessary to walk with this, as if I was some disabled old man or a deformed cripple?

Anyway, I was really hungry and went to the hospital cafeteria, where I ate like there was no tomorrow. I left the hospital and noticed I could not walk home. I would have to take a bus. That would be the first time I would ever take a bus; in Castelo Branco, I always go places by walking. It is a small town.

I went to the bus stop, limping. I checked the schedules, noticing a bus to Sé came by and I decided, on the go, to take it and go see my grandmother at the senior's home. It was annoying to take the trip standing up, the driver seemed to do it on purpose and would brake carelessly, take sharp turns like crazy. Besides that, they barely gave me enough time to climb off at the bus stop. A fellow without any human empathy for people with limited mobility like myself.

I went to see my grandmother, who was astonished to see me limping and with a crutch. I told her the story without too much detail. She laughed a lot. Then she made the same question as always:

"So, have you found a girlfriend?"

"Well, not yet. I like a lady from Lisbon, but she doesn't like me."

And I told her, without details, about my relationship with Luísa.

"Back in my days, the ladies wanted to get a lad to get married. Now they work and behave like goats. That has changed a lot, Son!"

We talked for quite a while, we even went for a snack and then I got on the bus again, heading to my uncles' neighborhood, luckily with a different driver.

I had dinner with my aunt and uncle and pondered not going out that night, but I went to the Burrow anyway. They were sober and also there was not a great will to go out, besides that, the band that would be playing was a piece of trash. Joey Nights had gone out to dinner with his girlfriend and her friends. I was sorry for him.

We went out for some coffee at the Society, somebody ordered a beer, and the others followed. Without even knowing how, the table was full of beers and the ashtray full of cigarette butts. We decided to go out in the night, from bar to bar. We went to the Emigrant Coffee, a small place, dark and depressing, but where there is some table soccer. We played and drank more beer. We went to the center of the city, I was walking slowly, with the help of the crutch. We stopped by the Black Tulip, a bar where the junkies from the Agricultural School usually drop by, and there we found some heavy scum: Ricardo, Mike, Gasolines and Madeiras. One time we got another beer, another time we smoked more hash. Everybody asked about what had happened to my leg. I told everyone different stories, one more surreal than the next.

We left the Black Tulip, staggering. We went to 5th Dynasty for a drink. It is a tradition to have a drink over there and skip the bill, although, when the bar is empty, we cannot keep this rule. However, this night, there was a huge confusion in the bar, a terrible mess, which led us to think we could drink and not pay. Eight drinks for eight big guys and what followed was to run away from the bar without paying, but there was a little detail, I was lame.

"Wait for the lame man, you motherfuckers!"

"Catch the lame!" – One of them yelled.

"The lame one shall pay!" – Another one yelled, while we were running towards the City Park.

Before we arrived at the park, we smoked another joint. I already had no pain in my knee at all, I even pondered jumping over the fence again.

When we arrived at the park, we settled near the trailer that was there. We ordered beers and Elói ordered some food. Bora Bora, Boni, Gasolines and Ricardo were gone to take a leak or something else and disappeared for a while. Meanwhile, Madeiras and Mike had a laughing attack and were stuck in the middle of the road, between the trailer and the entrance to the park. There were only a few cars riding at that time, but still enough to build up a little line. A couple, around their forties or fifties, started to honk so the guys would get out of the way, but they were so drunk they fell on the ground. The man opened the window and started to yell. The woman went out of the car and saw that they could not get up so she told me and Elói:

"Take these drunks off the road!"

"Ma'am" – I said, showing the crutch – "I am a handicapped person who has mobility troubles, I would really like to help, but, as you can see, I am unable."

The woman got furious and looked at Elói. He had his mouth full with a rissole and said some nonsense.

"Watch it, I will call the police!"

"Ouch, not the police, I have hemp in my pockets" – I said.

"We are friends with the cops, we have even ridden in their jeep" – Elói said.

And we both started laughing our asses off. The man from the trailer left his workstation and brought his clients, Madeiras and Mike, nearby. At that moment, while I was laughing my ass off, I came to notice that I am really happy when I am with my friends and everything burns down, which means, the further underground we go, the happier I am.

Since nobody liked the band that was playing that night, we stayed in the park by a little corner drinking beer and smoking joints. The group grew bigger and smaller as the night went by. Joey Nights showed up sober. I know my friend well and I saw that he needed to get in our vibe. I took a bunch of hashish from my pocket that I had bought from Hugo, my ex-workmate, and asked Célia, who had shown up as well, to make a fatty. I told Joey to hit it hard.

Way later, Isaura showed up.

"So, you are in town and don't say anything?"

"Ouch, hi, how are you?"

"What happened to you?"

"I work at a circus in Cacém now and a lion wounded my knee."

"Yeah, right. Look, has Boni told you?"

"About what?"

"That I have a boyfriend now."

"Ah! No... congratulations."

"Didn't he tell you anything? I told him to tell you."

"Yeah, Boni is a dude that does not talk about people's lives. He is an old-fashioned, respectful, honest hard worker."

"Yes, yes... he must be. Do you know who he is?"

"Who is what?"

"My boyfriend?"

"Ah, no. Tell me."

"Nuno. He got in one year after you, he knows you."

"Ah, right... nice. No idea who he is."

There was some silence and I thought of going back to my group of friends.

"Aren't you gonna say anything about my new hair?"

"Ah, I hadn't noticed, it's dark in here... yes, it looks good." I pondered if she was mocking me, because her hair looked exactly the same.

"You know, Gonga, sometimes we only notice things we've had when we lose them."

Seriously? Would I have to stand poor philosophy at two am? I changed the subject with a question about her course, which, actually, did not interest me at all, and then I patiently waited for her to finish her jibber-jabber and went away.

After a whole hour of drinking more beer and smoking hashish, Lídia showed up.

Really, I am a very weird guy, because I am not minimally attracted to Isaura who is actually a good-looking girl. While Lídia, who is very thin and not appealing at all, attracts me a lot. One must highlight that I had never noticed her until the day of the drinking record at Ti Jorge's.

Between the first and the second year of the course, me and Joey Nights decided it was high time someone would hit the record of drinking eight cups in a night, in that lair, by Gasolines and Elói. We prepared mentally and, by six pm, we went to Ti Jorge's with the objective of, not only surpassing this record, but also imposing a number that nobody could hit within the next ten years.

We drank and drank and drank, we ate peanuts, and lupines, and some hard and green snacks that had been in that hole for months. Around ten at night we already had hit the record and surpassed it by far, when Lídia and a friend, Sônia, looked inside while passing by the tavern, and saw us. I got up, staggered up to the door, opened it and told them to get in, they hesitated, the tavern had a bad aspect and the clients even worse, but they got in and said:

"What are you guys doing here? Tomorrow we have class!"

"Dear colleagues, you are looking at the holders of the new drinking record of Ti Jorge's. Including these ones, we are already counting ten cups" – I said proudly.

"But it's Tuesday!"

"And?"

"We worked a lot to reach this goal" – Joey Nights said.

After so much beer, any woman that would have gotten in that cave, would look pretty to me. And Lídia seemed incredibly beautiful to me.

"Eh, well, hey, Lídia, it's been a while, I have been wanting to talk to you, and Joey Nights won't let me lie. I have deep feelings for you."

She started to laugh and I saw that, though she did not like to be in that cave, she did like that I was hitting on her. Meanwhile, Joey Nights was trying his luck with Sônia.

"I have a boyfriend, Joey, it's not worth it."

"But you know he doesn't care for you, right, Susana?"

"I'm Sônia, Joey, my name is Sônia."

We were there for another good hour, two more cups came, we kept on trying to seduce them in a very corny fashion, they would laugh and, at times, would seem offended, however one could see they were enjoying themselves and had their egos quite high.

"Gonga, you have never even noticed me before" – Lídia complained.

"Yes, I have, but I am a shy fellow. And today, which is one of the most important days of my life, for I have hit a historical record, I wanted to ask you to marry me."

"How beautiful, I am moved" – Joey Nights said.

We all laughed, I tried to remain serious and to keep eye contact with Lídia.

"No, I don't want to, sorry" – she said laughing.

"You just broke my heart. At least give me a chance. If you want, I can go to your parents' house to ask them."

"You'd rather not, otherwise you would go guzzling all of my father's booze."

By eleven something we walked them home, they lived together in a house in a neighborhood kind of close to ours.

"It's not necessary, we can go alone just fine" – they said.

"Don't think about it, such good-looking ladies cannot go around alone this late, some drunks can come by and try to do mean things to you. We would rather go, so I won't worry" – I said.

We went to their house, they didn't want to let us in, but also, they didn't make much of an effort to avoid it. Unfortunately, we made a huge mess getting in and they got scared because they thought the landlady, who lived downstairs, would wake up and literally kick us out.

Since that day, I have always flirted with Lídia, deep in I saw right away that we had nothing in common, but I like to coquet around her and she plays along. Due to that, when I saw her in the park, I thought, perhaps, we could still make out.

"Check this out! If it isn't my future wife!"

"Ouch, Gonga, you're alive? I haven't seen you in such a long time, what happened to the leg?"

"I fought with a cop."

"Serious? What happened?"

"I am wanted because I am a Tibetan Buddhist."

"Yes, sure, you're a drunk who fell in some hole."

"Yes, close enough. So, wanna date me?"

"No" – she said as if it was the most absurd thing she had ever heard. - "I am looking for my friends, haven't you seen them?"

This situation got me thinking that with Lídia I have no shame, but towards a lady I care for, I shake like a green cane. Lídia only attracts me physically and, let us be honest, she is not a great beauty, which gets me thinking that in this game of seduction there is no steady rule.

"Hey, Lídia, but don't you see that I suffer from your rejection?"

"You're not my type."

"I'm not your type? What do I lack?"

"I like more manly men."

"Ouch, that one hurt. More manly? Things like hair on the chest? Worker's hands?"

"Like that, I don't like your style."

"Don't say that! Give me a chance. We could be very happy, or, at least, tonight."

"I'm not one of those."

"But I've already asked you to marry me."

She would laugh, but I knew she would not give in. Elói came around.

"Well, Elói, what about those eyes!" – Lídia said.

"It is from the contacts."

"Sure it must be..."

"Elói, Lídia doesn't want to make out tonight."

"Really, Lídia! If I was a girl I would certainly date Gonga."

"Shit, if you were a girl you would be too ugly, Elói" – I joked.

We laughed our asses off and Lídia took the time to go away.

I did not stay in the park for much longer, my cousin was around and I asked her to give me a ride when she went home. And that is how it was, I stayed a while longer, drinking and smoking with my friends, but, on the following day, there were things to do.

I woke up with a slight hangover, had lunch, and went to school to talk to the Physics teacher. Between my neighborhood and the school there are only two bus stops, but still I had to take the bus. Climbing up the stairs would make my leg hurt so, when I arrived at the school, in order to go up to the second floor, for the first time ever I used the elevator. The Physics teacher is a young man, a little weird, seems he is not really into fellowship with the students, but when he sees the student showing interest, he turns out to be quite a lovely character. He gave me copies of this year's exam. He asked me why I was using a crutch and I told him the truth, he did not laugh, quite the opposite, he threw me a censoring gaze.

I caught the bus again and headed to the train station. I bought a train ticket to Lisbon that would leave from Castelo Branco at five am. I would rather go for one more academic weeknight out and then go straight to the train station.

For the rest of the afternoon, I was packing up and then I had dinner with my aunt and uncle. The dinners always take place along with the TV news; this time they were saying we should not drop kitchen oils in the drain. My uncle argued like this:

"This is silly! Everything goes to STS. Just the other day, I changed the oil in my car and threw it into the sewer gutter."

My cousins disagreed almost in anger, they said it was an attack on the environment and that they could take the oils to the Eco-station themselves.

I got dressed for another night, although I was worried about losing the train, it was possible that I would get wasted and lose track of time, it would not be the first time.

I showed up at the Burrow and my partners were already considerably drunk. We smoked some playdough and went down to the Society. I started drinking some draft beer cups, I needed to keep up with those thugs' pace. Paula and Célia showed up. I asked Paula to take me to the station around four-thirty. She is quite responsible, even heavily drunk. I put my backpack in her car.

When we arrived at the party, even though I was already woozy, I was still kind of sober. That night the band playing was Bill's Farm. Joey Nights and Elói jumped over the wall again to skip the ticket. I decided, with much regret, to pay for it. I drank more beer, had a cigarette, talked to someone, and smoked some pot. At some point, the band was in the middle of the concert, the elements of the Burrow and the rest of the paltry friends were in the middle of the ballroom. And Elói started to stress out:

"That fellow, he is in the middle of the dance floor, looking for trouble."

I too had seen the same individual, an almost two-meter-tall guy, wide chested, looking like an armoire. He was right in the middle of the mess, and when anybody would touch him, he would vehemently push them away.

"Eh, well, I can't resist, I'm gonna teach him a lesson" – said Elói and we all tried to stop him, but he was already in the middle of the dance floor and, shortly after, he was all over that armoire, who was trying to slap him as one would cast away a fly.

It did not take long until the two-meter-tall guy lost it and went straight to Elói to request some explanation. The armoire's friends got in the fight and tried to catch Elói and the elements of the Burrow went out to defend their member. I threw the crutch on the floor and thought I could appease the scene, but when I was getting close to where they were, I saw one of the armoire friends taking advantage of the situation and slapping Elói around. I went faster, and on some impulse, gave him one of those pushes; I got him walking backward, he tripped over someone and fell on the ground. Meanwhile, the two-meter-tall giant was furious, he slapped Boni, pushed Joey and was trying to reach Elói at any cost. More people got in on the confusion, a pandemonium was set, the band stopped playing, the singer tried to calm down the hostiles:

"Guys, it's enough, calm down, this is a party."

Finally, someone stopped the giant, they took Elói from the site, I was looking for my crutch and the band started playing again. Where did I leave the damn crutch? I looked and looked, to the right, to the left, among the people, up and down. So, where is it? While I was seeking, I was making eye contact with people around me hoping someone would show up and say: "Here, Gonga, take your crutch, I was joking." However, that did not happen and, suddenly, I bumped into the armoire and the guy I pushed. I thought: "fuck it, I'd rather buzz off, where are my scumbag friends?" I buzzed off as quick as I could, limping, obviously.

I finally found my friends, they were in the middle of a jest, commenting on the scene with the giant.

"Eh, well, you're fucked up, even the band stopped" – Célia said, laughing.

"Elói is really crazy, don't give him any more booze" – someone sensible said.

"Did anybody see my crutch?"

Everybody started to laugh.

"I'm serious! Someone swiped my fucking crutch!"

I went back to the place where I thought I had left it, but it was gone forever. I kept on drinking beer and smoking hash until four am, when Paula told me I had rather get going.

At last, besides the Burrow, at the station, there were still Brígida, Gasolines, and Madeiras to say goodbye to me. I must confess I was really happy and moved to be with my friends. Everybody, with the help of the booze, told me they would miss me, that they felt my absence and that in September things would strongly be back to the way they were. I felt like I was in The Gonga Show, they would laugh heartily at any stupid thing I would say, "Eh, well, Gonga, you're the best" or "Eh, well, this fellow is really crazy". We smoked the last joint at the train station, I took my sneaker off and pretended I was calling my boss and telling her I would not show up to work. Someone snapped the sneaker from my hand and threw it on the railway. I complained, went down the railway and threw the sneaker back to the group while they were laughing as if there was no tomorrow.

The train came by, kisses, "see you, friends," I yelled and got in the wagon. I sat down, in front of me there were two ladies my age, one was beautiful. I remembered I was wearing contacts and should take them off, then I wanted to stretch my leg, but the two ladies were in my way and I could not do it. I used the seat beside me to lay the wounded leg and pondered once more about going to the restroom and taking the lenses off. Even though the train was shaky, I closed my eyes and, in a few seconds, I fell asleep. I woke up with somebody shaking me a bit. At first, I thought it was the train shaking, but the movement was getting more and more violent. I opened my eyes with some difficulty and saw the reader requesting my ticket. I took the paper and gave it to him, the ladies were still in front of me, kind of sleepy. I closed my eyes and fell asleep again.

I woke up startled, at first, I did not know where I was. After I had recognized the place, I looked out the window and we were arriving in Lisbon, the ladies were not there anymore. I looked at my backpack and nobody had stolen it and I remembered the damn crutch. Where would it be?

I went off at East Station and took another train to Cacém. I was hungry, sleepy and my leg was hurting. I was walking like a zombie, above all I still had to work by four pm. That was going to be a hard day.

When I arrived home, around eleven o'clock, I ate something and went to bed. My mother had washed the sheets and left some clean ones, folded for me to make the bed. I did not have enough strength for that, so I went back to sleep. I should point out however, that I did not make the bed for a whole week, until my mother, in a moment of rage, spoke these words:

"You filthy animal, you have been sleeping for a whole week without sheets! Aren't you ashamed? Go immediately make the bed!"

That day, when I went to work, I was tired, feeling like ending the journey and hibernating for many days. As I arrived at the store, there was the boss, Cristina, and snotty Christiane. They saw me limping and I had to tell the story. Obviously, I did not give details. It was a long and painful workday.

I have Said Goodbye to the Blockbuster
– Tuesday, August 21st, 2001

Last week I handed my resignation to Cristina. I knew she would be alone in the store on the morning of the 17th and I had been there on purpose to hand her the paper. She got sad, asked me to think about it, and if I changed my mind, the door to the store would be opened. I said I wanted to go out on vacation and then study for the Physics exam and, in case I flunked, I would be in touch.

I have an ambiguous feeling about leaving my job. On one hand, I really like the cinephile environment in the store, being able to watch so many movies, my workmates, the nice customers that come by, but, on the other hand, there is a negative part, which is the low salary, the arguments with the clients who do not want to pay fees when they bring back the tapes after the deadline, the scum that go to the store to steal and make me play cop. And, obviously, Luísa's possible presence.

Regarding Luísa, there is some doubt inside of me, and the more I want to forget her, knowing that she lives just a few meters away always gets me uneasy. I believe, the day I leave the store, I will quit feeling this anguish of being constantly under the expectation that she will show up at the movie rental. This even seems like a *déjà vu*. The same thing happened to me regarding Elsa, when I left the bar in Cacém Station.

Late June, she started showing up at the movie rental at the time I was out for dinner, coincidently or not. When I was back from dinner, Eduardo would always tell me:

"Look, your ex has been here."

I would be angry, I would check on her data and confirm her presence and the movie she was taking. There was a day I was not able to restrain myself and I have sent her an SMS:

"You don't have to come over only when I'm out for dinner. I promise I won't bite."

I thought the second sentence would appease the first one a little. I waited impatiently for her answer.

"I don't have the slightest idea of your dinner schedule."

I felt really bad reading her answer, she was so blunt and dry, and, possibly, it was true, she would not be waiting for my dinner time, she had better things to think about. Worse than that, was recalling Elsa and the way I had behaved towards her. I have come to notice that I played the same dirty game, playing the victim in the relationship. I wish to be a better person, a fellow that is happy with himself, not needing this kind of attitude. Therefore, I decided to answer:

"Sorry, forget the message."

She did not answer. From that day on, she quit showing up at the store and sent her brother to go and pick up movies. Sometimes, sporadically, I would tell him to say hello on my behalf. I have not seen her in quite a while, I even thought I was going to leave the movie rental without ever laying my eyes on her again, but, last Saturday, I took the morning shift, until four o'clock. When I was going home, I bumped into her with her brother and a friend. I greeted the three of them. I noticed that she was smiling and seemed happy to see me.

"So, it's been a while!"

"It's true" – she said – "how are you doing?"

"Well, fine, I have already handed in my resignation, on the 31st I leave Blockbuster."

"Really! And then?"

"I'm going on vacation for a few days in Holland and afterward to Castelo Branco to study for the Physics exam."

"How cool! You must be dying to go on your vacation to Holland."

"Yep, plus, two friends from Castelo Branco will go as well. It shall be very nice. And you? What have you been doing?"

"We have been to Algarve, in the first week of August." When she said "we", she was referring to her brother who was right by her side.

"I see, I see, you guys are tanned."

Truth to tell, she was really pretty.

"Ok well, see you, today I left early, I'll take the time to rest."

"Great, give me a sign when you come back from Holland."

We said goodbye with wide smiles. What did she mean by that last sentence? Would it be genuine? Did she really want me to talk to her? She really seemed happy to see me, she would not stop smiling. Why did she quit going to the movie rental?

What I have proven in this interaction is that I still like her, I barely saw her and my heart skipped a beat and my legs were shaking. Actually, I felt in her gaze that she likes me back. I remember our weekend and I know she was happy, so I do not understand why we cannot be together? Why does she not want to be with me? These kinds of thoughts and doubts eat me up, it haunts me all through the day, as if it was my own shadow. I would love to be able to talk to her openly and clear up everything.

Luísa's ghost has followed me lately, this one has been a complicated year in which I have been ditched by many girls. It is not that it affects my ego so much, but it always hurts a little. Besides Luísa, there was also Margaret, Lídia and, recently, Ângela.

Ângela's story holds a lot of resemblance with Luísa's. Ângela is a customer at the movie rental, who comes to the store weekly. We started with some shared glances. I saw that she liked corny romantic comedies and gave her some suggestions and she took some movies on my bill. She works at a bar in Massamá, where I have been a couple of times after work with my colleagues and she paid me a few drinks. It was obvious there was some mutual interest. Until the day I invited her to go to Sintra for a draft beer, as I did with Luísa. She accepted.

Ângela is a tall lady, almost my height and has her body a little hunched. She is not beautiful, but she is not ugly either, one of those girls that do not pop up. She has dark hair, but it is dyed blonde. It looks weird because her complexion does not go with that color.

We went to Sintra, in my dad's car, after work. While we were drinking some draft beers at the same bar I had been to with Luísa, I saw that I had nothing in common with her. She enjoys the paltriest pop, watches movies only to kill time, she is not a cinephile, she hates politics, likes to know about the gossip of the *jet set* and loves to spend a day in the shopping mall buying clothes.

She started telling me how she had remodeled her parents' kitchen, the furniture she had bought, the colors she had used and I quit listening, the conversation did not even slightly interest me and I started recalling the way I enjoyed being with Luísa, in that bar, of how interesting she was and how she had tastes similar to mine. I pondered, at that moment, making out with Ângela. On one hand, I thought she was attractive, on the other hand, she was not doing it for me, I would not want to go out with her again. I had an internal fight, while she kept on talking about the sorts of wood she had used in the kitchen. I got to the conclusion that I should make out with her, but I would need more alcohol.

The bar closed and I was not nearly drunk enough.

"Let's take a walk?" – She asked.

That seemed like a nightmare, we took exactly the same path I took with Luísa and we stopped by the fountain where me and Luísa kissed for the first time. I could not take her off my mind and

I knew I still liked her. By the fountain, I decided I would not go any further and if she wanted, she could step up and I would give in. But Ângela leaned against the wall of the fountain and waited for me to make a move. I took from my pocket a bunch of tobacco and smoked a cigarette, the momentum was gone and nothing happened. We went back to the car, in silence, with our heads down. I left her in Massamá and headed home, quite depressed. She keeps on coming to the movie rental, but I have quit going to her bar, the chemistry is lost.

It's times like these that I break down and remember the "mother of all the ditchings." And, curiously, it was not a ditch per se, but rather a demonstration of my own stupidity. I was in the middle of the first year and there was a fresh girl, about whom the simple fact of mentioning her name would make me lose sleep, who I have always believed to be a hell of a fox, one who is way out of my league. One day, for no reason, we talked about movies and she mentioned that she wanted to watch the movie: *Alien 4 – Resurrection*. I said I liked it too and I invited her to go watch it in the theater. She accepted.

Before going to the movies, I told Joey Nights and he said it was a mistake to go to the movies and then for a draft beer. He affirmed that I would rather get her drunk and make out with her. I should have listened to the great wise man of the night.

We met nearby the theater, she was beautiful with a really nice body and elegantly dressed. I thought: "this one is way out of your league, Gonga, what could a fox like that expect from you?"

That old theater in São Tiago shopping mall is quite mythical to me. It is where all of the Burrow and I watched *Funny Games* (1997), directed by Michael Haneke. After the movie, we discussed, in a cheerful cinematographic chat at Ti Jorge's, what the director's intention was because the movie was very masochistic. Me and Joey Nights watched *Titanic* with Leonardo DiCaprio and Kate Winstlet, and when, at the end of the movie, Leonardo dies, all the ladies started crying. I am sure that people around us thought me and Joey were a cute gay couple. It was also in that theater that we watched the Italian movie: *Life Is Beautiful* by Roberto Benigni. That movie is a masterpiece and at the end, when we got up, we noticed that Elói was crying, all moved. Poor him, he had to put up with us all over the night: "my cry baby, don't you see that's Jewish propaganda".

Anyway, I went into that mythical theater room with this beauty, quite nervous. We shared popcorn and made brief remarks while watching the movie, and in the end, we went for a drink at Patrimônio, a bar with quite a nice environment. I pondered for a while about what to drink, I couldn't decide between a beer, a Baileys whiskey or a natural juice. The beer seemed to me quite vulgar, the Baileys would be more like a lady's drink and I did not feel like having a natural juice at night. I ended up picking the Baileys and she had the orange juice. Since she was not a smoker, I decided not to take tobacco with me, but it was really hard not to have a smoke while I was drinking. We talked about the movie, she enjoyed it, though she did not find it anything special. I agreed with her and mentioned some movies that she would possibly like.

Afterward, she told me about her homeland, which was somewhere in the center of the country, about how beautiful the woods were, of the many rivers and streams that were there and she told me she loved wandering around the granges surrounded by nature. She talked superficially about her relationship with her sister and her parents and asked me questions related to this subject. Truth to tell, it was quite a nice conversation, she had an easy smile and would talk about feelings with no difficulty or shame. During the time we were there, I wondered if there was any chance of being with her. Maybe this was just our first date and I should take it easy, however, if I saw an opportunity, I would follow through and if she said no... patience, life goes on.

"I really enjoy checking out the origins of names and I have checked yours" – she smiled.

"Mine? Serious! So, tell me what it means."

"It's from Germanic origin, it means: willing to fight."

"Ok, how interesting. And yours?"

"Mine is Greek and means: the one who has wisdom."

"Cool!"

"The book also shows the origins of surnames. The most common ones."

"You must check mine up."

We left the bar, as a gentleman, I paid the bill and took the beautiful maiden home. She lived slightly close to the train station and as we were walking, I got an enormous urge to piss, but did not want to do it in the middle of the street. I wanted to give her a good impression, but the eagerness to relieve my bladder was getting bigger. When we arrived at the building, she invited me up to see that book. I accepted, hesitating a little because I was about to urinate right there.

She shared the house with another lady, who was already asleep and therefore she asked to keep the noise down. Her room was big, tidy, and smelled good; there was a desk nearby the window, with a computer, a high armoire and a double bed. She took the book from her nightstand and showed me. We sat on her bed.

"Look, here it says that Dias has a Roman origin."

I thought of asking to go to the bathroom, but I was in doubt, it would seem odd, I have barely got in her house and would already be asking to go to the bathroom. However, my desire to take a leak was higher than it all. We remained in silence.

"Well, so, I should get going..." – I said, heading for the door.

She showed me to the door and gave me a plastic smile.

Already by the door, I told her:

"We can set up another night like this, right?"

"Yes, sure, bye."

I climbed down the staircase and, in the first dark place I found in the street, I opened my fly and took out my vulture. An unparalleled pleasure ran through my body letting out that liquid, and while it took a while, it was an incomparable relief. Still, I was afraid some neighbor would see me urinating there, or even worse, if "the one whom the simple fact of mentioning her name would make me lose sleep" would be by her window watching me watering the herbs.

I went home wondering if I acted right. On one hand, I had shown I was a nice fellow, I did not smoke, did not take advantage of her, but on the other hand, maybe I took things too slowly, I should have tried something. It did not take long to see that she would ignore me. I invited her out again, and right away she said no, with an unfriendly face and a week later, in the disco, I was not wearing my contact lenses and could see almost nothing, but Elói told me:

"Check it out, there's 'that one who the simple fact of mentioning her name would make you lose sleep' with a fellow."

I blindly looked out to confirm if it was true and saw her with a lad, possibly from her homeland and who was maybe her new boyfriend.

I went home with my ego on the ground, really I am the most unlucky man in the whole town. Still, I didn't quite understand her attitude. I had been sleeping on this doubt until I told Maria João and she told me:

"The lady thought you did not like her and that is why you left her house."

"No, I respected her, I wanted it to be something more serious, that it would not happen right away on the first date."

"Women do not think like that, she took you home and was willing to be with you. As you took off, she felt hurt."

Fuck it, I am really a great sucker, that takes a dumb man! Women like "the one who the simple fact of mentioning her name would make you lose sleep" come by once in life.

Changing the subject, my parents went out on vacation and I had the house to myself. First I invited Nice and Rodas for a big dinner. Afterward, on another day, I invited Maria João, Rodas and his younger brother, whose name is Gonçalo too. We all had dinner, which I made, cod with anything and afterward, we went to the living room to play Risk, which is my favorite board game. However, some little insects were coming out from the game box, quite weird and disgusting.

"Check it out, Gonga, you must have those insects under your bed" – Rodas said.

"Ouch, how disgusting!" – Maria João said giving the impression she would puke quite soon.

We played until late, it was really fun. When Maria left, I stayed with the brothers drinking beer and wine and watching video clips that I had recorded on a VHS with the windows open, because it was very hot. One of the songs that played was Leonard Cohen: *Dance me to the end of love*, which is wonderful. But they were mocking, ranting and raving about the singer, there was no other option than to cast them out of my house. I said I was tired and wanted to sleep. I think they got fucking mad at me.

I decided to collect the board games, Risk and Monopoly, under my bed, and again I saw those insects wandering around my room. I have put the games in the attic. When my parents came back from vacation, I told them what was happening.

"And did you clean under the bed?" – My mother asked.

"No."

"And what are you waiting for?"

"I did not know what product to use."

"The one I put: floor cleaner" – I noticed my mother already did not have much patience left.

"Right, in a little while I will clean it up."

Although, I haven't had much time to clean up and, sincerely, I have never seen those insects again.

Back to my colleagues at the movie rental: Ana, the lady who would only work weekends, has resigned and now works in the shopping mall bookstore, which means, I still see her often.

Hugo shows up sometimes and we chat for a while after I close the store, he always scrounges some movies and sometimes we smoke a joint.

Vacation in Amsterdam – Thursday, September 27th, 2001

At this precise moment, I am taking a break from my Physics studies. I came back from Holland on September 14th, which was on a Friday and, on the following Sunday, I came back to Castelo Branco. On Monday, I started taking lessons from a Physics teacher, quite a nice guy who does his tutoring at his home, to me, Célia and Cláudia.

I am giving my all for this exam. I wake up early, around eight, and before nine I am already studying, I only stop for eating and smoking a cigarette. After lunch, I go out for some coffee with Célia and Cláudia and then we go together to our lessons, which take place every day in the middle of the afternoon. Afterward, we stick around for some chatting, later on, I have dinner with my aunt and uncle and at night I study for a few more hours. I am more than convinced that I will be approved, if the teacher doesn't make the exam too difficult.

Well, I think I ought to write about my vacation in Amsterdam. However, before telling of my adventures, I should mention that the 31st was my last workday at the movie rental. It was a special day, my former colleagues showed up to wish me luck and the cinephile customers from the neighborhood also wanted to greet me and exchange phone numbers. Even Luísa came by, she had been walking around the movie rental until she could have a moment alone with me, but, when she was there, I was talking to a customer and friend, who had brought me, from his personal collection, the Clockwork Orange by Kubrick. I enjoyed the movie so much that I went to the bookstore, where Ana works currently, to buy the book. Therefore,

Luísa, as she had seen I was surrounded by people, decided to only wish me a nice trip to Holland and asked me to give her a call when I was back. I felt sorry, when I closed the door to the movie rental for the last time and handed the keys to my friend and now former colleague Eduardo.

On the following day, September 1st, I went to the Magoito beach with Rodas and we spent the day laughing, because we invented an imaginary character: The King of the Beach. A hero who was irresistible to all the women, indeed, their own boyfriends would support and be proud if their partner had been shagged by The King of the Beach. Well, we made movies all afternoon with the character and it was quite amusing.

I promised to bring hemp to Rodas, so we would smoke together when I was back.

On the 2nd I went up and down with my luggage, my mother had bought lots of canned food for me to take and as I could only carry up to 25 kilos, I accepted and packed about a dozen cans of tuna and pilchard. I have noticed that my parents are nervous about me traveling and my father gave me an alert:

"Be careful, I heard that in Holland there are stores with whores and drugs! Do not lose yourself, instead you go to the museums."

On the 3rd, I had lunch early and took the train to East Station. Then, I waited for another train that would take me to Oporto. I noticed, since I was still in Cacém, that the case I was carrying was too heavy. Besides that, I had a small backpack with my documents and travel guides. The case is a Tommy Hilfiger and was offered to me when I bought a perfume. It is not practical, but it is stylish and that is mighty important.

During the trip to Oporto, I read a book about the life of the Dutch painter Vincent Van Gogh. I decided that I was going to visit the museum dedicated to him in the city of Amsterdam. The trip went well, from time to time I went to the bar to drink something and smoke a cigarette. When I arrived at the Campanhã Station, there he was, my good friend Elói, waiting for me. We gave a big hug and I was really happy to see him.

We took the bus up to his neighborhood, we talked the whole time as he showed me the significant points of the town. I have been to Oporto before, on a New Year's Eve with Marco, when I was 19 years old. Things didn't go well because an ATM ate my card and we did not have any money to come back to Lisbon, so we went to the Police Station, but they were overwhelmed and did not give a damn and my father ended up going to East Station to buy tickets so we could come back.

His neighborhood is not so different from the ones in Cacém, maybe there are more trees and grass. He lives in a tower. The house is cozy and quite tidy and Elói's room was way cleaner than mine. He lives with his father who, by that time, was out on vacation. We went to a supermarket to buy green wine for dinner.

"You know what, Gonga, this vacation I didn't have any alcohol."

I was not surprised, before Elói arrived at Castelo Branco he did not drink or smoke. However, the company wasn't not the best and, when he would go out, he started to drink as if he had no soul. He is a really intelligent guy, interested in informatics, movies and nature. This fascination for nature got him to enroll in environmentalist societies, he quit eating meat and he is a volunteer in the school bird recovery center. However, there is an animal side of him that is released when he drinks. He becomes extremely violent and totally out of control.

He made dinner. We obviously ate fish, a salmon. We drank two bottles of wine and right away I noticed that Elói started to change, as he was not used to drinking anymore, he took a different pace. We hit the night in Oporto. On the bus downtown, he told me:

"Today I want to go to a zone at Ribeira, where there is a paltry neighborhood. I have never gotten in there, but I want to go with you."

I became a little apprehensive, imagining how the shit could hit the fan, however, I did like the fact that he said that to me, because it was a demonstration that he believed in my bravery, possibly he believes in it more than me.

I felt like I had a debt with him since a violent episode that took place at Alternative. On a Thursday night, me and Elói were on the dance floor, filthy drunk; he told me he was going to the bathroom and I remained where I was. Suddenly, I heard some confusion. I saw Elói arguing with the nightclub bouncers and I headed to the disco door to check what was going on and saw a couple of doormen forcing him to the exit. I tried to talk to them and appease their nerves, meanwhile, I took the time to hand the ticket to the lady who was watching the coats. When I come back, I see Elói getting beaten up pretty hard by the two bouncers, still the guy knows how to defend himself pretty well and gave them some punches. The coat lady left the counter and pushed us out, then she yelled at the bouncers. What was I doing while my friend Elói was getting beaten? I was holding the coats... Fuck it, I really must be a wuss! Instead of not giving a fuck for the coats and helping my friend, I was watching two guys hitting one. Well, one must say Elói is no victim in this story, for what it seems, when he headed to the bathroom, there were some beer bottles there and he was throwing them against the wall. And a guy who was hit by some glass shards in the face complained to the doormen. Though in this situation I just stood there, it's worth pointing out that at Academic Week's concert I stood up for him.

There was another situation, at a bar nearby Alternative, in which a lady came to me very unsettled.

"Please, come with me! Your friend Elói is crazy and wants to beat someone."

I followed her, Elói and the rest of the scum were by the bar's door and I said right away:

"I don't know what's going on, but I stand by Elói."

At this point, the animal howled, he started to climb up the wall through a bindweed, the plant broke, and he fell on the ground and on his back, but he jumped back up, and started to scream at the group that was with the lady that called me. I stood by Elói's side, ready for the fight, even without the slightest idea of the subject matter. Afterward, I came to know that it was about a piece of skirt.

However, even with all the excuses I try to make up, the night in the disco is still a thorn in my side that I will not be able to take out so soon.

We got into Ribeira. It is an old neighborhood, looks like the old part of Lisbon. We went to a few taverns, one looking worse than the others. Almost all of them had pennants and scarves of Oporto Soccer Club, some would even have anti-Lisbon messages. I avoided talking to the people, they could notice my southern accent and that could go downhill and, instead of going to Holland, I would be going to jail. The customers were mainly old people and workers, the women looked hideous and some had bigger mustaches than me.

I had some drinks, mixed wine and beer and bitter almond liqueur, which could only go wrong. I left a bar as if I was Chuck Norris, in a faraway land, hostile, where freedom has been stunted. Not really knowing why, I hit the rearview mirror of a car that was going slow in the neighborhood. The vehicle stopped, the guy started to yell, I kept on walking like a bad nigger from Kzen, Elói stopped, apologized, said his friend was inebriated and came to talk to me.

"Man, you're crazy! Do you want to get in trouble with these people?"

"What the fuck? Where is Elói, the savage destroyer Worm?"

He started to howl, I did the same, then we laughed and headed to Douro River.

We walked down Ribeira, got fed up with walking, from time to time we would stop for a beer. When we arrived at Don Luís Bridge, which links the city of Oporto to Gaia, we sat outside a bar and stayed for a while, contemplating the beauty of the bridge.

"You don't have bridges like this one in Lisbon" – Elói said.

"Not in Lisbon, but in Cacém, over Jardas Riverside, there are quite a few like this one."

"I wanted to come here so you could see the bridge, but they are refurbishing it."

There were some scaffolds.

"We could climb up the scaffolds, Elói." – I threw the bomb.

"Do you think?"

"Is it forbidden?"

"Let's go."

We headed to the bridge and started to climb up the scaffold's stairs, drunk and laughing. When we were halfway up, a man showed up, the security guard, yelling.

"You're crazy, I'm gonna call the cops, come down right now!"

I stopped climbing, looked up and the river was dark, like there was no water, only a black hole. From where I was, I could see the lights of the city of Oporto and the walkway we had taken. The town looked so beautiful to me, I stayed still, hypnotized, contemplating it.

"Hey, Gonga, wake up, can you hear the man?"

I started making my way down, when I was about to reach the ground, the man was furious and yelling at Elói.

"What the fuck! You guys are crazy and come over here to kill yourselves! What the hell is that?"

Elói was trying to calm the guard down. I reached the ground, the guy threw me a furious gaze, I lowered my eyes like a kid who has been caught doing a prank and headed to the city of Gaia.

"Elói, let's see the city of Oporto from the other side?"

"Yep, we'd rather do it."

The man kept on saying obscenities and that got me thinking that Elói was sober, otherwise, he would have already slapped him around or even thrown him from the bridge.

From the other side of the river, the city did not look as beautiful as it did from up on the scaffolds, it was a different perspective.

"Gonga, we have already missed the last bus to my neighborhood."

"And what does that mean?"

"We have to make our way by walking."

"Is it too far?"

"Yep, over one hour."

"Fuck, it's the guard's fault."

"I agree."

The trip between Ribeira and Elói's house seemed like an eternity to me. In the beginning, I was looking at the city monuments with curiosity, but in the end, I was blaming Elói for not warning me about the distance accurately.

I spent the night in a sleeping bag, in his room, we left our sneakers on the window's parapet since they smelled. We fell asleep quickly though I woke up in the middle of the night to Elói's snoring. I was awake for a while and felt afraid of going to Holland alone. When he rolled over and stopped snoring, then I was able to sleep a little more.

On the 4th, I woke up nervous, worried that something would go wrong. We had breakfast, but it was hard for me to swallow. I decided to leave my mobile at Elói's, turned off. I never have any credit and, besides that, the roaming is too expensive, it would be cheaper to call from phone booths.

We left the house and took a bus to the airport. I was always afraid that we would be late. Elói, on the other hand, was laid-back and making jokes, I was sorry he only got tickets for the 10th. On the arrival at the airport, everything was a mess, with people coming and going with luggage. Once more, Elói was restful and led me through the airport. I handed my Tommy Hilfiger case to the counter and then we killed time until the boarding door opened. We were checking the book about Amsterdam and planning on places we would go.

When it was time to go, there was, by our side, a couple crying their goodbye. He was also heading to Holland while she would stay. The scene was very melodramatic, with hugs, kisses and tears. Meanwhile, Elói and I started imitating them, acting exaggeratedly when saying goodbye, pretending we were crying and saying silly things.

"Write to me, please."

"Don't you forget about me, we will always have Castelo Branco."

That scene freed me from my nervousness and I gained the courage to take a flight for the first time ever.

The aircraft was big, the rows on the left side had 3 seats, while the right side had two, it looked full. It took me a while to find my seat. I sat by the window, a northern Portuguese couple sat by my side.

Until the flight took off, I was getting more and more nervous. What if it falls? The probability is low, but once a while it happens. In how many pieces is this machine divided? More than a thousand certainly. And what if one of those fails? I started to sweat. I silently uttered a Buddhist mantra and the Lord's Prayer.

Oporto was hot, almost thirty degrees and the sky was clean. From the air, one could see the whole city, Douro River, and the sea. Afterward, more cities could be seen and finally the green was in sight, the groves, the mountains that looked flat. Bit by bit, I was relaxing, I put on my Walkman and was listening to music while looking out the window checking if I knew where I was. All the land looked the same, everything flat and the cities were little anthills. There were more clouds and I could not see the surface anymore.

The Captain announced we were about to arrive at the destination, though there was no city in sight, he said the temperature was 15 degrees and the sky was cloudy, which means, quite cooler than Oporto. When I began to tidy up my backpack, I asked the couple by my side where I should get my luggage.

"Are you Portuguese? We thought you were a foreigner."

"Oh, yes! Do I look like a foreigner?"

"Yes, you have something of the French about you."

My God, what an insult! Could they not choose any other people?

"I have never been to this airport, do you know where to pick up the luggage?"

Not to this airport or any airport, but I did not want to look like a peasant.

"We can help you."

They were really lovely, they knew the airport and walked me through many halls. I was surprised by the size of the place. They told me they were immigrants from Luxembourg and were going to take another flight. They were about thirty or forty years old and I asked if they had children.

"No, we cannot have them."

"And have you thought of adopting?"

I think I was a little indiscreet, but they were such good people that at the moment it seemed like a normal question. They did not look like they were offended by it and gave me an answer that seemed to me like they were pondering this possibility themselves.

I was very thankful to them, I wished them good luck and headed to the airport exit to catch the train to the Amsterdam Central Station. I asked a couple of people how one could get a train ticket and what was the line. I got on a double-deck train, climbed up to the 2nd floor and the carriage was kind of empty. I checked a railway map that was up on a wall but I did not understand anything, the names were incomprehensible. My tourist guide said the Central Station was the third stop after the airport. On the train there was a lad, who seemed to be about my age, of Indian or Pakistani origin and I asked if the next stop was the Central Station. He did not look away from his cell phone and said yes.

The station was enormous, with many lines, many trains and a fast-moving crowd. They were giving warnings through the loudspeaker, first in Dutch and then in English, about measures to take to prevent robbery. That alert got me even more unsettled. There I was with a very heavy case and a backpack with all my documents and money. I held tight to my belongings and left the station. I knew I had to take a bus or a tram.

There was a blond, tall man, with a Nordic aspect. I thought he was Dutch, so I asked him how to get to the address I had: Kloveniersburgwal. The name of the street was really weird, it looked like someone sneezed and then baptized the street. I did not even try to pronounce it. The man was quite friendly and walked me to a tram stop where he asked something to the driver in Dutch, then turned to me and said: "it's this one".

I got on the tram and asked the driver how much the ticket was. He told me I would have to get in from the back door, I looked to the other end of the vehicle and there was another employee on a counter charging the entrance. I crossed all the way to the other side of the carriage and I noticed the users of the tram looking at me thinking: "what hole did that rare bird come out of?".

"I'd like a ticket to..." – and I showed him the place in the note.

He told me the price, but I did not understand, and I gave him a 10 florins bill and hoped that would be enough. He gave me the change and said he would warn me when we got to my stop. I found a free seat, took it and looked out the window to see a bit of the town, but I could not enjoy the sights, I was too nervous and afraid the collector would not tell me where to get off. After three or four stops, he told me that was the one. I got out through the front door like the other passengers.

I got off the tram adrift. I was on a wide square where there were many streets in many directions. Which path should I take? I would rather not keep walking around, I would have to find someone to indicate the way to me. I asked many passers-by until one of them helped me with the correct instructions.

The Kloveniersburgwal street was a big one, perpendicular to a stream. I walked, checking the numbers on the doors, hoping to find what I was looking for or some sign of the hostel. The sky was getting more and more cloudy and it was going to rain at any moment.

I arrived at the hostel a little tired from carrying the luggage, however glad for arriving well at the lodge. The place did not even look like a hostel, it was just one of those three-or-four story buildings, with wide windows. I climbed up a few steps and rang the bell, a blond lad showed up and formally welcomed me and told me to get in. He took my reservation and started to talk about the rules and obligations of the place. I was too excited to pay much attention to the rules of the house.

He took me to the male dormitory on the second floor and gave me the keys to a locker. It was a relief to leave my case full of pickle cans in the locker and being able to go out free of the weight. I wanted to explore the streets surrounding the hostel.

I left the hostel. In front of me there was a stream of greenish water, to the left there was an iron bridge of weird constructions, the bridge had a ceiling that would form a square. Right by this bridge there was an old building, quite elegant, pink, it looked like a hotel. On the opposite side, the street was full of small businesses and some bars with tables on the sidewalk, although, with the rain threat, there was almost nobody there. The street was called Staalstraat. I walked down this street, checking the showcases, the buildings, the people and I crossed another bridge that was full of bicycles with locks. The street looked like it was made for the tourists, with stores full of souvenirs from the country and the city. At the end of this street, I got into a pedestrian zone, where there were a lot of people riding bikes and an ugly building that looked like it belonged to the government. There was a telephone booth and I wanted to call my mother. I felt like talking to someone. I put some coins in and dialed the number, it rang and rang and there was no answer. I checked my watch, it was six in Holland and five pm in Portugal, which meant my mother was now leaving work.

It started to rain some thin rain, so I decided to come back closer to the hostel and went in a bar. I ordered a beer from the bartender, he asked me if I had a favorite brand and I said:

"Give me some typical Dutch beer."

He smiled and served me some draft beer. There were a few people, one or another group of youngsters speaking in low tones. I took the beer to a window and enjoyed it while having a smoke and watched people passing by with their umbrellas. I pondered about my situation and felt proud of being able to save the money and take the trip alone. I had never been so far from home, the farthest has been Lloret de Mar, on the college freshmen trip.

This town was so different. Everything was different. There were a few cars on the streets and many bikes, the buildings were short and had wide windows, the people were tall and blond and there were bridges and water everywhere. I had more beer as more people came in and out of the coffee shop, the rain tamed down, the night came, and I went back to the hostel a little hungry.

I climbed up and down the many floors looking for a kitchen, but I did not find one. I found the dining hall that was also a bar, the bathrooms, the living room, but no sign of a kitchen. Due to that, I went to my locker, took some cans of tuna and pilchard in tomato sauce and sat down on the hallway floor, between the bathroom and the dormitory, to eat. Some guests passed by me and found it weird to see me there, but they smiled and I smiled back at them. I lacked some bread to eat with the pilchards in tomato sauce. I brushed my teeth and wandered around the hostel.

I wanted to go out in Amsterdam that night. However, I was a little afraid of going out alone at night in that big city. It was not the same as going out in Castelo Branco or Cacém. And what if I got lost? Or if I was robbed by some scum? But, fuck it, staying in the hostel on my very first night in Amsterdam was humiliating! Meanwhile, I heard someone talking Portuguese, by the bar's exit door. I stuck to them, literally.

"Are you Portuguese?"

"Yes!"

"So am I. I arrived today and wanted to go out, but I have no idea where to go."

"Come along with us, we already know some nice places."

The fellows were from Setúbal and were taking the interrail trip. They had been to Italy, Switzerland, Austria, Germany and on the following day they were going to France, then Spain and from there they would go back to Setúbal. They were bragging about taking the trip with very little money and told me about some mischiefs from their adventures. They said Italy was the best place to travel and eat.

We left the hostel and dived into the night. The weather was cool, a little over ten degrees and very humid. I must say that just a few steps away from the hostel I did not know where I was anymore and I just followed them. They wanted to tell me about their adventures and both of them kept talking at the same time.

We got to the famous Red Light District, which is a bunch of narrow lanes around an old church. There are coffee shops selling pot and many establishments selling human flesh, which means, strip-tease shows, group sex, prostitutes of all colors and ages. My chin dropped, the two Portuguese dudes had fun with my reaction. I felt small, a peasant coming out of the paltry suburbs from a held back country to a society that is some light-years ahead. There was a crowd walking through those alleys, they were mostly tourists, though one could see, there were many scoundrels, many vultures waiting for an absent-minded tourist. I do not recall seeing any policemen.

We got to a coffee shop. There was a stand where they had different sorts of hemp for sale. I did not know any of those names. My fellow countrymen said:

"Buy the Orange Sherbet, you'll go crazy right away."

I bought a baggy of a few grams, enough to make like five pot cigarettes.

We sat at a table and they ordered some crazy herb tea, while I ordered a coffee. They made their pot cigarettes and we started to smoke. The environment was dim, there were a lot of people and the music was loud and bad, it was some bad techno.

I got high right away, that herb was really good. They were talking loud, from time to time they would talk to me, but I could not hear or understand and they would keep on talking to each other and laughing. We went to another bar, they bought some herb called 4G. I gave them some of mine and asked them to make a joint. The new bar had hallucinogenic mushrooms and hashish cake.

"Have you guys ever tasted hashish cake?"

"Nope, we tried the mushrooms and I got sleepy, while he was on a trip."

I was hungry therefore, I ordered some hashish cake. It looked like a pastry cake, like one of those people sell in cafeterias.

I ate the cake while having another coffee and smoking more pot. And that is when it kicked in hard, such a hard kick that my head went around. Who were those guys sitting across from me? Then I recalled what I had seen all through the summer on the Portuguese news. Four Portuguese businessmen traveled to Brazil, according to them, to attend some business meetings, but actually they were there for the whores. They had been welcomed by a Portuguese man, who lived over there. He locked them up, robbed them and executed them by striking them in the head with a wooden stick. The bodies, still alive, were buried in a restaurant kitchen. The news was known all over Brazil as: "The Portuguese Men Slaughter".

I started to stress out, thinking those two individuals, seeming friendly, could be two cold blooded murderers preparing to kill me. Fuck, I would die right there, in a foreign country, surrounded by whores and drugs! I started to pay more attention to what they were saying, I was getting almost nothing, the music was loud, but they were laughing louder and louder and were looking at me. They must have been planning how to tear me apart and where to throw my body. The customers of those dim bars had a drug addict aspect and sinister faces. I was more and more sure they had a trap set up for me. On my left side I could feel some kind of breeze getting stronger, I do not know if it was the air conditioner or some hallucination, because my future killers felt nothing and were laughing at me.

We left that bar, all of the coffee-shops looked equally creepy, I wanted to go back to the hostel, I was stressing out worse every minute. They still wanted to wander around a bit more. I contemplated going back alone, but I was lost and high, I did not have the slightest idea of how to get to the hostel anymore. I could barely speak. We got in another bar, I ordered in Portuguese:

"*Dê uma cerveja, se faz favor.*" (Give me a beer, if you'd please.)

The two rascals laughed their asses off, the waiter, a young man of Hindu origin, threw me an unfriendly gaze. I did not understand what was going on, until the man asked me if I could speak English.

"Ah, sorry. A beer, please."

"So, you thought you were in Cacém, damn?" – one of them said laughing.

"Shit, I'm too stuck…"

And they started laughing their gruesome laughter again.

Finally, we headed back to the hostel; the night was cold, there was a mist and I was ready for a fight in case it was necessary. As soon as I saw the street with the sneeze name: Kloveniersburgwal, I was glad, my harbor was there, my home. They were lodged in a different dormitory and were going away on the following day. I didn't even say goodbye; they still expected me to say something, but I disappeared from their sight as soon as I had the chance. I went to the second floor, to the bathroom, took my clothes off, put the money in my locker and the keys under the pillow.

In the dormitory someone was snoring, there was a foot odor, but I was feeling safe then, far from the claws of those two. Time was passing by and I still had my eyes open. I realized that I would have to take it easy, I did not want to lose myself like that every day. I would rather watch out. I should not eat any cake or mushrooms. Bit by bit, I closed my eyes and fell asleep, cozy on my bed. I felt really small.

On September the 5th, I woke up to the noise of my dormitory mates, I got up, washed myself, put something on and walked like a zombie to the cafeteria. There were some kids, mostly from North America, talking loudly and seeming very cheerful for that early in the morning. There were not many options for breakfast, however I filled up. I headed to my locker and prepared for a cultural day.

I thought of going to the city museum that, according to the map, was close by. Still, I asked the clerk if it would be worth it to take a tram; they said no. It was not far at all, but I still got lost and had to ask some people for directions.

The visit to the museum was quite interesting, two things surprised me. One of them was the fact that Holland belonged to Spain many centuries ago, due to the marriage between a couple of princes. The other thing was how much sea territory that Amsterdam has stolen in order to spread its surface over the sea, building dikes and bridges.

I left at noon, hungry and I ate a ham sandwich at one of those trailers in a park. The sky was clear, the weather was neither hot or cold, the day was ideal to wander around, therefore I took a walk through the city streets all the way to the Royal Palace, which is huge, old, and quite beautiful; it seems to be the place where the royal family lives. I could have gone in, but I found the ticket to be a bit expensive and I decided to wander around the palace gardens instead.

I returned to wandering around the town without a steady destination, just checking the landscape and taking some pictures. I came to notice I needed a bike, almost everybody would get around town on a bike. Besides that, all the area is flat, which makes pedaling easier. One other thing that has called my attention is the beauty of the women. They are really good looking, tall, blonde, slim, I do not know if it is from so much bike riding, but one can see they are very healthy.

It still took me a while to arrive at the hostel and I went back to the same bar as the day before; the waiter was the same, who recognized me and smiled.

"Would you like a beer?"

"Yes, please."

"Where have you been today?"

"I have been to the city museum and then just wandering around."

"I have never been to the city museum" – he laughed – "Today was a great day to wander around."

We ran out of things to talk about, and I went to the outside of the bar and stayed there for a while enjoying some sun, along with a few other clients. On a table by my side, there was an Asian fellow. He had a map on the table and he asked me if I knew where something was.

"Sorry, but I am a tourist too."

"Ah, I thought you were Dutch."

"Ah, seriously? I don't look Dutch!"

"I cannot tell Europeans apart, you all look the same to me."

I was very surprised, to me the differences are clear and I tried to explain:

"The ones from the south are, in a general manner, brunette, with dark hair and eyes and they are shorter. The ones from the north, have a lighter complexion, hair and eyes."

He remained silent and, after some reflection, said:

"And you? Are you French?"

French again! I must look like a chauvinist baguette?

"Why do you think I am French?"

"You have dark hair and light eyes, which means, you're neither from the north or south."

I tried to explain to him a little of the different physical characteristics of Europeans, however, I noticed it was too hard. He asked:

"Are you able to tell apart a Greek from a German?"

"Yes, I think so. The Germans have a square face, while the Greeks are brunet and tall."

"It's hard on me. You too cannot tell the Asians apart, can you? To you we are all Chinese, right?"

Well, I tried to answer in a politically correct fashion, but, the truth is they actually do all look the same to me.

A few minutes later he went away with some of his countrymen and I went to the counter to pick up another beer.

Again I ate in the hallway, again pilchards and tomato, between the dormitory and the bathroom. I took a little walk through the streets, without going too far from the hostel or getting in the red area. Once I was back at the hostel, I took a shower and fell asleep, satisfied with my day.

The 6th was the day Joey Nights would arrive. Since I had left my cell phone at Elói's, there was no way we could make contact, but, before leaving Portugal, we had planned to meet on line 1 in Central Station, around 4 o'clock, which was the time his train was supposed to arrive.

I woke up glad, with the hope of having company and walking with him around the city. In the morning, I went to Dam Square which is a building area. They are really beautiful and old and there are always events on the street. The sky was almost clear, but it was getting cloudy bit by bit. I spent the whole day checking my watch, yearning to meet up with my friend.

For lunch I went to the Nieumarkt, which is a mixture between a market with many food stores and a grocery store. I bought chicken legs and a bottle of milk and I sat on a bench in a garden to have lunch. At three o'clock I headed for the Central Station. Step by step I was getting to know the city and it was not necessary to catch any tram.

At the Central Station there was the usual mess, people coming and going, trains arriving and leaving, the loudspeaker announcing the need to watch out for thieves. Before the scheduled time I was already at line 1, reading the arrivals monitor to see the train from the airport and I was looking all around to check if I could see Joey. Nothing. Not a sign of Joey. I stuck around for two or three hours, line after line to check if I could see a familiar face. Eventually, I went to the bathroom and a lady that was keeping and washing it asked me for money. I gave her two coins of 25 cents a florin. One thing that surprised me was the fact that the woman spoke English very well, like all the Dutch that came across my way, which made me think. I wonder if they speak more languages. German or French? Would the Dutch culture be facing a descent and within some years would Dutch quit being the main language of the country?

I left the station with my head down. Joey Nights did not come. I really wanted to see him. I walked down a street in the Red Light District. By the end of the afternoon, a bunch of black women with big asses and boobs were at a window, waiting for clients. They looked at me to see if I would go in. Although, paying for prostitutes is something totally against my few and low principles.

What was I going to do? I would rather call Joey, but I did not have the cell phone and I did not know his number. I would have to call my mother so she would look up his or his parents' number on my notes. I wondered about the possibility that something might have happened to him: might he have missed the flight; might he have missed the bus to the airport; might he be lost in the city? Would he know how to get by? He could have gotten sick or some relative may have died. The cast of possibilities was big. I decided to go back to the hostel with the remote hope of finding him there.

I intended to find the clerk and ask if a Portuguese lad has arrived within those last couple of hours, but the front desk was full of people and I decided to wander around the place and into the dining hall's bar, and there was Joey drinking a draft beer and contemplating the landscape of our sneeze street: Kloveniersburgwal.

"Shit, you're here!"

I was really glad to see him. It was as if I came out of an ugly place surrounded by cement and stepped into a green field full of life. We hugged.

"I arrived and waited for you on line 1" – he said.

"I was on line 1 myself. Are you sure it was line 1?"

"Yep, that's where the train stopped."

"But didn't the train from the airport stop at line 5?"

"I don't think so..."

"Well, fuck it. How did you get here?"

"Since I couldn't find you, I left the station to the taxi square and I caught one."

"But that's awfully expensive, isn't it?"

"Not so much, I gave the address, he put it on GPS and told me the price right away."

"Shit, how modern! In Lisbon they would go all around town only to take your money."

We chatted in the hostel bar, indeed between seven and eight pm it was Happy Hour, which consisted of way cheaper drinks, so we stayed there drinking beer. I told him how my arrival had been and about the two murderers from Setúbal with whom I had gone out.

When the happy hour was over, we ate some cans of tuna, octopus and pilchards in tomato sauce.

"But there must be a kitchen somewhere here" – Joey said.

"Yep, but since I haven't found it yet, I have been eating here."

And we ate, as usual, in the hall between the dormitories and the bathroom.

We went out so I could show him the surroundings, we crossed the Red Light District, saw the hustle and bustle that there was, but ended up coming back to our street. We crossed the square ceiling bridge and up Staalstraat Street, until we arrived at that ugly building. We sat on a bench from where we could have a view of the city half asleep with a light mist to snuggle it. Nearby our bench, there was a monument in homage to the Dutch Jewish people who died in World War II.

I wanted to smoke some weed I found in the hostel hall whilst having dinner. Since Joey does not know how to roll cigarettes, I had to do it myself. I mixed the herb with some tobacco in a pall, he made a filter and I rolled the joint, and this is the point where I usually have problems. I do not have much skill in this process and some of the product usually falls out, this turn it was fairly good and we

both smoked. The herb was good and we were contemplating the city while getting breezed. We sat in silence until I asked him:
"What are you thinking about?"
"About a time in which you saved my life."
"Me?"
"Yes, once we went to Ti Jorge's after some smoking, it was winter and it was freezing cold. I was already so high that I had forgotten to take a jacket. I arrived at Ti Jorge's, shivering from the cold, I wasn't able to speak or even think, I believe I was about to faint. When you saw me like that, you gave me your feather jacket and it warmed me up gradually, and just like that, you saved my life."
"Ah, I don't even remember that."
Although I did not remember that story, my mind flew to that puffer jacket I bought when I was like 16 or 17 years old, in a sportswear shop in downtown Cacém. I saved like 10 bucks and my mother gave me another 10 bucks to buy a winter jacket. But I did not want any one, I wanted a *Puffy* feather jacket, because at that time I cared a lot for the brand and having one of those jackets represented having style and money. However, the jacket was worth 25 bucks, which meant I was short of 5 bucks. The store employee, seeing the deception on my face, told me to come back on the following day with the money, but I told her that on the following day I would be off on vacation to my parents' land. Then, in order to not lose the sale, she said:
"Then, take the jacket, but you owe me 5 bucks. Leave me your data. Name, address and home phone."
At the moment, I really thought of giving her all the information correctly, but, at a glance, this goodwill was gone, and the scoundrel, suburban rascal came up and I provided the information all wrong. I gave the address and phone number of a schoolmate I did not like and invented a name: Jorge André Vinegar.

I left the store happy for having my feather jacket and for having that 5 buck discount. I was really proud of myself. To this day, I have never been to that store again.

While I was sitting on that bench, with the herb working on my head, I recalled how, at that age, I was such an insecure kid that would see in clothing brands a way of belonging to the majority. On another occasion, I went with my mother to the weekly fair that they had by the Agualva-Cacém firemen station and I wanted to buy a pair of pants with a false brand, since it was logical my mother would never buy me a brandy pair of pants for a fortune, so we had to go to the gypsy stands.

I found a pair of Levis pants, cheap, the symbols were perfect, and an excellent falsification job. They were worth like 5 bucks and I took them home so gladly. However, arriving home, I saw the brand was Lives. My God, how could I not see the letters were misplaced! My sister laughed her lungs off.

"What do you think?"

I came back to Amsterdam, Joey was talking, but I wasn't paying attention.

"Are you listening?"

"Come again, I'm sorry."

"How can I repay you for the fact that you saved my life?"

"Well, I don't know, let me think. Well, in the future, in case you have a son out of wedlock you must call him Gonçalo."

"A bastard child?" – he asked, laughing.

"Exactly."

"It seems fair. Deal."

There was silence again, each one alone with their thoughts.

"This herb is really good, right?"

"Yes, it can really bring some peace. What were you thinking about, Gonga?"

"That it would be nice to live here, but since I don't know how to speak Dutch, I would have to do shitty work."

"You'd have to learn."

"Yeah, but it would take years. It would be nice to live here and not have to work."

"You could request political exile."

"That's it, what a hell of an idea, Joey Nights. I can say I am a wanted man in Portugal because of my ideas, and they would pay me a monthly amount that I would spend on beer and pot."

"But you'd have to create a story so they would believe you are wanted for your political position."

"And I am! I am a Tibetan Buddhist and the Chinese lobby is trying to shut me up, besides that I am one of the most active voices in the fight for marijuana legalization in Portugal."

We both laughed, we were in a good mood and we went to the bar where I used to go, to have some beers.

The environment was the same as the previous days. By the entrance there were some smaller tables for couples or single people, while in front of the counter there were many tables, American style, for groups. Instead of the friendly lad, there was a lady about my age or maybe a little older, tall, round-faced, with light brown hair and blue eyes. She had huge breasts that caught the eye right away. The young woman's beauty got me a little unsettled, besides that, she knew she was beautiful and looked at us as if she was superior, knowing we were drooling for her. Since most of the places were taken, we sat by the counter. While having a beer and talking about random stuff, a very cheerful lady showed up by my side, and that is to avoid saying she was drunk as a skunk. She was talking loudly to the waitress and then, she looked at me and said:

"There you are again."

"Excuse me?"

"Yes, the other day, you came alone, but I was sober and didn't dare talk to you."

I looked at her with more attention, I had never seen her before. She was a typical Dutch woman: tall, blonde, blue eyed, small and round face, white skin with blushed cheeks, but that could be from the alcohol. She was talking close to my face and I could smell the alcohol and the tobacco she was exhaling. She was not a gorgeous lady, but she was perfectly doable.

"What did you want to tell me?" – I asked.

"I saw you and you immediately reminded me of Lee Van Cleef."

"The bad guy from *The Good, the Bad and the Ugly*?"

"Yes, that one."

I liked it way better when Luísa had said I looked like Edward Norton.

"But this dude is already quite old, besides that, he has an eagle nose and I don't."

"Yes, but your gaze is the same and, moreover, just like him, you have eyes of different colors: one is blue and the other is green."

"Gee, you shouldn't drink anymore, you're seeing things."

Then she yelled to the waitress and said something in Dutch, aiming at my eyes. They started to talk to each other cheerfully, laughing. It was getting awkward.

"See? She said yes, I was right."

"No, she said exactly the opposite."

She laughed exaggeratedly.

"You don't know Dutch! By the way, where are you from?"

"Where would you say I am from? And, please, don't say I'm French."

She laughed again.

"Curiously, I was gonna say French, but your English accent is hard to catch, maybe Italian or Spanish."

"Portuguese."

"Ah, I have already been to Portugal, more precisely Madrid."

And she laughed out loud, so loud and noisy I even felt secondhand embarrassment.

"Yes, I'm noticing that geography is not your strongest feature."

"Well, I will gather up with my friends" – she said, laughing.

"Right, it was a pleasure, what's your name?"

"Eva, I study here but I am from Utrecht. And your name?"

"Gonçalo."

"What? I'll never be able to pronounce it, I will call you Lee Van Cleef."

And she left, kind of staggering to her friends' table. I checked out her ass and it was not bad at all, no, sir.

"The lady is interested in you, Gonga."

"Do you think? To me it seems she likes the liquor better."

During the rest of the time I spent in the bar, I exchanged glances with her and she would make grimaces. Was she in an unbelievable soak or was she really like that? On one of my trips to the bathroom, to empty my bladder from so much beer, I had to pass by her table. She yelled:

"Do you need help?"

Was it just with me? The lady was quite daring, to the point I did not know how to react, she even got me a little disconcerted. In the end, when me and Joey were leaving because we wanted to wake up early to go to the Van Gogh museum, she came to talk to me:

"Hey, Lee Van, sorry, I didn't want to make you uncomfortable, I was only joking."

"Oh, right, no problem, I had fun. See you around, right?"

"Sure."

And she leaned towards me, kissed my cheek and left.

"What a dog, Gonga! You shouldn't be allowed to go out."

I got excited, the world should be like that, drunk ladies coming on to me, good herb and for free, I started to debate asking for political exile.

On September 7th, after breakfast in the hostel, we went to the museum of the Dutch painter. We went to the square where the buses and trams were and wondered which would be the quickest way to get to the museum. While we discussed, a Brazilian guy came around because he heard us talking in Portuguese and indicated to us which tram to catch. He was really friendly and we asked him if he was a tourist or if he lived there and he said he had been working in Holland for ten years.

We expected to find an enormous line to get into the museum but, since it was still early, there were just a few people and they were mostly old. We spent the morning there. There were many original pictures and others were replicas. There was a painting that even got me moved. Wheatfield with Crows. The painting captures a magnificent moment, the take-off of many crows on a yellowish grain field, and in this field, there are some brown and green paths. The crows seemed to be flying to a cloudy sky, threatening, in black and purple. The picture was so sad, but at the same time, so beautiful that I remained there for several minutes, hypnotized, moved, contemplating it. It is possibly the best picture I have ever seen.

By the exit, we dropped by the museum store, and I bought a picture from the painter: The Room, possibly the most famous of his career to give to my sister.

We had lunch in a place that served enormous and tasty sandwiches and Joey wanted to go to a coffee-shop in the Red Light District. This time, being there during the afternoon and already knowing a bit of the city, everything seemed different. The same prostitutes on the windows calling us with their eyes, the same fellows with the gangster style asking if we would care for some coke or opium, however, I did not find it as degrading as the first time.

We went into a random coffee-shop and the environment was not so dim nor the music so loud. On the contrary, it looked like a students' bar, a relaxed environment, with Jamaican music. We bought herbs, ordered a beer, but those places do not sell alcohol, then we chose a natural orange juice. We were talking, enjoying the effects of the pot and laughing at silly things. We did not want to get too high because that afternoon we wanted to rent bikes.

When leaving the coffee-shop, right in front of us a black lad had run over a lady that had been smoking at the table right by ours. The lady was raving in a language that seemed to be from the East; the lad tried to help her and he was saying she could not walk in the bike lane. Me and Joey stayed a while to watch the mishap. She did not seem to know how to speak English and would only strike insults in a weird language. I pondered if I should help the lady, who was holding her own leg, while the black dude hit the road, but when I asked her if she needed help, she threw me a furious gaze and said something that sounded aggressive. I decided to go and enjoy my good vibe on the way to the bike store and rent a couple.

The referred bike store was not so far from our neighborhood, it was a huge establishment, with two floors, and dozens of bikes showcased outside. The rent for the whole week was still expensive, but we were going to save the transportation money and it was the best way to get to know the city. The employee that tended to us gave us two options to choose from: either a bike with the brakes on the handlebars or on the pedals. With the pedals? I didn't even know that was possible! Those were way cheaper, but we did not want to die or kill anyone, even more so after the accident we had just watched and we both picked the ones with the brakes on the handlebars.

Riding through the city on a bike is a totally different experience. The bike lane is enormous and towards a car the bike always has priority. We pedaled with no steady destiny, from one place to another; we passed by different neighborhoods, many bridges, buildings of many shapes, one more beautiful than the other, and at the end of the afternoon, we went back to the sneeze street: Kloveniersburgwal.

One thing that I have quickly come to notice is the fact that Joey has been in the city for only two days and already knew the names of the streets better than I did, he has a sense of orientation way more developed than mine.

When we arrived at the hostel, we bumped into a problem, where were we going to leave the bikes? Perhaps we would have to buy locks. We went to ask the hostel employee. He was very friendly, and allowed us to put them in the building's basement, which was full of old stuff.

When I was already keyed up to dine on my cans of pilchards with tomato sauce and some bread, in the hall between the dormitories and the bathroom, Joey Nights came from somewhere and told me:

"Bring the food. Follow me."

I went after him and we climbed down many stairs, I got to an area of the hostel that I did not know and there was the kitchen.

"Fuck it! There is a kitchen in this place after all!"

"Sure, obviously, a place like this without a kitchen is totally stupid."

"And how did you find it, Joey?"

"Snooping."

There was some noise of clacking dishes and people talking loudly in many languages. We took a seat on a table, apart from the others, eating our cans and bread. Although now we had napkins, tableware, water, etc. Everything was more comfortable.

"Now I see why the guests would look at me weirdly, as if I was a tramp."

"While we are on this subject, have you noticed that there is a fellow that lives here who looks like a homeless man?"

"Yep, I noticed that too, I saw him looking for milk bottles in the garbage containers, I think they pay when you return those to the grocery store."

"Seriously? We can check on that and maybe change our tuna can diet."

"Excellent idea, Joey."

At night, we went out for a coffee in the usual place. Eva, the drunk, was not there. I was sorry I did not see her, but the famous waitress greeted us with a slight smile. After the coffee, we went to the usual place to smoke some pot, near the monument to the Jewish people chased by the Nazis.

It was cold and we were wearing mid-season coats. Mine was not so thick, however it had a turtleneck and a hood, which would protect me enough. It was gray with no pockets.

There was a moment, while contemplating the landscape, in which I saw a small shining star and reflected about the smallness of our planet and of humanity.

"Joey, do you think there is life after death?"

"I don't know, I don't think about it."

"Aren't you a Catholic?"

"Kind of."

"But you go to the service."

"Yeah, but that's a ritual."

"How come?"

"In the village we all go to the service, it's a way of knowing the news, to see the gals, after the service we go to the coffee for a vermouth and tell the latest gossip."

"Oh, right, so you just go to hit on the girls?"

"It's almost that."

He started to laugh at my dumb face. He still tried to explain something further about the ritual but I got lost in the middle. I was high and thinking about the possibility of our existence being this: growing up, procreating, taking care of the offspring, growing old and dying. It couldn't be just that! There must be more to it! And what if everything that I had read and learned about Buddhism is fake? I came to the conclusion that I would rather change the subject.

On September 8th, the plan was to go to the city park, the Vondelpark. When we were having breakfast, a single fellow took a seat next to us. You could tell right away he was Nordic; he was our height but with blond hair, almost white, cut like Kurt Cobain's, blue eyes and rosy cheeks. We started talking and I asked where he was from, he said he was from Canada.

"Blame Canada, blame Canada."

I sang a bit of *The South Park* series song, from the episode where they wanted to blame Canada because there were too many murders in the United States. He laughed and the three of us got along like a charm.

His name was Ted and he was from the city of Toronto. He had a couple of sisters and some nephews and would often talk about them. He liked movies and knew many European films. Regarding music he was a fan of rock, his favorite band was The Strokes and he had already seen them live in his town. He did not like soccer, but preferred ice hockey and football. He had worked for a year cleaning dishes in a kitchen, so he would be able to take a trip through Europe for a year and a half. He had started the trip in Ireland, had been to England and after Holland he intended to go to France and then Italy. He had no plans of going to Portugal, although we insisted that he come visit us. This was a guy who knew politics and was quite cultured. He knew some of Portugal's history and said that we had been the biggest slave dealers of the world. I answered that in school we learn that we made great discoveries, but we never approach the less positive side of those discoveries. He would prefer the way the Brazilians speak of the Portuguese. He was quite a curious fellow and would ask many questions about the relations between Europeans; if we were against the North Americans; if, in a general manner, people would consider Canadians as being the same as the Americans; if we knew anything about Canada; if it was only the North Americans who would eat at McDonald's in Europe; if we were for the Euro, etc. He loved those linguistic expressions that referred to Europeans, like: "richly like the French" or "From Spain neither good wind nor good wedding" or even "It's hard to please the Greeks and the Trojans at the same time." I explained to him that in Portugal we would say "Peniche's friends" referring to fake friends, which was because in fifteen hundred-something the English landed in Peniche to help Portugal against a Spanish invasion, however they actually came to pillage and plunder whatever they could. I told him that in Spanish there is an expression that goes: "pretend to be Swedish," which means pretending not to understand the language or the habits. He would laugh and try to use those expressions while he was drunk or high. He confessed he felt like a European and that he hoped to get to the Balkans and meet a lady because to him, the Balkans were the most beautiful women in the world. We tried to convince him that the Portuguese were also good looking, but he mocked us and said he'd heard they had mustaches. Since his surname was Anderson, I did my impression of the villain of the movie *Matrix* and yelled:

"Mister Anderson!"

He laughed and said I reminded him of his boss yelling at him.

That day, the 8th, me and Joey invited him to come with us to Vondelpark. Since he did not have a bike, we went with him to the store, so he could rent one. From there we headed to the park, which was huge, an almost 125 acre area. Gardens, walkways, child parks, small lakes, trees and more trees. People were running, doing yoga, martial arts, children playing, old people reading newspapers and books. We spent the morning there, took pictures and asked people to take pictures of the three of us on our bikes.

In the afternoon, we pedaled through the city, without a destination. We were adrift, stopping for a cigarette or to eat something. At some point it rained a bit and we had to take shelter in a coffee shop, where we kept up the conversation, there was always a theme. Joey spoke less, though he knows English, he is not very self-assured regarding his speaking, but bit by bit he was loosening up.

At night, he went to a restaurant for dinner and we went to the hostel's kitchen to eat chicken legs and milk that we had bought in the Nieumarkt. Afterward, we went to the Jewish monument, in the Amstel Square, as usual and we smoked pot and built philosophies about life, but it started to rain and we had to come back to the hostel earlier. Besides that, we were tired from pedaling so much.

On September 9th, we met Ted again at breakfast and we went around the town with him. The weather was better, it did not rain at all and the temperature was higher. We went to the Jordaan neighborhood, which is a very picturesque zone, with a lot of commerce and narrow streams. In the middle of the street there were some very original toilets, for men to piss in, but they were only halfway covered. We had lunch around there and planned to go near the Red Light District to smoke some pot. That afternoon was to me the point of no return, as I had come to notice, after that notorious afternoon, that I would have more fun if I drank some beers rather than spending the whole afternoon smoking pot.

We went into a coffee shop in the Red Light District, in the middle of the afternoon. It was a big place, ample, there were only a few clients. The owner was of Arab origin as well as his few clients. He gave us a menu with the herbs we could smoke and the teas we could drink. We filled our heads with smoke. I was so breezed that when the bill came, I could not think in florins, only shields. I looked at Joey Nights and saw those red, squinted eyes and knew he was in the same condition I was, or worse. Ted seemed to be made of iron, he would keep on talking and smoking as if it was just tobacco. My stress with the bill was so much that, at that moment, I was sure that the coffee owner was scamming us and I almost started to argue, however, the Canadian said the bill was right and I trusted him. I was in another dimension, so stoned I could barely speak.

Since we spent the whole afternoon in that coffee-shop smoking, we were hungry as hell and wanted to go to the hostel to fill our bellies, but Ted, who had more money, wanted to go to a restaurant.

"Does your budget not allow you to go to a restaurant?"

"That's not it, Ted, it's 'cause we're too high."

"But we can still smoke one before dinner, right?"

"This dude is a killer!"

And we smoked another one, on the hostel's street. While we smoked, I looked inside the windows that were big and wide, and I saw the residents start to turn the electric lights on, the boats sailing through the narrow streams and the cyclists passing by us, riding home. When we said goodbye, I noticed I was very stunned, with a dry mouth, the lights were too bright, the colors of the buildings too flashy, the sky was cloudy and it seemed like Van Gogh's painting of the crows.

We walked into the hostel and went to our lockers to pick up the cans of tuna and pilchard. We went down to the kitchen and suddenly, a group of Spanish or Italian guys who were speaking loudly shut up as soon as they saw us come in. We had such stoned faces that we were actually scary. When they heard us talk in Portuguese, they started talking loudly again. We opened the cans, shared the bread, but Joey Nights turned to me and said:

"Dude, I'm tripping, I'm gonna lie down."

And he left the kitchen. I kept on eating calmly, in a corner like a rat. I had the impression the Spanish or Italians were talking about me, however one could say that it might have been the herb making me paranoid. Before it was the two fellows from Setúbal who wanted to kill me, then it was the owner of the bar who wanted to scam me, and now there were those Spanish or Italians to insult me.

I left the kitchen, put my cans in the garbage, but Joey had left his can opened without touching the tuna. I decided to save it, because he could wake up hungry. Unfortunately, when I was climbing up the stairs, some of the oil dripped on my pants. "Fuck, Joey didn't drain the fucking oil." I went to the bathroom to see if I could clean up the mess. I laid water on it and the smudge got bigger. I tried to dry it, but more guests got in the room and were looking at me with surprise. I decided to leave the smudge and went for a coffee to see if it would wake me up. I went in the hostel's bar, the waiter came by and asked what I wanted:

"A coffee, please."

"Have you been smoking?"

"Excuse me?"

"Are you high?"

"Why?"

But what an impertinent question was that? Was it not legal to smoke pot? I was ordering a coffee and would pay for it. The waiter started talking to a Scottish man who was there. He was definitely Scottish because he was wearing a kilt and a t-shirt with the Scottish flag. He was huge, fat, red faced, drunk as a skunk and was gazing at me with an unfriendly face. I decided to leave the place, another paranoia, this time I started to think those guys would beat me up, only because I was high and ordered a coffee.

I went outside, the cold breeze hit me violently in the face, I had forgotten my coat and the night was dark and scary. I needed to walk to clear up my mind. The same way I would sometimes do when I was high, I started running through the bike path, I ran and ran, until some bike riders passed by me and yelled at me furiously, in a weird language. I imagined it was something like:

"This is for bikes, dumbass!"

I came back to the sidewalk. I looked around and did not know where I was. But how far had I run? There was a huge square, full of people and doves, with a monument in the middle and some stairs around it. How would I get back to the hostel? I could not pronounce the name of the sneeze street. I did not know the name of the hostel. I tried to think of any reference to come back to, a path to follow. While I was pondering exhaustively, I started to shiver because of the cold. I had to decide, I could not just stay there or I was going to die from the cold. Meanwhile, a group of Japanese tourists approached me and asked me to take a picture of them. I supposed they could not read in my face that I was lost and high, nor could they spot that grease stain on my pants. The weirdest part is that they were a group of about 10 people and they all wanted to take a picture with their own cameras and they would give me the machines so I would shoot the pictures. In the end, they thanked me in a subservient manner and asked if I was Dutch, when I said I was Portuguese they exchanged some words among them and told me they were from the south of Japan. When I finally got rid of them, I was very confused about which way to go, until I saw the police. I considered asking how I could get to the monument to the Jewish people, but I thought that they could be anti-Semite cops and they could think I was Jewish and throw me in the clink. Afterward, it came to mind the name of the bar where I used to go: Staalmeesters. When approaching the patrol-car, I wondered if I still looked high and if they would pick on me, however, I was just going to ask a simple question.

"Good night, which way is Stallmeesters bar, near Amstel River?"

They looked at me, one of them got out of the vehicle and started to tell me the streets I would have to take. Although, the other one said something in Dutch to his colleague and the one who was explaining the path to me told me they were going in the same direction and opened the back door of the car for me and put me inside. At the moment I thought: "you would need to be stupid to ask for directions, totally high, wearing not much clothing and dirty, to a couple of cops! And I say I'm from Cacém!" I imagined those two cops taking me to the police station, insulting me and hitting me mercilessly and carelessly. Calling me a tramp, homeless, telling me to go back to my land, etc., however the two cops were very friendly and asked me where I was from.

"From Portugal, from a land near Lisbon."

"Ah, I have been to Madeira" – one of them said.

"And me to Algarve, one can eat very well over there. The weather is excellent."

Those cops were so lovely. They told me they liked the south of Europe a lot because of the weather, the beaches and the food. One of them was learning Spanish and the other one was getting married that year. He was going to Brazil for his honeymoon and asked me how to say "thank you."

They left me near the bar, I still had the poker face to invite them to have a beer with me, they laughed and said no, the one who was going to Brazil said:

"Obrigado, obrigado (*thank you, thank you*), but we cannot drink on duty."

What a civilized country, I thought.

I went back to the hostel and decided that if it was possible, I would rather have some sleep. I went to the bathroom, took my clothes off and when I got to the dormitory Joey was coming out.

"So, you're going to sleep?"

"Yep, you chickened out!"

"Yep, I was too high. Let's go and drink something?"

"Yeah, sure, but not at the bar, there is a Scottish man there looking for a fight."

"What?"

We took the bikes and went to the Leidseplein neighborhood. It is an area with a lot of nightlife. There were street artists making pictures of the tourists, bars with tables on the outside and others with live music. We sat down, ordered a couple of beers and I told him what happened, he wondered if I was exaggerating, I, myself, thought the story was surreal.

September 10th was the day Elói would arrive, but he would only arrive by six pm.

That morning Ted was going to the Van Gogh museum. Since me and Joey Nights had already seen it, we went for a ride in the flower market, which was not too far from where we were lodged. It is a huge market, with countless stands for farmers, garden lovers and tourists. We wandered around the market looking for souvenirs to take home. I bought poppy seeds for my mother and my aunt from Castelo Branco and a mug for my father.

We went back to the grocery store in the Nieuwmarkt to buy our lunch. We learned that by returning the milk bottles we could earn some cash, so we were collecting the ones we would find around the garbage containers and actually some from inside the garbage containers, just like beggars. I commented to Joey that we could live like that for some time, eat canned food and chicken wings, drink milk and search for milk bottles to get by. He thought I was joking and laughed.

After lunch, we met Ted, exchanged impressions about the Van Gogh museum and drank some beers before going to the Central Station to pick up Elói. Before six o'clock we were already by line 1. But no sign of Elói. At times, me and Joey would go separate ways to try to find him, but there was no sign of him. During that afternoon, twice, two people approached us to ask for some directions in Dutch, and we would laugh and say we were tourists. Since there was no sign of Elói, we decided to go back to the hostel and call our parents so they could call Elói's home or his cell. Although, when we were leaving the station, there he was. He was carrying a couple of backpacks, had a scared face, and he was looking frantically in all directions, but did not see us. I got close and said:

"Give me the cash, scumbag!"

When he saw us, he took a deep breath of relief, laughed and hugged us. We introduced him to Ted.

"Shit, I could already see myself sleeping in the open."

"Didn't we say line 1?"

"Did we set that up? I didn't remember."

Then, Elói told us that when he arrived and did not see us, he went to the tourist shop that was beside the station, but he neither had the address or the name of the hostel. He had left his notes at home. He started to freak out, since he had brought his cell but did not have any credit, therefore he would have to call from a booth. But his father wouldn't be at home, so he couldn't help with the address, and he would have to call Joey's home or mine, but he did not have the home numbers. The longer it would take, the more he imagined himself having to pay for a hotel or any inn. The tourism shop was already closed and he was getting more and more desperate.

We went laughing all the way to the hostel, passed by the Red Light District and Joey Nights showed Elói a prostitute that he wanted to take back to his homeland; she was a tall and brunette woman, with prominent breasts about whom we used to joke and say she would be Joey's helper in the graduation internship. When we arrived at our street, Ted wanted to smoke some pot so the four of us stopped near the stream. We were all in a good mood, laughing and talking loud. I was trying to keep Ted from feeling apart from the group, because we would talk in Portuguese and he would not understand anything but I tried, from time to time, to keep the conversation in English.

The pot helped us to be even happier and we went to the hostel's bar, where it was happy hour and took the time to drink. While the four of us were cheerily talking next to a window with a view to the stream, a Brazilian couple showed up at the counter and they ordered two coffees. The waiter, the same one that did not want to attend me the other night, did not understand anything they were saying and the couple could only speak Portuguese. I pondered if I should help or not. I recalled that in my first days a Brazilian had helped me and Joey with the directions to the Van Gogh museum, so I thought I should do the same. I got up and told the waiter that they wanted a couple of coffees and wanted to pay with a debit card, the waiter said the bar did not accept cards and they would have to go and cash out. I informed the couple that there was an ATM nearby, but I would like to pay for their coffee. They thanked me plenty and told me they were from São Paulo and were on their honeymoon. I wished them good luck and joined my friends again. I was glad about my good deed.

We had dinner in the kitchen and, for the first time, we cooked. Ted was a good cook and we put together the food we had to make a good meal. Meanwhile, we were talking to the many guests that were around the place. It was a lot of fun, the place seemed like The Tower of Babel.

At night, we went to the same bar as usual, we kept on drinking beer and soon enough we started to smoke pot. It was weird not to have to hide in a dark corner, like we used to do in Castelo Branco and we smoke carelessly in the middle of the street. At some point, Eva passed by me and, this time, she was sober and I was drunk, and she ran her hand on the back of my head.

"Hi, Lee Van Cleef."

"Hi, Eva" – and I winked at her.

Elói and Ted were astonished and I had my ego quite high.

"But, what a dog! You already have a girlfriend here?"

I did not say anything, and only smiled.

"This fellow shouldn't be allowed out" – Joey said.

Later, the four of us ended up smoking more pot near the monument to the Jewish people and talking until late at night.

I believe September 11th will remain forever in the history of humankind. Two weeks have passed already since that day and the news keeps on showing the images of the twin towers being torn down by two aircraft. Although, we only found out about the attack at the end of the afternoon.

In the morning, after breakfast, we said goodbye to Ted, who was leaving that day. We exchanged e-mail addresses and wished him good luck. We went with Elói to the bike store so he could rent one, we kind of already knew the employees in the store. He chose one without the brake in the handlebars, those cheaper ones that are halted by the pedals. The lad that tended to us still tried to dissuade Elói from renting one of those, because he thought all the foreign tourists are dumb and we are not used to the brakes that way, but Elói is a bike expert and took it anyway.

I must confess I felt some exasperation that morning. Elói had all this energy to see the city, while I had been there for a week already and would prefer to be relaxed at a random bar drinking beer and watching the Dutch women pass by. However, I had to take to pedaling, literally. We passed by almost all the villages I have already visited and afterward, we passed through the city square and went to the grocery store for lunch, as usual, at the Nieuwmarkt. We took some milk bottles to trade for money and, this way, buy food. Meanwhile, a black man, possibly homeless, saw us and said something in Dutch, we answered any bullshit in Portuguese and he started to yell.

"I'm fighting for my land."

We spent the rest of the day repeating that sentence and laughing, one would say something stupid and the other one would answer: "I'm fighting for my land."

In the afternoon, there was more of the same, pedaling through town, stopping to take pictures, eating something, smoking a cigarette and going through the alleys, enjoying Amsterdam. At no point did we take notice of the terrorist attack, it is true that I recall seeing in a coffee house a bunch of people gathering up in front of a television, however, I did not give it much thought. There was a point in which we got lost, and we saw a city map, Elói got close and was checking it and we told him:

"Hey, Elói, up there it says: Gay Map."

Which means, it was a map with a gay itinerary, however Elói was so concentrated on seeing the map that he didn't pay us any mind at all. I, in a quick action like a cat, took a photo of Elói reading a gay map in Amsterdam, unfortunately my camera is a piece of junk and the picture did not come out well. This picture would be worth millions. Still, how much we mocked him that afternoon must be told.

By seven pm, already tired from so much pedaling, we got to the bar as usual, nearby the hostel and then we saw the images. I had never noticed there was a TV set in that bar, but, when we walked in, all the heads were turned in that direction. A Dutch channel broadcasting the news and showing the images from CNN, with the following subtitle:

"America under attack."

The images astonished me as much as Elói's reaction, who, when seeing them, let out a sinister laugh. One has to highlight that he is anti-American, anti-capitalist and anti-imperialist. Even still, his reaction was so unreasonable that he realized it. It seemed as if this was a science fiction movie, it could not be true and, moreover, a second aircraft struck while some channels were already broadcasting straight from the place. There was no doubt that it had been a terrorist attack. But who? How? I felt that if that could be happening in the heart of the USA, then nobody was safe, it could happen the following day in Amsterdam. Afterward, someone said that there were more aircraft that were heading to the pentagon. How? But who would be behind it? The news was as shocking as engaging. At that moment, I came to realize there would be a before and after that attack. The United States would retaliate and that revenge would be painful. The channel was then talking only in Dutch.

"Man! What the hell is that!" – I said.

"This looks like a movie" – one of them said.

"Within three days we are going to catch a flight, will there be any trouble?" – said another.

We went to the hostel for dinner, Elói made some soy and me and Joey dined on some pilchards in tomato sauce and tuna, for a change. I will not be able to eat canned pilchard for a while. Every conversation in the kitchen was around the same thing: the attack. More news, more rumors, everything was uncertain and at the same time attention worthy. We went, for the first time, to the living room, which was full of youngsters like us, from all nationalities, watching the news straight from CNN and the images of the aircraft against the towers, time and again.

We left the hostel heading to the bar to drink some beers and check how the environment was in the city. As I walked in I saw Eva, who got close to me and said:

"You cannot go back to Portugal anymore, you will have to stick around here."

"It seems so, may I stay with you?"

"You wanna come and live with me, Lee Van Cleef?"

"Yes, if you can support me."

She laughed and I smelled alcohol and tobacco on her breath, she was already clearly inside a bottle. She was with a friend who came to sit at our table. One must say the friend was even hotter than her, but Eva was actually interested in this tall drink of water. On one of the trips to the counter, she got near me and I kissed her. We started to have fun right there at the bar, we went to one of the more reserved tables and there we made out before stopping to have another beer, smoke another cigarette and talk:

"I don't believe you don't have a girlfriend."

"I mean it, seriously, I don't."

"With those eyes, there must be some girls after you."

"Well, I can't complain. And what about you? Don't you have a boyfriend?"

"No, I broke up with a lad a short time ago and I have been kind of depressed."

Some more kissing.

"You came to Holland to smoke and drink every day?"

"No, I came to see the town. I visited some museums and things like that. I have also smoked and I am even taking some pot for my friends over there."

"Are you going to the airport carrying hemp? Are you crazy? Above all, after what has happened today, you are gonna get arrested!"

"No, it will be only three small bags, they are not going to arrest me for that, but if I go to prison, you're going to visit me, right?"

"Yes, sure, and I will bring you tobacco. Have you tried the mushrooms?"

"No, only pot, I also ate a hashish cake, but it got me sick."

"Then you don't know what drugs are, boy!"

She made me feel like a kid, as if I was an amateur regarding drugs, but actually, for me there was always the limit of joints. I never wanted to cross over that line, nor do I have any curiosity about the sensation that any other kind of drug might provide.

The bar closed, the waitress, the pretty one with the brown hair and ample bosom, was Eva's friend and we went to another bar. Me and Eva went to a corner and kept on making out. My friends picked two Dutch women, however, they did not have any luck, another guy came around and spoiled their flirtation.

"I would like to know Lisbon" – Eva said.

"I come from an ugly part of Lisbon, but I could show you the touristic zones of the capital."

She lived with some friends, one of them was at the table, she studied in the university and was in her third year of Law. She used to go often to her homeland, Utrecht, which was nearby. We talked about movies and she thought *Pulp Fiction* was overrated. She did not tell me what her favorite movie was, she thought it was childish to choose a favorite movie or song.

We have went to yet another bar and, this one, absurd as it sounds, was a gay bar, and was one of those Elói had seen on that map. We laughed a lot until Eva pulled me into a corner and we kept on making out. That was still a little bit of a scandal, all the eyes turned to us. At that moment, neither of us gave a shit about the situation and would not be stopped for anything. I laid my hands all over her body which she not only accepted but encouraged. I could already picture myself having sex in an Amsterdam gay bar, it would be a story worthy of telling to my grandkids. And I said to her:

"Let's go to your apartment?"

"I cannot, I live with some friends and it's not allowed."

That sounded like a lie.

"Then let's go to an inn or a hotel."

"Wait, I want to, but let's get to know each other better, maybe I can go to Lisbon."

Seriously? I did not want to have a relationship with her, there was no chemistry, at least not from my side. I just wanted to get laid.

"Tomorrow, I am going with my friends to a little village, we want to see Holland's countryside, wanna come along?"

"I can't, I'm going to Utrecht to have lunch with my parents, but at night I'll be here. Would you show up?"

"Yes, I think so."

"And don't you want to come to meet my parents?"

I laughed.

"Like in the movie: *Meet the Parents* with Robert DeNiro."

She smiled.

"My parents are very open minded, they would like to meet you."

Was she serious? I, at least, did not take the conversations seriously and kept joking around with the subject.

The gay bar closed. Outside it was raining cats and dogs. I still insisted that we go somewhere, but she went home with her friend and it looked like she was sad, almost crying. I came back to my friends who enviously insulted me.

On the following day, in the morning, Joey told me he still tried to talk to Eva's friend, but his English is limited and he only told her he had a farm in the north of Portugal, she did not show much interest and it was a long and uncomfortable night.

We went to catch the train in the Nieuwmarkt Station, which was close to the market where we used to buy chicken wings and return the milk bottles. There was a direct train that took over an hour to arrive at the Naardermeer Natural Park area. During the trip we contemplated the landscape. The further away we got from the town, the more we would see forests and pastures, with huge cows. The houses got rarer and once in a while we would see the famous Dutch mills. Everything was green, one could see it rained often and there was heavy rain that day.

We arrived in the middle of the morning and wandered through the park, where there was a lot of flora and fauna and we saw many birds that we could not identify. We bought food and ate in the middle of a beech forest, with a lot of underbrush. Afterward, we got to a small town with only a few streets. We popped up to the site, the inhabitants were all tall, we, which are 6 feet tall on average, were the shortest. They were all blond and with a rosy complexion and they looked at us curiously.

We went into an ice-cream parlor and ordered a big double ice-cream. We sat down to see the movement of the street, which was not much and after ice-cream, me and Joey Nights smoked a cigarette, Elói always looks at this addiction with disapproval. Then, I felt like going to a bar and sticking around, drinking some beers and smoking some cigarettes until it was time for the train. However, Elói as well as Joey did not want it, so I had to follow them, a little annoyed.

We decided that we would go back to Amsterdam by bike, it was like twenty kilometers. In the beginning, I complained but now, I must confess it was a magnificent trip, through the woods and pasture camps. The landscapes were very beautiful and we saw a lot of birds. At some point along the way, I asked Joey subtly, as if I had no further intention, about a hot blonde, called Ruth, who I had my eye on and took the same course as his girlfriend.

"She's very conceited. Nobody can stand her."

"But does she have a boyfriend?"

"I don't know, I think so. She has been in many arguments with her colleagues. Don't waste your time."

What a pity!

In the middle of the way, Elói's bike chain fell off track and he almost fell. We were there for quite a while until we managed to fix it, and it was already twilight.

"Elói, I would like to stay here and help you, but a Dutch woman is waiting for me and I don't give a shit for you. Try to survive the way you can in this forest. You can do some kind of *Blair Witch Project* thing."

"I could be part of the Elói Garbage Project." – Joey said laughing.

Elói was stressed about the bike, but he managed to fix it. When we arrived at Amsterdam, we were near the Ajax soccer field. It looked like Cacém, there were many towers and a dangerous environment. It was the least touristy part of town. Since we were lost, we asked a lady that was passing by how we could get downtown. She answered that she did not speak English and we noticed she was Brazilian.

"Are you Brazilian, ma'am?"

"Yes, I am!"

"We are Portuguese!"

And we laughed.

The lady was very friendly and gave us directions. In the end, we thanked her and wished her good luck. She smiled a lot and one could see she enjoyed using her language in a foreign country. While pedaling, I wondered where that lady worked? She was certainly a humble person, who lived in a poor neighborhood. She probably came from Brazil for a more dignified life, maybe to send some money for her children or parents. Afterward, I remembered that couple I helped in the hostel's bar and I thought that karma had paid me back. I helped a couple and later that lady helped me. Everything was making sense.

It was already night time when we arrived at the hostel. We were tired and hungry. I took a shower, put on some dry clothes and ate something. I still thought of going to see Eva at the bar but I was very tired and, actually, she did not interest me enough for me to make any bigger effort. My conscience became a little heavy because we had set it up and I did not show. Although, when I laid down, I fell asleep in just a few seconds.

September 13th was our last day in the city, therefore, I barely woke up. I felt sorry for leaving Amsterdam. I would have stayed some more days if I could and I would even have liked to get a job so I could stay and know the country better.

That day we pedaled up to the waterfront zone of the city. We saw, from outside, the Nemo museum, which is an enormous building that looks like a boat. We crossed many bridges and visited many small islands that could be found in the middle of the river. We talked to the inhabitants, ate local food in a trailer and, at the end of the afternoon, we had to return the bikes. We packed up and had dinner.

I wanted to go to the Staalmeesters bar one last time, maybe to talk and have a good time with Eva. I took a shower, shaved my beard, put my contact lenses in, and got dressed in some not-so-tight clothes, but tight enough to display my muscles. I looked at myself in the mirror, and thought I looked attractive, my skin was tanned because of summertime, any my wavy hair that was messy on purpose and light eyes would contrast with the color of my complexion. "Today, you are going to get laid, Gonga!"- I motivated myself.

However, Eva was not there and we drank a couple of beers. When I realized she was not coming, I talked to the pretty waitress.

"Hi, do you know if Eva will be around tonight?"

"I don't think so, she was waiting for you last night."

"In the end, I could not come, could you hand her this?"

I gave her a note:

"Gonçalo – Lee Van Cleef gongadias@hotmail.com"

Deep down, I felt bad for not showing up the previous night and the note was like an apology, although I did not really care if she did not write to me, we didn't have much in common. It was only a physical attraction.

We sat next to the monument in the memory of the Jewish people, at the Amstel riverside and from there we contemplated, for the last time, the street lights and smoked our last joint in Amsterdam. The herb was good and we were soon happy and laughing.

"But did you have to choose this place? Next to this monument?" – Elói complained.

"Do you have a problem with it?"

"The Jewish invaded Palestine and they are occupying more and more territories."

"But you cried in the theater when you watched *Life is Beautiful*" – Joey said and we all laughed.

"Yeah, Elói, and that was pure Jewish propaganda."

"Don't you guys remind me of that."

"Besides that, you have a big nose and you are brunette, who can say you are not a descendant of the New Christians and are actually Jewish?"

"Then things would be different, you would support the occupation of Palestine and say your people had rights on that land."

We all laughed and joked about the theme.

"Hey, Elói, Gonga a few days ago had some existential questions" – Joey Nights said in a sarcastic tone.

"Gonga, there is nothing after death. Science cannot find anything."

One thing that has always annoyed me about Elói is that superior posture he assumes when talking about this subject. He is an atheist and considers everyone that has any faith as ignorant. We have already had many arguments about this theme and, that night, I did not feel like getting into the subject. He went on:

"You talk about reincarnation, but how do you explain that the men reincarnate if earlier the world population was little, less than a billion and now we are seven billion?"

"Who said you are going to reincarnate as a man, on this planet or in this galaxy? Saying that all the life and evolution that this planet already had was by chance seems ridiculous to me."

The discussion went on for a little longer, but, actually, I wanted to laugh and enjoy the last night in town and did not want to get into theological themes.

The following day, at five in the morning, we left the hostel and walked to the Central Station. We passed by the Red Light District, the ladies had the curtains closed, they were either sleeping or cleaning up the house. My luggage was way lighter, without the cans of pilchard and tuna.

As we got near the airport, I was getting more nervous. I was carrying three bags of pot; it was a small amount, but I could still be taken in and have problems. Besides that, with September 11's paranoia there could be a more detailed inspection. They were joking around with me and saying that I was going to jail and they would tell my parents and our colleagues in Castelo Branco that I was arrested for a different reason, for killing a prostitute.

"No, don't do it, say I have requested political exile."

At the airport there were more police, more dogs, more control. I thought of throwing the drugs in the toilet, in any bathroom, but it was just a few grams, some memories from Amsterdam. I left the herb in my bag in the middle of my dirty clothes.

We still had to wait a bit until boarding time, there were some florins left that were not worth enough to exchange in Portugal, so we decided to buy something at the airport by putting our money together, but Elói, a fanatic anti-smoker, said right away that it could not be tobacco which, by the way, was what I wanted. In the end, we bought some Dutch candy, so sweet that it was impossible to eat it.

Passing by the security, I noticed in my tobacco there were a couple of hashish cigarettes, that I didn't even remember where there. I did not give it much thought and the cops did not pick up on it either, actually, I think they did not even open the pack.

When I took a seat in the aircraft, I requested to go by the window, but just like the others, I fell asleep. When we got to Oporto, nobody picked on my luggage and I was glad for passing three baggies of pot. Joey Nights took a bus to Guimarães, while I went to Elói's house to pick up my cell phone and some other belongings. Elói complained that his trip was the shortest, basically only three days, because the travel over there itself already took two days. I had lunch with him and, when it was time, I took a bus in his neighborhood up to the train station.

"Well, Elói, see you in Castelo Branco, when will you go over there?"

"I have to go and take an exam, but I am waiting for your visit in Salamanca."

"You can count on it, I will check up on the cash situation and we will schedule a good day for me to pay you a visit."

We hugged, I thanked him for his hospitality and took the trip to Cacém.

On Sunday the 16th, I took the trip to Castelo Branco, which means I stayed only a short time in Cacém. There was enough time to do my laundry, sleep many hours in my own bed, and set up to meet Maria João and Rodas, to whom I gave one of the baggies. He was very glad and wanted to smoke the pot with me, but I told him to smoke it with his friends, and that I had already smoked plenty. The remaining two bags I gave to Célia and Toxic. They thanked me a lot and told me that I was crazy for bringing that from Holland.

I haven't been smoking pot, I have decided that from now on, I will only smoke if the idea is to drink some beers and to go out. I have come to notice that smoking, even if it is a good quality herb, makes me paranoid and sleepless, therefore, I will avoid smoking pot.

I received an e-mail from Eva, who turned out to be very glad that I left the note, because she was thinking she would never speak to me again. She told me a little of her day-by-day and invited herself to come, during the Christmas vacation, to spend some days with me. I answered that it was fine by me, although I had some difficulty to find other themes to write about, I put some trivialities to build up a couple of paragraphs.

One of those days, while I was studying, Luísa called me. My heart skipped a beat, I felt my mouth dry and butterflies in my stomach. She was very friendly.

"So, how about Holland?"

"Very nice, it was spectacular. It is a very developed country."

"Didn't we agree that you would call me when you arrived back?" – She said jokingly, but I noticed she was kind of charging me on that.

"I thought you only said that to be polite."

She laughed.

"I meant it. When are you coming over?"

"I will have an exam on October 3rd, and on the 6th I'm going over there. Would you like to set anything up?"

"Yes, of course. When you arrive, you call me. Don't forget."

My eyes were shining with joy. In the end, she still remembered me and she may have pondered further and might want to be with me now. I feel I still like her a lot.

The End of the Burrow – Sunday, November 25th, 2001

Before talking about the disbandment of the Burrow, I have to reflect on the fact that I was approved in Physics with 14 points. The grade filled me with pride, after so many hours of work and dedication. It was the second-best grade, someone got 15. Célia was approved too, with 11 points, but, unfortunately, Cláudia flunked. Moreover, she called to ask if the grades were already published and I had to give her the bad news, which obviously contrasted with my happiness for having been approved. The day I knew that I was approved, Celia and I filled our heads with hashish and we drank until late at night.

The disbandment of the burrow was something I was already expecting, so it did not take anyone by surprise. Bora Bora, who got in two years earlier, was already doing his internship for the conclusion of the course; he still pays for the room but he seldom comes over. Elói went to Salamanca to take an Erasmus program. Joey Nights spends a lot of time at his girlfriend's house. Meanwhile, Boni, to avoid staying alone at home, either comes to our house, which we call the Lair as an homage to the Burrow, or he goes to his homeland.

It was an announced death and one would say a little agonizing, to see how that house, that one day was full of life and cheerfulness, then was kind of empty. But that is how life is, everything changes, everything is in permanent flux.

The Society's coffee has also changed management, Teodoro left the tavern and now there is someone else exploiting it. According to the rumor mill, Teodoro was caught cheating on his wife with a neighbor. His wife found out and the marriage almost fell apart but Teodoro managed to convince her with some soft talking. Although, one of the conditions that his wife demanded to save the marriage was that he leave the Society and get a job far from the neighborhood. I was quite sad when I found out about it. When I saw him in the neighborhood, I asked if it was true and he said yes: "the flesh is weak, comrade."

"Tell me about it, friend" – I confirmed.

Changing the subject. My uncle's attic, where I live with my cousin Toxic and three other students who are preparing for entrance exams, all between 17 and 19 years old, has gotten more important in my social life. Most of the time we spend the nights at home, playing cards and drinking beer. They do not belong to the *Legalize It* crew and prefer beer. Sometimes we go out, but they prefer going out with the people from their school and me with the people from mine, so we usually don't run into each other at night.

I have quit smoking joints when the plan is to stay at home, which means, if I do not go out at night I do not smoke. Besides that, I quit buying hashish and herb. It all came down to the constant paranoias that I used to have when I would only smoke and not drink anything. Furthermore, I realize that when I stay at home smoking, I have insomnia. I feel like I have more fun if I drink some beers than if I spend the night smoking and creating paranoid movies. However, my cousin Toxic thinks I am just going through a bad phase and every night he encourages me to smoke some hashish, for he does not like to smoke alone. I always tell him no and he already understands that something has changed. Now, to get me to smoke, he always invites me to go to Ti Jorge's or to some bar to drink some draft beer.

Naturally I feel that my behavior has changed since I came back, not only from Holland, but from Blockbuster, and obviously, that influenced the Burrow's decay. I want to finish my course and get into the work market as quickly as possible. Therefore, now I attend the classes, take notes and, at home, I review and study.

One has to mention that those boys that live in the Lair are some real rascals. One of them has a jalopy and since he never has any money, they steal gasoline from construction sites: from plowing machines and things like that. That went on for a while, the guys would always brag about never buying gasoline, I even went along with them a couple of nights to see how they did it. They studied in an area where there were some construction sites, so they would go over there at night with a hose and a bucket, open the machine's tank, shove one end of the hose in there, suck on the other end and proceed to steal the liquid. Although, a certain night, when they were out for one more stealth, the cops showed up with a lot of police cars. They had to spend the night in jail, until they were presented to the judge who allowed parole, but in case they were caught another time, they would be behind bars. The news was exaggerated, there was even a small article on the national news saying:

"Dangerous Gas Gang Caught"

Dangerous Gas Gang? They were only two small crooks that would play swindler and when they got caught they shat their pants in fear!

The other day, one of them brought a cell phone he had gotten in a bargain that already came with a thousand shields of credit. Since we all had cell phones, nobody showed any interest in keeping it, however we agreed we could spend the credit. On a night of beer and cards, someone suggested calling the girls whose phone numbers we had. Since I did not want to involve any of my friends, I looked for any lady in my contacts and I noticed I had kept the number of a certain Filipa, a monitor of a summer camp where I worked. She was a shapely girl who had a boyfriend, but, for some reason, we exchanged numbers.

We sent many messages that night and to Filipa I have sent the following SMS:

"I cannot forget that kiss."

All of us were laughing like rogues and waiting for the answers that could come. On the following day, checking on the phone, there were many calls and messages, however, there were a couple of numbers that would call almost nonstop: Filipa's number and another one that later, we came to know, was her boyfriend.

It went from bad to worse; the boyfriend was a jealous, insecure fellow, paltry and paranoid. He kept on calling again and again and, when we would answer, he wanted to know who we were, how did we have his girlfriend's number, where we were, he said he would call the cops and kill us all. And we kept on sending more messages to Filipa: "I wanna be with you again" or "I still smell your perfume."

In the end, the joke got old and we gave the phone away to someone.

On the subject of dating, my relationship with Luísa has had some development.

Early October, when I already knew I had been approved in Physics, I went to Cacém to spend the weekend. As we had planned, I called her and we met on Sunday, the day I would go back to Castelo Branco. She picked me up at home, I already had my backpack with me and she would leave me at the East Station afterward. We greeted like old friends. She was thinner, I mentioned it and she was glad I noticed. Luísa talked about her work, of the stress she had been building up and of a couple of workmates she had at the company that treated her badly, almost enough to call bullying. I told her about my vacation in Holland.

"So, did you meet any Dutch ladies?"

She had asked the question as if she would have the right to charge me for anything, as if she was my girlfriend. I hesitated; I was not going to tell her the truth, but what had caught me off guard was the way the question was asked. By what rule did she have the right to ask it? She noticed I had flinched and said:

"I don't believe it! You had someone there?"

"No, I did not, but why do you ask?"

She noticed she had crossed a line and tried to find a way out.

"Just curious…"

I was silent for a moment.

"No, I haven't met anyone. I remain without a girlfriend."

She smiled and I noticed she was glad. I also noticed that I did like her jealous reaction and got even more nervous.

"Where should we go?" – I asked.

"To the beach."

"Really? It's a little cold to be at the beach, isn't it?"

"I love to be at the beach when there are not many people and we can hear the ocean in peace."

"I did not know this sensitive profile of you."

"Maybe it is because you don't know me as well as you think you do."

"You don't let me" – I said and we both laughed.

She was glad and would look at me almost always smiling. I was shaking like a leaf. How does she do this to me?

"Don't tell me we are going to the beach in Oeiras?"

"Yes, why?"

"I have a huge connection with this beach."

"Tell me" – she requested.

I told her when I was 16 or 17 years old, I used to go to that beach with my friends from Mira-Sintra, the Mill Boys. In the Summer, every week, my father would buy me three round trip tickets to the beach. "Only three?" I would complain, I wanted to go at least five times. Then, I decided I would hitch my way to the beach and use the tickets to come back, this way three days would become six. And that is how it was, almost every morning, me and a few more boys would hitch beyond the IC19 bridge. There was always someone to stop and, in a general manner, people were friendly and would give us advice. Until one day the person who stopped was a neighbor and friend of my father's, who told him. My father forbade me from going to the beach and sent me to Lentiscais, to spend the summer with my grandparents.

"Gee, you were a menace to society!" – Luísa said laughing.

"I remember we would go by bus and nobody wanted to sit near us."

"Why?"

"Imagine, 10 to 20 lads, teenagers, with hormones hopping up and down, we would make an impressive mess, we could not see any woman. On the bus as well as on the beach, a circle would form around us, nobody wanted to sit near us. Once, the bus driver threatened to call the police in case we did not calm down."

"How awful! And did you calm down?"

"Yes, but, at the end of the trip, we name-called and spit on him."

"Gross! What a scumbag!"

"Yes, a horde from a housing project" – I said proudly. I remember I had the habit of carrying some markers and writing: "Mill Boys" everywhere: buses, coffee houses, bus stops, walls, etc. There was a friend who also liked writing and he would tell me: "Hey, we'd rather write Mill Nazis, it's stronger." But I would answer: "Dude, I think the Nazis didn't really care for gypsies or blacks." And since half of the gang was either gypsy or black, he stopped writing Nazis, but kept on drawing the swastika.

The two of us took a walk by the shore, barefoot, without holding hands. She told me, again, about the relationship she had before. She was playing the victim again and blaming the ex-boyfriend for everything. I pondered if Elsa would do the same. Afterward, she told me the story of a friend she had lost, a year ago, because her boyfriend was trying to hit on Luísa, she told her and she did not believe her. I notice she always plays the poor little thing. We sat on the sand and stayed there contemplating the horizon, we talked about the movies we'd watched lately, the music we'd been listening to and who was currently working at Blockbuster. It was marvelous!

Before taking me to the train station, we met her half-sister, who has a tavern in Camarate. There is definitely a resemblance; the half-sister is short and brunette too, but she is way fatter and one can see she does not take care of herself. I did not understand the reason she took me there, she got in only to greet her and it seemed she was showing me off. I noticed they did not have a close relationship, as opposed to me and my sister, and in a short while, they ran out of subjects. Luísa's brother-in-law, who has the authentic aspect of a caveman tavern tender, barely gave her any attention. It was weird.

We headed to the East Station and she waited for the train with me. When it arrived, before boarding, I grabbed her and kissed her. She did not push me away, far from that, she held the back of my neck, bit my lip and sucked my neck.

"Well, you are gonna leave a mark!"

"That was the intention."

I took the trip very happily. I like her, I want to be with her, with all her melancholy, victimizing and concerns. By the middle of the trip, I sent her an SMS:

"I loved the kiss."

She answered right away:

"What a pity we started so late."

I did not want to put any pressure on the relationship at any point, without knowing its nature. We exchanged messages, mostly they were short, not very important subjects. When we talked on the phone, my heart would beat fast and my palms would get sweaty.

By the middle of October, I was back to Cacém, with a high expectation of seeing her. On Saturday, we scheduled to have lunch at a restaurant in Cacém. We greeted each other with a long kiss. We had a very pleasant and cheerful lunch, and did not stop talking and telling each other about funny things that had happened to us.

"Check this, Gonçalo, my brother is spending the weekend with my father, while my mother is out with a friend and will only be back at night."

"And..."

"Let's go to my place?"

"Let's go" – I said, laughing, really looking forward.

We went to her house, but we were making out before that in the restaurant's parking lot. Her building is tall, there must be like 8 or 10 floors, and there are two elevators. We were kissing and touching in one of them.

"Shall we do it here?" – I asked.

"We'd rather not, a neighbor might come around."

Luísa's house looked big and modern, however, actually, I have practically only seen her room, since she quickly pushed me in there. She pulled the shades down, we were under dim light and soon she took her clothes off and was naked in front of me. My God, what a beautiful body she has! It is not perfect, quite the opposite, her breasts are small and she has prominent hips, but it is this imperfection that attracts me and looks perfect to me. Since, once again, we did not have any contraceptives, she went to her brother's room to steal some and later she told me she thought he was still a virgin.

We made love twice that afternoon. We talked and made out on her one-person bed. The bedroom was tidy and smelled nice, it was painted purple and dark blue. There were some pictures of landscapes and some photos of her with friends and family. She picked a photograph from a drawer in which I was in Sines, with a baseball cap turned around and in the background the ocean and the castle.

"I used to have this one on my night-stand, but it bothered me too much and I took it out."

"I am not that ugly" – I joked.

"Silly, it's 'cause I love you" - she said shyly.

"I love you too, Luísa."

"I know" – she kissed me - "but I need you to wait a while, I am having a hard time at work."

At least I appreciate her honesty when she talks about us. I already did not know very well what our relationship was anymore. Are we a couple? Are we friends with benefits? And obviously I am willing to wait, I really like her.

Afterward, we were making love again, and we got exhausted and fell asleep within half an hour. She woke me up and asked if I would like to have dinner at her place, I said I wanted to go to the movie rental to talk to Eduardo and I would catch the train later. We said goodbye for like twenty minutes among hugs and kisses, I felt we were both in love. And what a great and beautiful feeling, even more when it is reciprocal.

I had a coffee with Eduardo, who told me Christiane had been caught stealing and was fired, my chin dropped. I never liked her. I told him about my comeback with Luísa and took a movie on his bill. It was a little bit weird to come back to the movie rental. There were already employees that I did not know and I did not recognize any of the customers.

On Sunday, Luísa took me again to the East Station, but this time, we walked hand in hand through the Park of the Nations and made out while waiting for the train. We scheduled to see each other within 15 days, when I was back.

During those fifteen days we kept in touch, I did not want to be boring or to pressure her, so I would wait for her to call.

On the first weekend of November, we were together again, however, she worked on Saturday and we could only see each other on Sunday, the very day I would have to go back to Castelo Branco. I was a little down for not spending more time with her, but I did not want my disappointment to show. We could have met on Friday night or Saturday, though she complained she was tired and wanted to be with me on Sunday when she would be fresh.

We had lunch at a restaurant nearby Rossio and went to Saldanha's theater afterward. She looked very attractive and waited for me to compliment her clothes and told me she had lost a few pounds. She was sweet the whole time and we spent most of it kissing.

"I wanna watch your newest movie."

"My newest movie! What do you mean?" – I asked.

"Edward Norton's new movie" – she laughed.

"Ah, that's right!" – I laughed to myself – "Check it out, do you know who Lee Van Cleef is?"

"No, it doesn't ring a bell."

"He is an actor, do you remember *The Good, the Bad and the Ugly*?"

"Yes."

"The bad one is Lee Van Cleef. Someone said I looked like him."

"Oh, yes... maybe a little. Who said that to you?"

"It was in Holland."

"But who?"

"Some Japanese guy who was staying in the hostel" – I lied.

The movie was *The Score*. A thriller with Robert De Niro, Edward Norton and Marlon Brando. It is a bad movie, unoriginal and predictable, so we ended up not watching it and making out instead. There were not many people and there was nobody in our row. The environment started to warm up.

"It would be better if we went to a hotel" – I told her.

"Yes, without a doubt."

She tasted like salt and popcorn. She opened her shirt a little and put my hand on her breast, while she was caressing my whole body.

"Take it out..." - she whispered.

I pulled my pants down a little, opened the fly and my "vulture" popped out. She started jerking me off, but I noticed she did not have a lot of practice in the procedure, she was doing it too hard and one of her rings was hurting me.

"Slow down" – I asked.

She calmed down, found her way on the task and I was kissing her and caressing her breasts. And then the volcano blew out, a wave of lava was spread over the next seats, on my legs, her hand and who knows where else. We cleaned ourselves as best we could, with not much effort and she was whispering again.

"Did you enjoy it?"

"A lot."

She was glad and we intertwined fingers while watching the rest of the movie.

We said goodbye at the station among kisses and caresses.

"See you in 15 days?" – she asked.

"I think so. Don't you want to show up in Castelo Branco?"

"And bump into the girlfriend you have over there?" – she said laughing.

"Come on, you are going to like the city. We can go to my parents' village."

"Right, it might be a good idea."

We kept in contact, two or three times a week, most of the time she would be the one to call. Every time I would call, I was afraid she would think I was pressuring her. I even talked to Eduardo to check if he would see her around the movie rental and I was afraid he would tell me he had seen her with another lad, but that did not happen.

On November 15th, she called me saying her car broke down and she could not come. Honestly, the excuse sounded weak. I noticed she was being cold, as if she did not want to spend much time talking to me. I told her there was no trouble and when I would spend a weekend in Cacém I would give her a call. That call got me thinking, something has changed. I wanted to believe it was nothing, that is the way she is, she was very busy with work, and maybe her car was broken for real.

Then, that weekend, I arrived and called her. I was nervous about the possibility that she was not going to answer, we had not been talking on the phone for a few days. She seemed glad to talk to me and told me she was going to try to see me, although, on Saturday she would have to go to Oporto due to some work matter and promised me she would call me when she was back. I spent the whole weekend checking my phone. With whom would she have gone to Oporto? Would it be true? In the end, she called me when I was getting on the train back to Castelo Branco. She apologized, but she had been tired from working too much; she gave me a few details from her trip and we planned to meet when I was back in Cacém or she would go to Castelo Branco to see me. We will see each other next time, but with her I have ups and downs like a roller coaster, at times I am up on the clouds, so in love and happy, other times I am down to the ground, afraid she will not call me anymore and does not want to be with me. I do not understand why she does not want to open up to me. In her house, she said she loved me... so why does she leave me so loose?

Last weekend, I went to Lentiscais with my father to harvest some olives. It is a task I do not enjoy. We woke up too early, around seven, and it was freezing cold. We carried the ladders and spent the whole day picking olives. We only stopped for lunch. In the afternoon, we had to clean the olives, which is not so much work. This is a tradition that has its days counted. I, in the future, will not be doing this anymore, it is not profitable and I will not spend my vacation days doing it like my father, who enjoys it. I know he likes spending time with me, he asks about a lot of things but, actually, I feel he always treats me like his son and not as an adult, he keeps on giving me advice as if I was a kid. We argue all the time regarding the environment and social issues. It seems to me he has a very negative perspective towards the world, he says he is a realist. One of the things that costs me the most when I am with him is that I cannot smoke, because if I do, he starts criticizing me right away.

A situation that annoyed me that weekend was meeting my uncle Basilio, who I actually like, and he asked me if my course had any future, he always does that kind of commentary and it even seems he wants me to be unemployed. I know he wishes me well however, since his children decided not to go to college, he tries to put mine down. He used to do the same to my sister too, but she is already employed and earning good money and that bothers him. He, like the rest of the inhabitants of the village, values people depending on their economic level, their income, not their principles and actions. Afterward, we discussed what some news was broadcasting about a sheepherder who was complaining that the wolves kept on attacking his sheep.

"They all should be killed!" – he yelled.

"Well, but don't the wolves have the right to live?"

"But all they do is damage!"

"The sheepherder should work on better fencing. Humans don't have the right to exterminate a species only because it harms us."

"Of course we have. Out of what should the sheepherder make his living? I would like to see if it was you."

The rest of the family, who were hearing the discussion, took his side.

I went to see my grandmother in the nursing home and since it was olive season, I took the opportunity to take her from the home to her house. She liked it and gave me a thousand shields. I have noticed her becoming more worn out, it seems she has difficulty speaking. She is quieter, I do not know if she is sad or if it is natural for old people.

The following day Elói came to see us. Having him over was like a party. Since he does not pay for the room at the Burrow, he slept in the Lair's kitchen, on an old couch we have. I was glad to see him, it was really fun to go out at night with him again, like old times. He was telling me about adapting to Salamanca, he said he had some acquaintances, that the guys are nice and they try to help him. The university nightlife is crazy, with way more partying than in Castelo Branco. He is learning Spanish and can already sustain some conversations but he confessed that in the beginning no one could understand him and he was kind of lost. He insisted that I go visit him. I said that maybe the beginning of the next year would be a good time for that.

"Hey, Gonga, you have to do an Erasmus, it is a very cool thing."

"I don't know, Elói, I like to be known in the school, to know the corners of the house. Going to a new place and just when you begin to adapt, you have to come back... I don't know..."

"The guys wanted to know me, right away they wanted to welcome me and help me. Listen to me."

"And the gals?"

"There are a lot of them and they are way cheekier than here."

"Have you found one for yourself?"

"Not yet, but I have my eye on one that is going down for sure."

"Good, don't make a bad name for the Nation."

I have been going out at night less often, although the College nightlife is sacred. Which means, every Thursday, at night, I go out. Many times I go alone and I never get there high. I start drinking some beers at the neighborhood taverns and when I arrive at the bars downtown I am already a bit tipsy, but far from being drunk. Since I have adopted this behavior, I can say I have been talking to more people. I am more willing to meet new people, however, most of those nights I end up with my old junkie friends.

One of those Thursday nights, I went out alone. I went to Rubro and Caffe with Milk, drinking, smoking some cigarettes and talking to one person or another. Meanwhile, Rita walked into the bar with some friends. At first, I thought she would not greet me, since the last time I saw her on the Academic Week, she shut me down big time. Although, this time that is not what happened and she came straight to me.

"Check this out! If it isn't the great Gongas!"

"Hi, Rita."

We kissed twice and she got so close to me I felt her breast.

"So, what have you been doing? I haven't heard from you!"

"Well, on the Academic Week you shut me down so hard."

"On the Academic Week? Did we see each other?"

"Yeah, you were with your friend, I had fallen and had an injured knee."

"Ah, yes, that's it, I remember…"

She smelled like tobacco and wine, she had dinner with her friends and was already inside of the bottle. She started to get too close to me, I felt her body, her breast, her legs rubbing against mine. I had seen this movie before!

"You know what, Gongas, me and Alice had a matter to solve that night and we couldn't give you attention."

"Alice? Your friend's name is Alice?"

She started to laugh hard.

"Don't you tell me you didn't know her name?"

"Yes, I knew… It's just that I didn't remember."

"Well, well, you didn't know and you still have taken her to bed."

"Did she tell you?"

"Sure, we are best friends. We tell each other everything. I even know she scratched your back."

"Yeah... well, that was..."

"That is the way she is when she reaches orgasm."

"Ah, yes? How do you know? Did she tell you?"

"No, I have seen it. We have been to bed together many times."

I must have opened my eyes like an owl, because she started laughing like there was no tomorrow. I felt a little warm, I was sweating. She grabbed me by the collar and kissed me, I felt her humid tongue and her tobacco breath. I tried to think. This was not right, I liked Luísa, I was going out with her, we made love a short time ago, in her bedroom, and she confessed she loved me. Although, I was not her boyfriend, which means, I was not officially her boyfriend, she was always saying "at this moment I cannot," this way I was not doing anything wrong. Indeed, she would never know, just like it was in Holland.

Rita started kissing me again, I allowed it and started to touch her bottom, right in the middle of the Coffee with Milk, with the people watching and laughing. After a few more minutes on the task, she went to the counter to pick up some beers and I went to the bathroom. I was very doubtful. Should I have fun with her and maybe even get laid or cut it? I felt like John Travolta in *Pulp Fiction*, when he is at the head man's house and does not know if he should fuck his boss's wife or not. On one hand, I wanted to, she physically attracted me and did not want anything more than a crazy night, so why not? However, on the other hand, I liked another lady. I remembered my Buddhist roots and decided not to take her to bed, because the karma law was going to punish me. I would not like Luísa to go to bed with another guy. Although, one must point out that I am a weak being, feeble for a good piece of butt and a pair of tits.

I came out of the bathroom and still did not know which way to go. I walked around the pool and soccer tables, pondering what to do. Meanwhile, Madeiras has shown up.

"Yeah, kinda cool, Gonga, you around here?"

"What's up, Madeiras, how are you?"

While Madeiras was talking about something unintelligible, because he had gone over his limits, I reflected that he was a sign from the Gods for me to decide not to frolic with Rita. He told me to go to Black Tulip because Ricardo and Mike were there and we could smoke a joint. I accepted. I walked across the bar on tiptoes so Rita would not see me, because if she saw me and came after me, it was possible I would not have the strength to say no. We went to Black Tulip, chatting, though I was disconnected and wondered if I was acting well.

As Madeiras had said, Ricardo and Mike were at the Black Tulip. I admire those two guys. The two of them, when they got to school, were anti-prank, which means, they refused to take part in this stupid tradition and did not show any fear of the pressure they suffered. They are vegetarians and fought for putting an option for them in the school cafeteria, but they do not at any moment try to convince the rest of us to be vegetarians. They founded the recovery center for wounded birds in the school; they got in the course because it is their vocation, not by chance like me. They understand the fauna and flora, they love to wander by the mountains and rural paths, they know animals by their Latin name and they are always ready to help with whatever is the matter regarding the environment.

Ricardo is a very popular fellow among the potheads, because, besides always being cheerful, he has principles and he is active in the defense of those principles. One day, I commented with him about the upcoming of the Left Wing Block, a new party, of a modern left-wing and he told me:

"In my opinion, Gonga, the parties exist to defend their own interests, not ours. They are only going to put in public offices the ones who have the party credentials."

"Maybe you are right, the party democracy is rotten."

He is an anarchist. He always carries a spray can in his pocket and writes short anarchist sentences on the streets walls, things like: "let it be, son, they take care of everything" or "the big ones only seem big because we are on our knees. Let us stand up" or even "if there is no justice for the people, there shall be no peace for the government."

Ricardo thinks, and I believe he is right, that our course is full of subjects in which the teachers give the lessons to be learned by heart, without proposing any problem or any conflict solving situation. That night, I told him about Amsterdam and the adventures I had over there, he laughed a lot and, afterward, he told me he wished he had come along, but to the most rural part, to the natural parks, to be surrounded by nature.

The Black Tulip is in Cansado Village, in the old part of town, with old two-story houses among buildings from the eighties of seven or eight floors. Next to the bar there is a church, which is a huge building with some weird architecture, there are no windows and it is painted pink and white, with many nonsense arches and many crosses. The church is on the top of a slope and in the courtyard there is a garden, mostly paved; there is only a little green area and a fountain in the middle. The access to the church takes two flights of stairs on the side and one on the front. The ones on the side are limited by the church wall itself and by a high cement gantry. And it is there, in one of those staircases, where we used to smoke joints, a perfect place because it is protected from the cold winter wind and it hides us from obtrusive eyes.

In one of those trips between the Black Tulip and the church staircases, a spray can fell from Ricardo's pocket when he was sitting on one of the stairs, it rolled through the steps and fell on my feet.

"Geez, what does this happen to be?" – I imitated the accent of a cop from the North.

"This is not mine, officer" – Ricardo said, laughing.

"Don't tell me it's you who has been writing shit around the city, mister. Besides that, you are a deadbeat with a junkie aspect."

We all laughed and, afterward, more seriously, I asked:

"How do you draw such perfect letters on the sentences you spread around town?"

"We have a mold at home, we build the sentences, then all we have to do is to put the mold on the wall and paint. Gonga, keep this spray can, we have many at home."

"Really? Thank you, I have always been an excellent painter."

Then, in an act of poor judgment, I shook the spray can and, on the church wall next to the staircases, I decided to write: "legalize it." Or, at least, it was the main idea, I was already so drunk and high that I did not know if the word "Legalize" ended in "ZE" or "SE." I hesitated for a moment, my brain was quite damaged, I could not sustain any logical reasoning and decided to go with "ZE." However, since I had poorly measured the size of the letters, the "IT" did not fit. The three other junkies were laughing their asses off.

"Well, Gonga, now I know why they call you Crazy Gonga!" – Mike said, laughing.

"Yeah, kinda cool, dude, this fellow is a real nutcase" – Madeiras said.

"Friends and fight comrades" – I said, trying to impose a serious look - "this has been the highest moment, the apogee of my fight for legalizing marijuana. Here, on the walls of a decaying institution, an unstoppable action for legalizing marijuana right now will arise."

"Bravo, Gonga, Bravo!" – Ricardo had a good chuckle.

I have always liked to graffiti on the walls with spray paint, I have a long history in this field. When I used to live in Mira-Sintra and we would go to the beach or to play soccer in the next village or simply wander around with no destination, I would always carry a spray can around and paint on the walls: Mill Boys. I must have painted over 30 places in Cacém, some are still there and when I pass by, they fill me with pride. I was caught only once. We were playing in a village in Cacém, beautifully named *Casal do Cotão* (Fluff Block). It is a village full of slopes, with many buildings of all colors, a really ugly neighborhood. I decided to paint on a garage that the mill boys had been there. However, the garage owner showed up scolding me and did not allow me to finish my work, so it looked like: "Mill Bo." Many times I have wondered about going back to that place and doing my creation over and, a random day, casually, I passed by it with a friend in his car. I asked him to go to the garage but the owner had painted over the letters. He certainly had no artistic sensitivity.

This weekend, I have been to Cacém, not being able to see Luísa, I met Rodas and I took the spray can with me. We had been drinking the whole night in the same place: a very Portuguese tavern, full of old men playing cards and smoking. Me and Rodas were the youngest there and we never saw a woman in that cow-house. During that night, I had been meditating exhaustively about how I should use the spray. On a ramp to my neighborhood, the Tapada Mount, more precisely on Raul Brandão Street, there is a huge building, with like ten floors. Next to this building there are some staircases, which are, possibly, the worst staircases in Cacém. The stairs are unleveled, full of holes and without a rail. On the wall of those staircases someone wrote: "Long Live Commonism." That misspelling has always intrigued me. What kind of person would write this kind of thing without knowing that communism is written with a "U" instead of an "O?" Perhaps some kind of ignorant? Some larky kid? A workman who did not have the time to read the communist propaganda? Or who knows, maybe it was the masterpiece of someone who wanted to shock the passers-by.

That night, while I was with Rodas, I had the chance to correct the misspelling and write a "U." Although, it would also be nice if I could draw the sickle and the hammer on the typo. Afterward, another idea came up, putting a Nazi swastika on that "O." It was not a bad idea, it would be like indicating that the two ideologic limits: fascism and communism were not so far apart from each other. However, when I arrived at the place, it was cold and windy. I was drunk, but not enough to make me not care about the neighborhood. I analyzed if it would be worth painting the wall, for being caught would be embarrassing. I decided not to mess with the "Long Live Commonism" and a little lower I wrote: "Long Live Kazen."

Every time I pass by my most recent paintings: "Long Live Kazen" and "Legalize" I feel inexplicably proud, I imagine it is like what Van Gogh felt when finishing and looking at his paintings.

My Grandmother's Death – Thursday, January 17th, 2002

The death of my grandmother is clearly the most significant news of recent times and since evil never sleeps, her death was the peak of various horrible situations, like Murphy's law says: "Anything that can go wrong, will go wrong, at the worst possible moment."

But before telling about my grandmother's death, one has to make a review of the terrible end of the year that I have had. Well, it was not terrible in every field, regarding school I was approved in almost every subject, without the need to take recovery exams, something that has never happened before. But I will tell everything that happened in chronological order.

In December, on a weekend in which I came to Cacém, I planned to go Christmas shopping with Maria João. One has to highlight that I hate shopping, above all in the middle of the Christmas season, when the stores are full of people. I decided I would only lose one day on this torturing task of buying presents for my parents and sister. Maria João came along and, in between one store and another, we had a coffee and smoked a cigarette. I must say I even enjoyed the day, because I love to spend time with my friend and I even bought a gift for my aunt and uncle in Castelo Branco and another for Luísa.

On that weekend in which I went shopping, I went out for dinner with Luísa in Massamá. I noticed she was tired and stressed out, she complained about work, about her colleagues, her father, etc. At the end of the meal, we had some kisses in her car and said goodbye. She seemed colder, with less patience for my stories, quieter and one would even say it looked like she was forced to make plans with me.

"Do you already have plans for this New Year's Eve?" – I asked.

"Yes, I am going with some friends to Algarve, just the girls" – she laughed. – "I really need to get out of here, be with my friends and dance until I fall down."

I got jealous, we could have gone somewhere together, only the two of us, as a loving couple, but it seemed more and more that our feelings were not identical.

Eva, the Dutch, quit writing to me and I thank her for that. Our emails were getting shorter and shorter and pointless. Although I did not want to be the one to quit writing, since Luísa would be spending New Year's Eve with her friends, it would not have been bad if I spent it with Eva, as she had suggested.

During December I was receiving the grades of the tests I had taken on many subjects and I was approved in all of them, except for one in which I have to take an exam. I could say that this success is due to the fact I was attending the classes, taking notes, studying more at home, going out at night with less frequency, however the truth is I am a crook and I cheated to be approved.

I have always used cheats or any trickery that would make my life easier. In my student life I have been caught three times, and the last one was in December, which is why I have to take the exam.

The first time I was caught copying I was in third grade, my teacher would say before the break:

"Study page 23 of the book, because afterward you are going to take a spelling test on this text."

I had the brilliant idea of not only studying the page but also copying the essay in my notebook. When the teacher would say the text, I would write what she was saying, but I already had it written on the other page. Something ingenious for an eight-year-old boy. That worked out and I came down from 10 mistakes per text to 1 or none. The teacher complimented me and told me I was making great progress, although, one fine day, she caught the trick and struck me twice with a ruler in front of everybody. A few days later, she called my parents, not for this cheat, but because I was caught in another scam. At the end of the classes, my teacher would go away and some of the students would stay in the classroom gathering their material or finishing some activity. I had the habit of going to the board, grabbing the chalk and writing in big letters, nice words like: "shit" of "dick" or even "pussy." Why would I do that? I actually do not know, maybe a psychologist could explain this deviation. I think I simply had fun scandalizing.

The cleaning lady, who would clean the room after the class was over, saw that time and time again and complained to my teacher. There was a witch hunt in the classroom and a snitch let the cat out of the bag and told on me.

"The stains fall on the best piece of cloth" – the teacher said when she knew it was me.

Therefore, she called my parents to the school, told them everything and I expected to take some vigorous whipping from my father, but he did not even touch me and just forbade me from going out to play soccer for a month, which ended up hurting me more than a beating.

The second time I was caught cheating I was already in high school, in a countability test, in which we had to know by heart some weird formulas. The teacher was smart and heard me crumpling the notes when I took them from among the test pages and shoved them into my pocket, hence she asked to see what I had in my pocket and caught me. Since that day I have only used plasticized cheats.

The third time, and I hope it to be the last one, was now. In a subject about rural and environmental hotel development. Just like Ricardo says: "the teachers give the lessons to be learned by heart" and this teacher wanted us to know how many beds there must be in the rural hotels or how many bedrooms, plus a cast of stupidities that we could only learn by heart. So I made some notes with all those numbers and used them. I thought I was being subtle but, at the end of the test, the teacher, who is young and has a sharp face, said:

"Did you use the cheats a lot?"

"I ended up not needing them."

"You are a rascal and a swindler" – he said without laughing.

"Do you think so, teacher? Then watch out for your wallet" – I said laughing, but he did not find it funny and I thought it might have been better if I had hushed.

He reproved me with an eight, I have to memorize that shit to go to the exam.

I enjoy cheating, I love the moment in which I catch the teacher distracted and, with my heart pumping, I lay my notes between the pages of the test.

Deep inside the teacher is right, I am a swindler, a crook, but it is my nature, why should I hide it? I have always enjoyed cheating when playing Monopoly, it is more than the simple act of winning the game, what I like is cheating on it without being caught, that is the fun part.

When I came back to my parents' house for Christmas Vacation, I was expecting to meet Luísa regularly, but that was not what happened. I only saw her once, which was one day before New Year's. We went to North Massamá's garden and we had been making out for an hour.

"Afterward, when you arrive at Algarve, say anything."

"Yes, of course. "

"It would even be nice, if we went to Almograve again..."

"Yeah, but I already had it set up with my friends. With whom are you going to spend New Year's Eve?"

"I will be with Nice and Rodas, we are going to the High Village. Can we still see each other before you go?"

"Maybe, I'll call you."

I felt she was happier with her plans of going with her friends on a vacation than being with me. That got me depressed and I opened up to Maria João. I told her everything about this story because she knows how to listen and gives me the perspective of a woman. She also does not understand Luísa's behavior very well, but she believes that she likes me, though she is afraid of getting hurt. I noticed I have been confused, I constantly check on my cell phone waiting for her to write or call. I go through our relationship and I cannot understand what we mean to each other. Sometimes she gives in and tells me she wants me, other times she does not talk to me for days and seems to get annoyed by me. All of that eats me up inside, I take those doubts to the pillow, I roll over and over on my bed thinking about it and every time I wake up, hoping to have a message from her.

New Year's Eve was a prelude to the terrible get-go of 2002.

After having dinner with my parents, I planned to gather up with Nice and Rodas. This year, Nice wanted to take the car, she did not want to wait for the first train to come by like last year. As opposed to last year, it was not raining, but it was freezing cold. However, there were not so many people in the High Village and the Beer House was almost empty. The atmosphere was sad. I was hoping Luísa would call me at any time. She did not keep her promise and did not call me when she arrived at Algarve. I noticed that Nice too was uncomfortable, she does not drink or smoke and she had to put up with two drunk junkies. Rodas and I drank and smoked a lot. I think he was having fun, but I was in deep pain. Though both of them were my good friends, I wanted to be with Luísa, not with them. Even with all the drinking and smoking, I was not able to enjoy myself and I wanted to go away and sleep deeply for days or weeks on end.

That night, we saw the first Euro coins. We all wanted to see how the coins looked and what pictures the other countries had put on them. So that is it, now we are Europeans.

From the High Village we went to Terreiro do Paço, on this occasion instead of hundreds of cars parked in the middle of the square there was a disco, covered with techno music and fireworks. The ticket to the disco was free and we got in. It looked like a house party, there were 10 men for each lady. Moreover, one could see it was paltry people. Nice was not feeling so good and wanted to go home. I understood and I also did not want to stay, Rodas was the only one who was enjoying the music and the surroundings and kept on saying the same sentence from last year: "Legalize it, comrade." He did not understand that Nice was not feeling well and started to yell at her for wanting to go back to Cacém so early.

"Come on, I don't understand, aren't you having fun?"

"Can't you see I'm not?"

It is in those situations that I think Rodas does not have the sensitivity to see when his friends are not well, to me it was clear that Nice was not enjoying the night. For sure she would also prefer to spend the night with someone else. She did not tell me anything and I also did not tell her that I was depressed because of Luísa.

"Look, Gonga, what if we take her to the car and the two of us stay here?"

"Nope, Rodas, I'm going with her."

We were silent in the car almost all the way. Rodas still complained about going home so early and said the trouble was Nice not being in the mood. She said she did not have the patience to put up with drunks and scumbags. There was an argument between the two of them, in which I tried to calm them down and I took Nice's side. In the end, she left us near the gas station at *Bons Amigos* (Good Friends) Avenue.

We bought some beers at the station and had them in the little garden behind it.

"Well, man, I don't understand Nice" – Rodas complained.

"Rodas, she wasn't feeling well."

"But she should have changed her attitude and enjoyed the night. She was carrying a long face the whole time."

"Maybe there is something wrong, perhaps she wanted to be with someone."

Afterward, I tried to open up to him about my relationship with Luísa, the fact that she did not say a word to me that night, I wanted to unburden a little, but Rodas is not a good listener, he always drags the love themes to his own ground. He started to talk about his ex-girlfriend from when he was 17, of how much chemistry there still is between the two of them and practically did not even hear me. Afterward, he wanted to talk about soccer and I thought it was time to go home and sleep. It would have been enough if Luísa had sent me a simple text for my mood to have changed radically.

And since evil never sleeps, a few days later, my grandmother passed away at Castelo Branco Hospital. There were some breathing complications, but at her age, 92, it could have been anything.

When we knew about her death, we all packed up and left for Lentiscais, where the wake and funeral took place. I took the car trip with my sister and my parents. I was driving with my sister by my side and we were talking to each other, our mother reprimanded us for not mourning and remaining quiet. We disagreed, saying we were not disrespecting anyone, however, to avoid hurting her feelings, we kept in silence the rest of the way and asked her to not scream and cry out loud as it was usual in Lentiscais.

We arrived at Lentiscais at dusk and went right away to the backside of the church, which is where the wakes take place. It had been raining most of the day, there was fog and the temperature was around three or four degrees. Getting in the wake, we saw some people sitting around the casket, which was halfway opened. We started greeting the people there, who were mostly relatives. Half of them I didn't know, but I did what my parents and sister did and greeted them all. Some people who were closer to the family would hug me, saying things like: "there goes our grandmother" or "that is how life is."

My mother had a crying attack when she saw her mother in a coffin, she screamed and was hugged by my aunt from Castelo Branco. The situation was moving but, at the same time, awkward, because her screams for pain cut the sepulchral silence installed in the place.

I preferred not to look at my grandmother's face, which was covered with a little kerchief. I did not want my last memory of her to be a dead face. I took a seat in one of the chairs that were around the casket. The temperature in the wake was quite low, nobody took off their jackets or overcoats. Whenever someone would open the door to the outside, an icy breeze would blow in and quench the place even more. There were a few heaters however, in a general manner, the place was not prepared to hold a wake.

I never really know how to behave in situations like this and I basically imitate others. Everybody in the room had their heads down, some women prayed, others went in and out to smoke a cigarette or go to the coffee place. I sat in a corner and did not get up from the bench for a long time, I would only get up when someone would come to me to give me condolences, I did not know most of the people and they would introduce themselves like distant uncles and cousins.

I left the room a few times to smoke a cigarette with my cousins; we were all sad. I sent a message to Luísa asking her to call me when she could. I wanted to unburden myself a little with her, tell her about my grandmother's death, but she did not call me all night.

That night, while I was sitting in that corner of the room, I imagined what all those people, around the casket, were thinking. Some about the deceased's life, others maybe about their own death, others would be remembering their own dead relatives, some people were thinking about the inheritance for sure and still some others thinking about what they were going to do for their next vacation.

At that moment, I started praying the Lord's Prayer and some Buddhist mantras and then I remembered the many books I had read about death from the Tibetan Buddhist point of view. According to the sacred books her soul would be right now surrounded by beings that had already reached nirvana. They were comforting her and would teach her the path to enlightenment. She would be in this state for about a week and then would reincarnate again in another being. That reincarnation would depend on the karma cumulated from this latest life of hers. As to me, personally, it always seemed she was a good grandmother, affectionate and caring. I think her children as well as her husband would not have enough reasons to complain about her, her next life was set to be blessed. Although, during this night, it also occurred to me that all I have read could be wrong, that she died and on the following day she would be buried and there was nothing else to it. There might be no soul, no heaven, nor reincarnation.

Afterward, it came to my mind the idea of what legacy she was leaving behind? What influence did she have in this world or on the people that surrounded her? What influence did she have on me? I recalled one time, when she was still living in the village, and I passed by her by car, stopped and told her I was going to show her some ostrich, which she had never seen before and would call them big bugs. There was a farmer who had a small land where he would grow and sell ostriches and we went there. She was astonished looking at those huge birds with long necks and big strong beaks. When we got back home, she gave me 500 shields.

"Thank you, son, for taking me there, nobody has ever had the idea of doing that."

I was moved to remember that story. Afterward, I recalled the summers I used to spend with her and my grandfather, and how they treated me so well, although I was a stupid teenager who many times would show up high at dinner time and would laugh like a dumbass about everything.

"The kid is nuts" – they would say.

I felt ashamed.

I recalled many of the moments the two of us spent together; near the fireplace, when she would warm up my hands and toast a piece of bread for breakfast. When we used to go to the vegetable garden with my grandfather on his donkey cart. When we were in her room in the nursing home, near the window, and she would give me her big hands with spots and marks while she was listening to my stories. She would always give me practical advice and tell stories about her past, which I would always imagine in black and white.

She had a harsh past, almost miserable. She did not go to school, did not know how to read or write. She would work from sunrise to sundown for a picayune that was barely enough to buy shoes for her children. My grandfather fell for the fantasies people would tell about France. They would say over there everybody is rich, that there was a lot of abundance, that in the future he would have a car and my grandmother would have a fur coat. So he went to France, left his family behind and crossed over the Iberian Peninsula on the sly, almost died from exhaustion when crossing the Pyrenees and, when he finally arrived in France he had to work from sunrise to sundown, and live in a muddy slum in the Paris suburbs, and hide his money in his underpants because there were fellow countrymen that would try to steal it. Afterward, he would send money monthly to aid his wife and kids who had stayed in Lentiscais and he would only come home once a year. What a hard life!

I remembered my grandmother telling me that during the Spanish Civil War, many Spanish people would flee to the neighboring Portuguese villages. They would come only with the clothes on their backs and would only ask for a bit of bread and water. All she had for lunch was a loaf of bread and some bacon. So, she would share her bread with the adults and give the bacon to the children. That memory made me sorrowful; she was such a poor person and had no trouble in sharing and now, we, who live in abundance, look at the poor and the refugees with contempt. This thought got me even more desolated and I started to cry quietly, I thought nobody had noticed, but soon someone came to comfort me with the typical line that: "we all have to die and she was already old." However, old as she was, that would not draw a comma from the fact that I had lost a friend.

I kept checking my phone, waiting for Luísa to call, but she didn't. I started recalling the conversations I had with my grandmother about the weird relationship I had with Luísa. My gramma had a negative opinion of her and thought I was letting her treat me like her puppy, all she had to do was throw a bone and I would come running right away. I concluded she was right, the problem was not that the time was not right for a relationship, it was that I wasn't the right person, because, otherwise, she wouldn't treat me like that. It was like I was drunk and, in that moment, I had a glimpse of lucidity and understood that there would never be a proper time for Luísa because I was not the proper lad. She, someday, would meet someone that would be the right person for her and would make him a priority. I decided it was high time to quit running after the bone, I had to break free from her, this kind of relationship was not healthy for me. Therefore, I decided it was high time to cut Luísa off.

My mother and some aunts stayed all night at the wake. I went to sleep for a couple of hours and, on the following day, after the service, the casket was taken to the cemetery and left in a grave which was already opened. It's always a sorrowful moment, me and my sister were hugging and crying. My aunt from Castelo Branco said a sentence that got stuck in my memory: "the next generation is us." Someday it will be my turn. Someday it will be me.

In the following days, I had no news from Luísa, I do not know if she did not see my message or simply saw and did not want to talk to me. One thing is for sure, I had decided to end whatever this was. I wrote her an email. It was a three-paragraph email and in the first, I told her about my grandmother's death. In the second paragraph I told her that I had been feeling for months like that Bob Marley song: *Waiting in Vain*. I was always waiting for "the moment to go by" when she would want to give me a little more visibility in her life and I would not be waiting in vain. I knew that if I had finished the email at this point, it would leave an open door for her to call me, convince me to take her back and throw the bone again, so I decided to write a third and decisive paragraph. I said I had met a lady, that she helped me with my grandmother's death and that now we were dating.

I knew that with that paragraph I would be cutting the evil by the root. I would like to know what she felt when reading the email, if she felt betrayed, misled or if it was simply trivial to her, including the relief of not having to say "at this moment I cannot" or "the problem is not you" one more time. On the night I sent her the email, I still waited for her to call me, to ask me for forgiveness, a chance, but that did not happen. On the following day, in the morning, I nervously went to check my email to see if she had already answered and she did.

"Hello, Gonçalo, I am sorry for your loss. At this moment, I cannot give you priority in my life."

Two sentences, that is all she said to me, no more. That was all I was worth to her. And once more those stupid words saying "at this moment," making me believe that the problem was not me, the problem was the moment that was really terrible and would always be terrible.

It has been a terrible beginning of a year, but, at least, my relationship with Luísa was cleared up. Let us give the future a more positive look, because after the storm comes a calm.

Trip to Salamanca – Saturday, February 16th, 2002

Before the beginning of the second semester, I went to visit Elói in Salamanca, since he told me that in March he would have to leave the house where he was staying and take the end of course internship in Valência through a scholarship. I got jealous of the trips he was taking, the places he knew and I thought, if I liked Salamanca, perhaps I would still go there for an Erasmus.

On February 7th, a Thursday, I went to catch the train at Santa Apolónia Station. The ticket was still expensive and I only bought it one way, because on my way back I was not going to Lisbon, I was going straight to Castelo Branco. I was really ready to see my great friend Elói, to know about the news in his life.

The train left the station at dusk, on a clear-sky winter day, but with the temperature around eight degrees. The wagons were divided into compartments and in mine there was only a man around 30 years old who was a bricklayer and was going to Paris. The train is called Sudexpress and goes from Lisbon to Paris. The man was an immigrant; we talked about soccer and then he invited me to have a beer at the bar. I declined, I told him maybe I would go later. I did not feel like beginning to drink so early and, besides that, the drinks at the train bar are always very expensive.

At one of the following stations, a Spanish couple showed up, around 40 or 50 years old, going to the city of Rodrigo, one stop before Salamanca, and they were carrying some cages with parakeets. There was also an Asian man from the country of Sri Lanka, an island located in the South of India. We talked in English and he told me he was traveling across Europe by train and had a lot of curiosity to know Portugal.

"Really! Why?"

"Because in my country you are known as the boogeyman."

"The boogeyman!"

"Yes, when the Portuguese sailors arrived on our island, they stole, burnt and killed a lot of people. Since then, when a child does not want to eat, we say: 'Watch it, I'm gonna call the Portuguese.'"

I am not a nationalist, nor a patriotic guy, but when I hear those stories about our ancestors, I feel so much pride. It fills my heart up and I get the urge to get up, put my hand on my chest and sing the anthem out loud. How is it possible that such a small nation was able to screw up so many times? It is really impressive.

The lad asked to take a picture with me and said:

"I will show this picture to my mom and say, at the end of the day, the boogeyman is not that bad."

Soon it was dark and, bit by bit, the passengers of my compartment were quieting down. The bricklayer did not come back from the bar, the Spanish couple was napping and the lad from Sri Lanka was playing some video game. I started to read, but I could not concentrate. Then I recalled a school trip I had taken with the course group, in 1999, to a Spanish village, lost in Sierra da Gata. A random environmentalist organization, with aid from the government, had set up a convention to discuss environmental problems and opportunities taking place among the border areas between Portugal and Spain. It was a bargain to us, the students, because we only had to pay to attend the convention and food and accommodation were covered for us.

Of course, the Burrow and the rest of the scumbags enrolled right away. They took us by bus to a camping site among the mountains, a very green and humid area, away from the township. The camping site had bungalows and a big cafeteria. Me, Joey Nights,

Elói and Boni were all together in the same bungalow, while Bora Bora, Célia and Paula were in another.

On the first night it rained torrentially; we all stayed in our bungalow smoking hashish, there was no bar around so we had to get by without beer. We spent the night playing Pictionary; people would go in and out of our bungalow, commenting that there was a tremendous load of smoke in our house. I recall a Spanish dude who got in trying to be friendly, but we were so high and would only say nonsense. I started to howl and called him a bear, the poor lad took off as soon as he saw an opportunity.

It was fun to play Pictionary being so high, Joey Nights had to describe a word through gestures; he would aim at Elói and dance like a snake. We yelled: "drunk, junkie, traitor, dancing pig, snake, poisonous, dick." Elói did not find it funny, until Joey turned the card and it was a worm. Since then, Elói has been known as Worm, he even likes it because he is a fan of Dennis Rodman, a Chicago Bulls player whose nickname is the worm. As an act of revenge or a joke, when Joey Nights went to the bathroom, Elói, or rather, the Worm locked him in with the key. Then Joey got the idea of jumping out a minuscule window that was in the bathroom. He went outside, fell in the mud and came knocking on our door shivering from the cold, barefoot. Bizarre and stupid situations would occur all the time and Worm, in a moment of rage, threw the ashtray against the window and broke the glass.

"Shit, Elói! Are you fucking crazy?"

"Shit, I didn't want to break the glass."

"Now it's gonna be cold" – I complained.

We put some cardboard up to mask the damage and above all to avoid freezing to death in that bungalow.

Though I currently go to class, prepare for tests and pay attention to the lessons, back then all I wanted to do was smoke pot, drink a lot of beer and be surrounded by the Burrow so I could laugh until

I dropped. Hence, I barely saw any of the convention, possibly I did not spend more than twenty minutes hearing the experts talking about environmental themes and I was always at some tavern in that Spanish village. I remember one particular Spanish tavern, where they were watching some bulls race, and the floor next to the counter was covered with sawdust. We smoked hashish playdough, not knowing exactly how the tavern keeper would react. He was a young man who smiled and turned the fan on so the hashish smell would not be too intense. The customers were lovely and tried to teach us to say beer in Spanish.

When we would go to the cafeteria for dinner, we were always very high and anyone could tell. What mattered was that the teachers who were there, possibly tired of their day-to-day lives, had been drinking way more than us. Some of the teachers were trying to hit on the students. Some drunk students were insulting the teachers. It was pandemonium! But one of the things that shocked me the most was that the Spanish eat yogurt for dessert.

Another funny thing was Vasco and a few more scoundrels in our course, got in our bungalow, messed it all up and stole our pillows. Vasco was mocking the situation the whole day, and since we did not know what he was referring to, we did not care. Besides that, he has such a hard accent from Madeira that one can barely understand what he says. When we arrived at the house and saw that, Elói and I got furious. One has to highlight we had drank and smoked a lot, hence we did not even think about the consequences. We went straight to Vasco's bungalow, where, thank God, he was not, because he is stronger than a bull, and started kicking the door. His colleagues didn't open right away, but when they saw the lock was almost breaking under the strength of the kicks, they did. We got in as if we were two dangerous gangsters, nobody stopped us, searched for our pillows and took them back. Afterward, they told Vasco that Elói and I were very high with our eyes rolled up.

When we were going away, we were in a room waiting for the bus to take us back to Castelo Branco, Paula got near me and said:

"Hey, Gonga, did you see my dossier? I think I lost it!"

"But did you have any notes?"

"No."

"Then why do you want it?"

"I would like to keep a memory."

I saw a bunch of dossiers on a table, got close as if I did not want anything, took one and gave it to Paula.

"Thank you, Gonga" – she said, laughing – "You are really crazy."

"You're welcome. I'm always happy to help a friend" – I said, smiling.

I did not give it another thought, until Lopes started asking around if anyone knew about his dossier.

I want to believe Lopes is my antithesis. He got in like two years before me and was always an exemplary student. He never misses classes, does not drink, does not smoke, does not say bullshit. He is honest and I never understood why he is friends with Bora Bora; so, on some occasions we bump into each other. He is from a city in the back of beyond and, like many others, hates people from Lisbon and sees me as if I was some rich boy from the capital. Lopes dresses as if he is already a 40-year-old engineer, I have a feeling he is a homosexual but he is one of those who is never coming out of the closet. On a certain occasion, he told Bora Bora I was a bad influence, a dangerous fellow.

"Did you see my dossier, Gonçalo?" – Lopes asked me.

"Nope" – I said, uninterested.

We got on the bus and I was sleepy, so I leaned against a window and went most of the trip sleeping or pretending I was sleeping. Lopes was agitated, asking everybody about his dossier, because he had taken many important notes. Somebody told him they saw me going near his dossier and he did not let me go anymore.

"But, look, Gonçalo, are you sure you did not see my dossier? 'Cause that is really very important to me."

"I told you already, I haven't seen it, but if you want you can keep mine."

"It's not that, I took many notes and wanted to study them."

That guy is really presumptuous and a dumbass. Worried about not having some notes from a paltry convention to study. Where do you see things like that?

That same afternoon, before getting home, Bora came to talk to me.

"Hey, Gonga, but it was you who stole the dossier, right?"

"Stealing, *moi*? Are you calling me a thief?"

"Yes, you are a prowler with no compunction, come on, where did you leave the dossier?"

"Paula has it, she lost hers and I, as a gentleman, gave her one that I found lying around, which was coincidently Lopes'. Too bad."

"Well, what do we do?"

"Let's get soaked in the Association and forget about it."

I know Bora was kind of sad about the situation, because Lopes is his friend and, besides that, he kept on bothering him over the following days.

I arrived at the Salamanca Station a little after midnight. I was welcomed with an icy breeze and by Elói. We gave a big hug and went to his house. He was telling me the news.

"So, Gonga, I have a girlfriend" – he said, laughing.

"Really? What a dog!"

"Yeah, tomorrow I will introduce her to you, it's already late today."

"But we are still going out, right?" – I asked. I wanted to party.

"Sure, let's just go to my room and leave your backpack."

He had rented a room at a huge apartment, living with a lad and two ladies. He asked me to keep the noise down and we went to the kitchen to eat something. One of the housemates was there to grab something. She was short, brunette and had a nice round backside.

"That is quite a round ass that your friend's got there, Elói."

He made signs for me to shut up and I was ashamed, because I didn't think she understood Portuguese. When she left, I said:

"So, does she speak Portuguese?"

"No actually, but the Spanish used to go to the border to buy towels and bedsheets. She may understand a little."

"They go there to buy towels and bedsheets?"

"Yeah, it's really weird, but that is what they say."

"Well, we usually come to Spain to buy candy, perhaps they also don't know we have this habit."

We went to many bars, all full of youth, noise, alcohol, music and the smell of pot. Elói really liked a bar decorated under the style of the architect Antoni Gaudí. It was a very sui generis place, where it was worth paying attention to the details, but it was dark and full of people. We drank a lot, laughed, hit on some girls, some hit on us and we partied hard.

I could see right away on that first night that the academic environment in Salamanca was way better than in Castelo Branco, it was like they were two different leagues. Besides that, I was hoping to listen to some paltry Spanish music like: *Macarena*, or *El Toro Enamorado de la Luna* or even *El Venao*, but strangely enough the music playing was nice, modern Spanish rock music and some foreign music. There were more students, many were foreigners, the people seemed open-minded and willing to make friends. Another detail I liked was the fact of, for the first time, using the Euro outside of Portugal and that made all the sense. We were finally Europeans, not like some months ago when I would stress out between the Shield and the Florin. Since the first night, I thought of getting some information about the Erasmus program.

We arrived home, already drunk, his room was small and I slept in a sleeping bag on the floor next to his bed. I was afraid Elói would snore all night long but I was so tired and drunk I fell asleep right away.

On the following day, Friday the 8th, we woke up with a huge hangover. He had a high lamp, where the light was aiming at his pillow and the button was at the floor level.

"Elói, open your eyes wide and take a look at the ceiling. Can you see that?"

"What? I see nothing."

Then I turned the button on and the light struck him right in the eye.

"Oh, what a huge asshole!" – he complained. – "I will cast you out of my house."

I was laughing my ass off. I have always loved laughing over someone else's misfortune.

I went to take a shower, but Elói asked me not to use his shampoo, because it was expensive. We had breakfast, while watching the Eurosport channel, which broadcasted winter sports. Afterward, he showed me around town and introduced me to his girlfriend.

"You will like her, she is such a cool lady."

"And how long have you been with her?"

"For a month. It sounds like a lie, but I am her first boyfriend."

"Really? But how old is she? Like 14 or 15?"

We laughed.

"No, she is 21."

"Is she ugly, then?"

"Not at all, you'll see her soon."

He showed me the *Cueva de Salamanca* (Cave of Salamanca), the *Torre Clavero*, and the *Casa de las Conchas* (House of the Shells), etc., etc., and then, there she was. She was not ugly, no sir, nor was she any astonishing beauty. She was a normal lady, tall, with a huge smile. She was very friendly. Elói told her about our night and we made plans to meet again that afternoon, because she had some affairs to take care of.

We got to *Plaza Mayor* and my jaw dropped from the beauty of the square. It was huge, full of life, the architecture was fantastic, the balconies, as well as the windows, were very unique. While I was enjoying the views, two acquaintances of Elói showed up. One of them was a chubby brunette with curly hair and the other was blonde with a rosy, round face and blue eyes. They were very lovely too and we exchanged a few words. The brunette was called Verónica or Vanessa, I didn't learn her name, while the second one was Enara, whose name I didn't even catch at first and I even thought she was English for she had some Nordic features. I found her very good-looking, dressed with class, she had a style that was not too flashy; she wore some bracelets and rings with symbols I did not know, but I am sure they had some meaning. She had a very beautiful smile, like a shy child. She had two piercings: one next to her left eye and another under the lip. I was really fascinated by her beauty and friendliness.

When we split up and headed to the *Palácio de Anaya*, I asked about her:

"What a gorgeous woman!"

"Forget it, she has a boyfriend and he is quite a nice fellow."

"I'm not jealous."

"I know you, rascal, you didn't come all the way here to screw up. These people are nice and they are my friends."

"But you are going away to Valência within a month! You are never going to see these people again."

He took a deep breath and looked sad.

"Yeah, it's true, now that I have managed to build a small group of friends, I'll go away. The worst is the relationship with Elena."

"Do you like her?"

"Yep, I do. We get along, she is quite nice."

"Ouch, the Worm is in love" – I said in a sarcastic tone. – "Is València too far from here?"

"Yes, more than 500 kilometers."

"Well... You can see each other from time to time..." – I did not know how to cheer him up.

Afterward, we went to the Roman Bridge that is over the Tormes River.

We had lunch in a tavern that he knew and that had good prices. The Spanish serve two courses, the first one can be a soup or a salad, while the second dish is either meat or fish. Then we went to meet Elena, Elói's girlfriend, at a midtown bar.

The bar was in a two-story building, with iron tables contrasting with the old wooden house. There were only a few free tables and we climbed up to the second floor. Most of the customers were young, there was some buzz and the smell of hashish in the air. We had been talking all afternoon, Elena was talking slowly so I could understand and when I did not, Elói would try to translate. I was astonished that the people could smoke hashish in the bar, no trouble, it felt like we were in Holland. Elói confirmed he was also surprised on his first days here. In Castelo Branco it was totally out of question, they would call the police. The only public place where, sometimes, we could smoke was the disco Alternative, already drunk in the middle of the mess on the dance floor.

By the end of the afternoon, we went to the house of a friend of theirs. The apartment was full of youngsters, an impressive buzz with a lot of smoke and more beer. The ladies that had been introduced to me at *Plaza Mayor* were there and Elói insisted on introducing me to a lot of people whose names I quickly forgot. A big circle was made and we all sat in chairs, passing the pot around, while some drank and others talked loudly. I had already drunk enough to feel extroverted, but the language was a big boundary, so I preferred to talk low to Elói and Elena and hope nobody noticed my presence.

It was a well-spent afternoon. Elena is an excellent person, very lovely and cheerful. She stayed for dinner at those friends' house, while the two of us went back to Elói's house. Elói still does not eat meat, so he made a vegetarian meal. I helped him while we drank some beers. The lady with the round backside who lives with him showed up, she was making dinner too. We talked a little, she asked some questions about which monuments we had visited and which bars we had been to, etc. When we ran out of subjects, the spirit in the kitchen got a little awkward so, right after dinner, she went to her room.

Around 10 at night, we went back to the house where Elena was, this time the huge group had shrunk to half a dozen people. The owner of the house was there with her boyfriend, they spent the night curled up on the couch. The two ladies from *Plaza Mayor* were still there. They were drinking a mixture of red wine and coke which they called Calimocho. The goddamn drink was good, cool and sweet and I had quite a few glasses. The place was nice, the laughter was easy, I questioned why there were so few people, to which they answered that many had gone to their homeland to spend the weekend.

"How come you didn't go?" – I asked the blond lady, the one called Enara.

"No, my land is too far."

"Where are you from?" – Elói had already told me she was Basque.

"I'm from the Basque Country, 500 kilometers from here."

One could see she had been drinking, because her cheeks were already reddish. She had a beautiful face, with gleaming light blue eyes. She was still dressed elegantly, without being flashy, and with class. Her gestures were feminine and she had a shy smile.

In the end, only about five of us went out. Enara was all the way next to me and we talked the whole time.

"I have never known anyone from the Basque Country" – I told her.

"Well, I have been to Portugal a few times and, besides that, many Portuguese truck drivers pass by the zone where I live. You are terrible drivers!"

"Truck drivers are weirdos."

We talked the whole time, when there was a word we did not know we would either ask Elói or say it in English. I questioned if she was for the independence of the Basque Country and she hesitated.

"It depends on the country they want to create, but, at first, I think so."

"Then why did you come to study in deep Spain? To spend the money of the Spanish taxpayers?"

"They didn't have my course in the Basque Country, besides that, I have nothing against Spain. Actually, my father is from Burgos."

Since I did not know where Burgos was, and also because I didn't want to sound ignorant, I didn't take the subject any further.

"But are you for ETA?"

"No, of course not" – she answered right away. "The conflict must be solved by talking."

I told her I had watched a Portuguese documentary on television, where they showed the two main cities of the Basque Country: San Sebastian and Bilbao. In this documentary, two groups of youngsters were talking about their perspectives. In Bilbao they complained that the state persecuted the Basque culture and would not let them decide their future in a self-determination referendum. As for San Sebastian, another group was complaining that they could not wear the Spanish national soccer team shirt on the street because they would be insulted and there was no tolerance toward those who felt Spanish. I remember, at the time, I was watching the documentary with my sister. We commented about how lucky we were to have been born in a peaceful country like Portugal. Enara said neither of those tales are true and that the media exaggerates everything.

We walked from chapel to chapel, from bar to bar. In one of those bars I went to the counter to order a beer and, since I did not know the Spanish beers, I went for a Heineken. The bartender did not understand me and I repeated again and again:

"A Heineken beer."

Enara saw me in trouble, got close and told the employee:

"*Una Reinaken.*"

"Reinaken, but it does not start with an R!"

She laughed and I found her smile delicious, afterwards, she looked at me and I knew she wasn't just paying attention to me to be friendly, she was attracted.

We chatted for a moment at the counter. She told me she went to the movies alone to watch *The Lord of the Rings* and that she liked it a lot, indeed she had already read the book when she was a teenager. I said I worked in a movie rental during last year and that I preferred Star Wars. Afterward, we talked about literature and found out we both liked Anne Rice vampire books. We talked about the various characters that fascinated us in the series and at that moment I felt like kissing her, however, she had a boyfriend. I was only passing by and did not want to cause any trouble, but moreover I still was not drunk enough.

We also talked about music and I noticed right away, by the way she dressed, that she was a rocker, she surely did not like hip-hop. We coincided on one band that we both liked: Him, from Finland. I said I liked it a lot, but, actually, I only know a couple of songs. She listened to a lot of Spanish and Basque music and was telling me the bands that played at the bar where we were:

"Check this out, this is *Platero Y Tú*; this is *Extremoduro*; this is *Marea*, etc., etc."

One could notice this kind of band does not play in Portugal, at the bars and on the radio they only play the most festive and paltry music that comes from *nuestros hermanos*.

She confessed she did not like *fado* and that the Portuguese music she knew carried the Brazilian accent and it was samba, which she also did not like.

"Don't worry, I don't like *fado* either, it's too dark. In Brazil they make a lot of good music, but here you only have samba for carnival."

When we came back to the table where Elói and Elena were, we told them the Reinaken joke.

"Yes, yes, they put an R in all the words that begin with H. For example, they say Ralloween instead of Halloween or Rappy Rour instead of Happy Hour" – Elói said and we all laughed.

"And we, the Basque, we even put another R, we say Rralloween" – said Enara.

After that, they found an excuse by saying that English was poorly spoken in Spain because they dubbed all the movies and series.

"However, we have the best dubbers in Europe" – one of the girls said.

"The best and possibly the only ones, since only a few countries in Europe sustain the habit of dubbing movies" – I mocked a little.

We went to another bar that looked more like a disco. There was less light, louder music and a lot of people dancing. We went to the middle of the room and danced. Enara went to get a couple of beers and when she gave me mine, she hit it on the neck with her bottle and I chugged the beer.

"*Hey, chica vasca loca* (Hey, crazy Basque girl)" – I said with my terrible Spanish accent. She laughed a lot and maliciously looked at me.

I got close to her ear and said:

"You are very beautiful, can I kiss you?"

"Not here" – she said.

We kept on dancing, but the tension between the two of us was increasing, when there was some Spanish band on, she would tell me which one it was and, when she leaned in, we would hold hands. Elói was watching out of the corners of his eyes.

In the end, when we left the bar to go home, climbing up the bar's staircase, I held her hand, she turned around and we had a long and desired kiss. I stayed there with Enara, but Elói and his girlfriend were already waiting for us and we followed them. At the bar's door, there was a little more awkward goodbye. Elói tried to avoid bigger troubles and pushed me, literally.

"Let's go home, see you tomorrow."

I kept looking back at Enara and thinking about a miraculous way of seeing each other somewhere else.

"Shit, Gonga, you fuck up everything, you are really a dog! This will have big repercussions on the friend group. The guys are gonna tell her boyfriend."

"So...?"

"So they are my friends, and they are going to ask for explanations, and I am the one who invited you and you just screwed things up."

"Elói, you are going away to Valência, they are not your friends, they are your acquaintances. I, on the other hand, am your friend."

"Yep..."

He did not seem very convinced however, I was not very worried about it. How I felt about the Basque girl had been something special, not just one more flirtation, like with Rita or the Dutch Eva. No, there was something else there. I connected with her in a manner that I have not felt many times before. She had everything I liked in a woman: she was curious regarding music, movies and literature. She knew about politics and history. And besides that, she was pretty, she had a feminine non-vulgar charm. She was even kind of out of my league. What could she see in me?

It took me a while to fall asleep, I pondered if tomorrow she might want to straighten things up and tell me all of that was a mistake and that I should forget the kiss. I planned on going away on Sunday afternoon, but Elói was asking me to stay until Monday morning but, after what happened, it was possible he would throw me out as soon as possible.

Saturday morning, after eating breakfast, we went shopping. The temperature was low, the sky was clean. We saw Elena and talked to her at a supermarket. On our way back home, Elói wanted to drop by some herbalist to buy soy and other vegetarian products. I was wandering around the store, without paying real attention to anything, when someone caressed my back. I turned around and it was Enara. I was surprised she was there, at that very time. She told me she had an appointment with the nutritionist of the store.

"Ah, really? Why?"

"To try to eat better because I tend to grow fat."

To me it seemed it was a woman thing, for she was thin, curvy indeed, and very attractive.

The three of us left the store and walked, Elói a little further ahead, giving us a little privacy. We talked about unimportant things, without mentioning the previous night.

"Elói, invite her for lunch at your house" – I said to him in Portuguese.

"Fuck off, don't involve me in your affairs. You are a troublemaker!"

"Come on, do it and shut up."

He invited her and she accepted.

She was wearing light pants, a little tight, some Doc Martens red boots. Her coat was almost white and she had an Arabian style black and white scarf. Her hair was straight, blonde down to the shoulders.

Elói made lunch, me and Enara helped a little, we were sitting side by side and talking cheerfully. I told her about my life in Castelo Branco.

"This is a lucky fellow, he does not have to cook, he eats at his aunt's house. He does not even wash his own clothes."

"But do you know how to cook?" – she asked me.

"Not really, I don't like to cook."

"Are you from Lisbon?"

"Well, I am from nearby, I come from a town called Agualva-Cacém."

"Yes, his city is often seen on television because of the robberies and delinquency" – Elói said, laughing and she could not tell if it was true or not.

"Where do you live in the Basque Country?"

"Right on the border with France."

"It is for sure more beautiful than Cacém" – Elói said.

"We have a lot of mountains and they are always green, because it rains all year round."

"Then it looks like Cacém" – I said, joking. – "My parents live in a neighborhood called Tapada Mount, which is a mountain with almost no trees, only undergrowth and a lot of rubble from the construction sites that people avoid instead of taking to recycling."

In the middle of the conversation, the lady with the round ass showed up. She started to talk to Elói and Enara, but I did not get much of anything because they were talking fast. However, she had noticed Enara was Basque.

"How did she know?" – I asked.

"Maybe the accent, but I think the scarf gives me away."

"Oh, yeah! It looks Arab, doesn't it?"

"Yes, in the Basque country it's very common, like a revindication symbol."

While we were talking, we exchanged complicit glances. I felt like kissing her again, or talking, only the two of us. After lunch, we straightened up the kitchen and went to Elói's room. His room had a little balcony and she and I went there to smoke a cigarette. Elói laid on his bed and closed the blinds to give us some privacy so the two of us could be alone on the balcony. She complained, without great conviction.

We made out for a good part of the afternoon. We stopped to talk and see the people and cars on the street coming and going. The breeze was cold, but neither of us wanted to get out of there.

"Are the Basque usually as beautiful as you are: blonde and blue-eyed?"

"No" – she laughed – "in a general manner they are all brunet with aquiline noses and prominent cheekbones."

"And do you speak Basque?"

"Yes, I do, I learned in school. It's very hard, they say it's the oldest language in Europe."

"Ah, yes! And on the streets do people speak Spanish too?"

"Here we say *Castellano*. And yes, most people speak *Castellano* on the streets."

"And what is the difference between *Castellano* and Spanish?"

"It's because in Spain there are a lot of languages, so it's more correct to say *Castellano*."

"What a weird country!"

I did not want to talk about the future, I did not know what she wanted. Maybe this was just some flirtation. Even though I asked her:

"Have you ever thought of taking part in an Erasmus Programme?"

"No, not really."

"You could go to Castelo Branco. I would welcome you there…"
"Or you could come here."

We exchanged some more kisses and caresses, got off of the balcony and joined Elói.

I imagined there was an internal fight in her head. This was not right, she had a boyfriend, he would certainly end up knowing, either through her or someone else. I could see she wore an anguished face at times and I tried to calm her down, but I did not know what to say.

We spent the rest of the afternoon and night at Elói's girlfriend's house, who lived with some friends, where we played cards, listened to music, drank beer and smoked cigarettes. She gave me a little sheet of paper with her email, phone and address in the Basque Country. I pondered if that meant she wanted to keep in touch. I was really glad, because I wished the same, indeed each minute I felt more like I was falling in love, but it was a different kind of love. I noticed this time I already knew better how to control the feeling, it was not new to me; and maybe that is the reason it was less bright, it blinded me less than with Elsa or Luísa. However, it was more solid than the two previous ones. The feeling was more mature, I knew exactly what I wanted and thought, at that moment, the feeling was reciprocal.

We went to some bars, but there were always people with us and nothing special happened. I told her I would only go away on Monday morning and I noticed she was glad.

On Sunday morning, we planned to go see an exhibition of the French sculptor Auguste Rodin, which was on show only for that weekend, nearby Salamanca Cathedral. Only five of us went, besides me, Enara, Elói and Elena, there was also a lady called Carmen, who was very talkative and friendly. I wore the same jeans as the previous day, and a gray and black shirt with my old leather jacket. I put on my contact lenses and messed up my hair.

We had breakfast at a coffee shop downtown, there were hundreds of delicious cakes. I ate two and had some coffee with milk, it was very weak coffee. I sat beside Enara; our legs were touching and at times we would hold hands. When leaving the place, in front of the cathedral, which is impressive, Carmen took a picture of us and I got close to Enara and smelt her Vanilla perfume.

I am quite ignorant regarding fine arts, I knew neither Rodin nor his most famous work: *The Thinker*. I contemplated the piece for some time, it is a burly man, sitting, meditating about something. Enara was by my side the whole time and knew much more about the sculptor's work than I did.

I had lunch alone with Elói and as time was passing, I was getting more taciturn. I felt like I was living in a storm that was growing bit by bit. Would I see her ever again? Or would this day be the last? And if we saw each other again, what kind of relationship could we have? We are 500 kilometers apart. And in the middle of it all, she had a boyfriend. Would she tell him? Would he be a violent fellow and maybe even beat her? Elói, maybe noticing the state I was in, cut the silence:

"Hey, Gonga, before going to Valência I might be going to see my brother. He is working in Lisbon, we could set something up if you will be in Cacém."

"Yep, we could go to Sintra."

"That would be nice, I will check if Elena wants to go."

"Great, we could take a path through Sintra's Mountains, first go to the village and afterward we could go up to the Moorish Castle and then to the Pena Palace."

"That would be very nice."

If the afternoon was hard to get through, the night was painful. Her boyfriend came by and we decided to all go together to have some coffee to say goodbye to me. It was a very embarrassing situation, he was a really friendly lad, who knew a lot about soccer, followed the Portugal national team and would like to see the team play in the finals. One could see he was a good person, that he did not even imagine that I had something with his girlfriend. I would look at her and see her glance guiltily and that did not make me feel good at all. I pondered if maybe for her this game was normal, making a fool out of him and perhaps he did not mind. When saying goodbye to Enara we exchanged two kisses and our lips got so close any blind man could see there was something there.

I went home with my head down.

"He is even a cool dude" – I said.

"Yep, poor him" – Elói confirmed.

Elói fell asleep right away, but I was far from being able to sleep. What would happen? Why does everything have to be so hard? It was already complicated to find such a special girl, with so much in common and up above this she lived far away and had a boyfriend. Shit, love is really fucked up!

I woke up with only a few hours of sleep; the bus would leave at eight in the morning from Salamanca so we had to wake up early. I ate something, but I had a lump in my throat that was quite big. I went out nervous and all the way to the station there was tension. Elói tried to cheer me up with anything, but I could barely hear him. We passed by the showcase of a store and I saw my reflection. I was pale with tired eyes, and looked like I had been smoking pot. What had happened the day before? Would her boyfriend already know? Might they have made up? Would she be waiting for me at the station?

"Did you hear what I said?"

"Oh, sorry, Elói, I was distracted, come again."

"I need to go to Castelo Branco to take an exam, may I stay at your house?"

"Sure, *bro*, no need to ask."

Who was at the station, waiting for me, was her boyfriend, not looking very friendly. I cursed my luck. Elói said:

"Shit, don't tell me there will be a fight."

One could see that he, as well as I, had had a bad night. He spoke fast, gesticulating aggressively. I believe he came intending to tear my face apart, but he was smart enough to know he was at a disadvantage, he was shorter and smaller than me, besides that, he knew Elói would not let it happen. I did not show him fear or regret. I frowned. He said something like this:

"Well, yesterday you guys made a fool out of me. Do you think you did well?"

"I didn't know you."

He shut up and I sincerely felt sorry for him. His ego was low and if he liked her, which looked like he did, it was bad luck. I said goodbye to Elói with a hug and tried to shake his hand, but he refused.

"Seriously? After what you've done?"

I got on the bus, willing to disappear from that place as soon as possible. It was an old vehicle, smelled like gasoline and the curtains were dirty. I felt even worse. I put a cassette on my walkman and tried to enjoy the trip. However, I had so many contradictory feelings, so many uncertainties, I could not see anything clearly. It started playing "*Será*" (I wonder) by Pedro Abrunhosa and I could not hold back my tears.

"I wonder if you remember the color of the gaze
When together the night seems endless.
I wonder if you feel this hand that grabs you
And holds you with the strength of the sea against the bay.
I wonder if you can hear me say
That I love you as much as any other day.
I know you will always be there for me,
There is no night without a day nor a day without an end.

I know you want me and love me too
You desire me now like nobody ever did.
Don't go away, don't leave me alone,
I will kiss the floor you step and cry over the way.
I wonder."

We stopped at the border between Portugal and Spain. I took the note Enara had given me, with her phone and tried to call her. It was off.

The bus arrived at the city of Guarda. I waited for around two hours for another bus to Castelo Branco to arrive and took the time to have a sandwich from a machine at the station, which I knew was disgusting and moreover expensive. The trip to Castelo Branco was better, I started to cheer up, thinking about my friends from the Burrow and the Lair, the academic nights, staying late at Ti Jorge's, etc.

When I arrived at Castelo Branco, I showed up at the Burrow. I told the news to Joey Nights and Boni, they told me their affairs too. This is their last semester in Castelo Branco and I noticed they want to make the most of it, although the Burrow is going downhill, with Elói and Bora Bora moving out the place is losing power. The Lair is the one getting the main role with people coming in and out.

One day after I arrived, I received an email from Enara apologizing for her boyfriend's attitude, but she could not wait anymore and told him the truth that same night. She questioned me if what happened between us was just an adventure, a flirtation or something else. I answered right away; I did not even mention the scene at the bus station and told her I felt there was some strong chemistry between us and I wished to see her again soon. I was willing to go to Salamanca or to welcome her in Castelo Branco with open arms. However, a few days later, she wrote to me saying she was confused, she needed to think. Where have I seen this movie? I answered that I would respect and understand her decision and nothing else. I could have promised her the world, sent her roses, many love letters, and showed up by surprise in Salamanca, however, I am not like that. I am not going to force anything, if it's not clear to her, the way it is to me, then we would rather go separate ways. But I am sorry, really sorry. Sometimes I wonder if her relationship has any future after a betrayal and I have no answer. Perhaps I came to show they needed to strengthen the relationship, or maybe sooner or later the relationship will end and she'll happen to remember me.

I sought out some information about the Erasmus program with a teacher from school. She was very lovely and told me I could take a semester in Salamanca or in Prague, in the Czech Republic.

"Which one do you prefer?" – she asked.

I was in doubt. Going to Salamanca would surely mean my adaptation would be easier, for the language as well as the culture are alike, I would also be closer to home, but if Enara went back to her boyfriend the situation would be embarrassing. How could I face them? However, if she decided to stay with me, it would be the best option, with no shadow of a doubt. Going to the Czech Republic would be more of a complicated change, but also very pleasant. I faltered.

"May I think for a while?"

"Of course you can! You have until May to think. There is nobody enrolled yet, you are the first."

It seemed clear that I would move on very shortly, I just had to know where to.

The other day, while I was studying and listening to the radio, they played the Bob Marley song, *Waiting in Vain* and remembered Luísa. It had been a while since I thought about her and, when I heard the song, I felt she already belonged in my past, just like Elsa. Looking back at the weird relationship I had with her, I feel like I am not the same person anymore, the weekend in Salamanca changed me, now I see more clearly she never really gave herself to me, because

I was not "the one" and, deep in my heart, I hope she finds this so-called "the one," without any grudge. A finished chapter in my life, just like Elsa; when remembering the relationship, it even seems it was in another lifetime. Buddhists say everything is in constant change, nothing is forever and I feel I am the best example of that.

I expect, with some anxiety, to soon receive an email from Enara telling me about her decision. I would like her to bet on the underdog, and take a chance with a foreign lad who lives five hundred kilometers away. I would like to show her the part of Portugal that is not shown in the tourist guides. My homeland, the beautiful Cacém; introduce her to my friends from over there, take her to my childhood neighborhood: Mira-Sintra. She might like small villages, like my parents'. She would take me to the Basque Country and show me the mountains she told me about, the typical cities and villages of the region. Maybe she would teach me some words in Basque.

While I write these lines, I look out the window and see how the trees have already started to change the leaves and receive the first spring breezes. The temperature is rising and it seems spring is coming without warning, which gives me the will to do some running again with my uncles' dog, Penguin. The two of us go through the grove that's in the School, an old dumping ground that they have managed to turn into a grove, full of green trees with flowers blooming. This transformation, from a dumping ground to a grove, gives me hope that everything is possible, that the boundaries are us and we are the ones who place them, our minds. This is the reason I constantly remember Tom Hanks' line in the movie *Cast Away*: "I have to keep on breathing, tomorrow the sun is going up, nobody knows what the tide will bring." Yes, I do not know what tomorrow will bring, but I want to live it with enthusiasm.

Gonçalo JN Dias was born in 1977, in Lisbon (because there are no maternities in Cacém), he lived and grew up on the streets of Kzen until he was 19 years old when he went to Castelo Branco to study. He has lived in the Basque Country since 2007. He is married and has two children. He still considers himself a Buddhist, but he does not smoke pot anymore.

Thanks for reading the book, if you can leave an honest review I appreciate it

Other books by this author:
The Good Dictator
Part I – The Birth of an Empire
Part II – The Expansion
Part III – The Succession
Manual for a Murder
Love and Fear on the Santiago Path